DISCOmbobulated

Dispatches from the Wrong Side

Simon A. Morrison

www.headpress.com

50 beats from the Wrong Side

CELEBS

SPOOFS

REALLY RATHER WRONG

A SIDEWAYS GLANCE
AT CULTURE

THE MOST WRONGEST

HOW IT STARTED &
HOW IT ENDED

Dedicated to the Ravers of Revesby and
Veterans of the Disco Wars

A few years ago, I spent an eventful period living on the Wrong Side in LA. I have since managed to pull myself back from the edge because, as nice a place as the Wrong Side is, I wouldn't necessarily want to live there again.

But I do like to visit occasionally and these Dispatches form a record of such excursions...

1
Pikes

CHECKING INTO IBIZA'S INFAMOUS HOTEL; TALKING TO TONY
PIKE; WEARING ANOTHER MAN'S SPEEDOS TO RECREATE THE
VIDEO TO WHAM'S CLUB TROPICANA

I'm in the business of stories. I'm kind of a dealer in narrative — I
hear stories and I pass them on — at street level — maybe cut some,
maybe stamped some, but as pure as I can make 'em. Same with these
Dispatches. I swear on Satan's toenails I wish half the things I write
about hadn't happened to me, just as I wish I could tell the whole
story; because these Dispatches are like icebergs, with ten per cent
above the surface and ninety per cent of the real rancid indulgence
lying underneath.

Clubland is an amazing environment for characters, for storytell-
ers and their mad stories. Fuck *Jackanory* — some of the best stories
I've ever heard have been back in someone's hotel room on a post-
club-mash-up-meltdown, passing the baton of storytelling as you
pass the joint, trying to make new pals laugh with tales of ever more
ridiculous daring do, revealing the scars and bumps and bruises you
wear as badges of honour from the Disco Wars.

And this kind of segueways with all the mellifluous grace of a DJ's
mix into the last Dispatch when I was out in Ibiza with the first ever
Antipodean holiday to the Rock. With barely the chance to wash my
smalls I found myself back on the island, this time trying to avoid
work. I was attending my best mate's stag/hen combined do. And
it was like some plot from a wrong sitcom because wait for it: I am
his best man, I used to go out with both bridesmaids, and sure as

1

Discombobulated

love eggs is love eggs on about the third day one of them bridesmaids exploded and threatened me with my own shoes. And you should NEVER threaten a man with his own shoes. As is usual in these situations I ran away and took recourse in stories, and those of possibly the first Antipodean on the island, the pseudo-Australian Tony Pike, from Pikes Hotel, one of the most fabulous places to lay one's head this planet has to offer.

Where strangers take you by the hand, and welcome you to wonderland / From beneath their panamas...

Tony Pike has got some stories. If you're ever lucky enough to be at Pikes Hotel, offer to buy him a drink, try to manoeuvre him into conversation, sit back and prepare to be enthralled. Take your pick — owning the island of Eoini in Papua New Guinea (long before the Future Sound of London laid claim to the place); interfering with more females (many famous) than is polite; owning a marina in the south of France; sailing around the world; building the hotel that bears his very own name with his very own hands; welcoming just about every pop star and DJ worth their ego through the doors. "The reason why famous people like it here, is that no one intrudes on your privacy," he detailed when I last sat down with him, in a gravely growl that makes his stories so enduring. "It doesn't matter who they are, how much money they've got or whether they're black or white or famous or not famous — they just come here and relax."

Castaways and lovers meet, then kiss in Tropicana's heat / Watch waves break on the bay...

"We've always had famous people coming here. Last year Grace Jones phoned up. She hadn't been here for... well, I can't remember how many years since Grace was here. She said she wanted to come for ten days. I said, 'Grace, I can't even put you up for one day.' She said, 'Pike, you're a cunt.' Grace always had such a way with words."

And all that when, according to rumours, Pike and Mrs Jones had a thing... go... ing... on. Kylie Minogue wanted to stay ten days but

Pike could only find her room at the inn for one night. And you know what, she went and stayed there, for that one night. But it's not all about being starfucky and fawning to the celebs that litter the island of Ibiza like fancy glitter dropped from the stars. You can be a star and not shine: "Geri Halliwell is the opposite — she's a snob. She thinks she's a star but she's not. Kylie is a star, same as Grace."

Soft white sands, a blue lagoon, cocktail time, a summer's tune /
A whole night's holiday...

And then of course there was the video that put Pikes on the map. "It was Wham! that kicked it off in 82 when they shot Club Tropicana," says Tony, who appeared in the video as Gringo, the be-tached barman serving drinks to George and Andrew and Pepsi and Shirley, still amused at the memory of Andrew Ridgeley doing a bunk without paying his bill. Wham! may not mean much to teenage trainee DJs, but it was a turning point for Pikes, and made the hotel a "must do" for the planet's glamour glitterati.

A couple of years ago I figured (through another fog of inebriation) that it would be a laugh to recreate that video for a magazine I was editing on the island. I have absolutely no idea what inspired this idea, just as I have no idea how I was persuaded to climb into someone else's lime green speedos and play George Michael... it just seemed like a good idea at the time. Pike was generous enough to resurrect his role as Gringo, we reconstructed key moments from the video and I haven't laughed so much since Sol Campbell signed for Arsenal. Kookily, a remix of Club Tropicana has returned to haunt the island's dancefloors once again this summer.

With everyone from Spandau Ballet to Carl Cox using the place as a base on the island, you have to wonder who Pike's favourite guest might be? "Freddie Mercury," he replied, before the question is even finished. "He was the best guy I ever met in my life. I don't care whether he was gay, or what he was, he was just a wonderful person."

Of course everyone has now swapped guitars for decks, exchanged Freddie's big fat slug of a 'tasche for the ubiquitous cropped hair and goatees of clubland. So if you want starfucky, get on this — I was at

Discombobulated

Pikes with Paul Van Dyk when he was putting the finishing touches to a track on his laptop. It appeared on his last album as Pikes. Yup, DJs are the new rock stars and just like the old guard they all want to lay their weary heads at Tony's. But Pike, as always, is ready to have them sign their names in at reception, whoever they are.

"I couldn't understand the DJ thing at first," he explained. "But now I know a lot of them personally, get involved and talk to them, I realise that they're wonderful people and they've got a lot of skill and knowledge of the music industry. This place was a great favourite of Frederick Goulder's*. I remember he asked me one day, 'Is that Sven Väth over there?' I said yes. He said, 'Oh I'd love to meet him' and I said, 'Frederick, you want to meet Sven Väth?' He replied, 'Yes, music has no barriers, I'd like to meet him and talk to him.' So I went over and I said to him, the old guy over there is Frederick Goulder and he'd like to meet you. So I get the two of them together and they got on famously. Frederick changed his whole idea of music — he was still stuck with playing Mozart but he also went into disco. Poor old bugger, he was never the same after that."

Pike, at sixty seven, is a hardy example of an open minded rapscallion of the old school, the kind of guy you aim to be at his age. He doesn't care what you do with two bits of vinyl; he cares about what's between your ears, about who you are when you climb back down off the decks, off your pedestal. He has had to endure serious illness, and the brutal experience of losing his son, who was murdered in Miami over a dispute regarding the hotel. Similarly, as people half his age moan that Ibiza ain't not wot it used to be, he thinks the reverse: "Yeah, it's getting better and it's going to get more and more so. What's happened now is the music culture is bringing people together. Back then it didn't exist — you had to make your own. Therefore it's changed for the best I think. There was nothing exclusive about Ibiza then, it was all hippies. As time goes by the population increases and people travel more and have more money than when I was young. Which I can just about remember. I'm older than God now."

Indeed. And if God had a hotel, I would still prefer to stay at Pikes.

* A famous pianist who has since died. | *July 2001*

4

2
Smugglers Run

ADVENTURES OF DARING DO WITH SALTY SEA DOGS ON THE HIGH
SEAS (WELL, THE MANCHESTER SHIP CANAL); WATERBORNE
ANARCHY AND FLAGONS OF ALE

Question: Why are pirates called pirates?
    Answer: They just *arrrrrrrrrrrrrrrrrrrrrr...*
    And that, my too too gorgeous amigos, is comedy you can cash at
the bank. Original pirate material.
    It also leads rather neatly onto this Dispatch — a tale of daring
do on the high seas, set amongst salty sea dogs and one legged pirates with cutlasses between their teeth and pure evil on their minds,
whose only thought is to swing onto your galleon and swipe your
booty. *Rrrr.*
    It started innocently enough, with your intrepid pen pirate in his
shack in Manchester. The building superintendent is called Ken, a
man with grey hair and blue tattoos that speak of more seafaring adventure than a library full of books ever could. Ken the Koncierge I
call him, and this particular morning he was wearing a black T-shirt
adorned with the skull & crossbones. I remarked upon it as I passed
him on the stairs and he explained it was the mark of his time spent
on submarines. He then took me to one side and into his confidence,
whispering of another apartment in the building. Where the smugglers live.
    Fly Guy and Mad Dog.

5

Discombobulated

He had given them his skull & crossbones flag to fly on their vessel — a canal barge by the name of the *L.S. Lowry* — which they commandeer on a monthly basis to smuggle revellers out of reality and over the Wrong Side of the horizon. They call it... the Smugglers Run. I sucked a whistle through my teeth and into the back of my throat — I had no idea such ne'er-do-wells and lowlife lived amongst me and my respectable landlubbing neighbours. A regular rum bunch by all accounts, they gathered by the docks (always the site of wrong goings on, is the docks) — a hardcore of vagabonds and vagrants who would soon as slit their own mother's throat for a gold doubloon and flagon of ale. Mercenaries of both high seas and high times.

I packed a handkerchief with some provisions, tied it by the corners to the end of a stick, swung it over my shoulder and, humming a merry tune, headed for the docks of Castlefield — a dangerous and ominous place, even in the warmth of a late summer afternoon. To mingle in, and appear part of the tapestry of this seascape, I holed up in a nearby hostelry and ordered ale. Soon, I overheard talk of the *Lowry*, and then... there she blows... appearing through the mists, chugging down the canal to moor up by the entrance to the saloon. Pirates began to emerge from the nooks and crannies of the alehouse, sinking their jars and walking in a line to the ship, as though ghosts on some otherworldly pilgrimage, a black skull & crossbones flittering in the wind as though wafting its evil across the surface of the water. I joined the human trail and soon I had smuggled myself aboard; human cargo.

Up anchor, splice the main brace, break open the rum and Roger the cabin boy. Something there was about leaving shore... *arr*... it soon sent everyone disco doolally, as though the very act of setting sail was like freeing yourself from the moorings of morality. This was my kind of deep sea depravity — a pirate odyssey — where the goods we were smuggling were good times themselves.

Time to find Mad Dog and Fly Guy. I revel in the company of kinky thinkers; tinkers with healthy dents in their cerebral cortex. Straight thinking is anathema to my warped soul. I found them soon enough, swigging rum and jigging in the rigging. These flatmates and shipmates came to the decision some two years ago (for this was the second birthday) that landlocked clubs were staler than a pirate's privates; that there was only so much you could do with two decks and a dancefloor... unless you added a third deck, the deck of a ship. "It's escapism, isn't it," said Mad Dog. "An escape from Manchester out onto the sea, getting away from it all."

Ah yes, the pure and simple joy of running away to sea, hightailing it for the high seas, swapping the shoreline for lines of an altogether more exotic dimension. Once in international waters (well, the Rochdale Canal at least) all bets are off. The barge at capacity holds sixty. "Sixty of you are getting away from it all," said Fly Guy. "And you just feel part of something. You feel like you're up to mischief." Mischief was indeed the order of the day. The pirate promoters had offered free tickets to anyone with crabs or scurvy. Nice of promoters to put something back. "Yep, we give 'em the crabs and scurvy," Fly Guy grizzled, Mad Dog whispering a note of caution: "we do advise people to bring their own lemon and lime."

As we pootled our way into the Manchester Ship Canal the music fired up, greeted by a combination of cheers and people banging the underside of the low roof of the barge. The flyer indicated the music policy was "vermin bass-driven shanty house music" and by the looks of if there may well have been love rats, rave rats and all manner of vermin aboard. Fly Guy lowered his patch over one eye and raised his cutlass to the heavens: "Once the sea shanties get going, everyone hits the roof," he grinned maniacally and threw himself into the action.

Swashbuckling is in my blood and soon I did the same, adding my own dimension by staggering from the cubicles and knocking over a speaker stack. Mad Dog had a magazine: *Canal Boat and Inland Waterways*, which he poured over as if it were pornography. "No seriously, I get it every month," he said, turning to the centre page pullout. "We're just downright vermin. Dirty sea rats at the front and salty sea whores at the back."

Daring to venture further into the barge, I fell upon the rum revellers forming this smugglers' huddle. Truly it was waterborne anarchy — the owners of the boat had given Mad Dog and Fly Guy a wide berth (if you'll excuse the nautical tomfoolery) and allowed the party

Discombobulated

pirates to get away with some salty shit. A random poll was taken of the swashbuckling revellers and our scurvy says: it were proper off the hook. These pirates weren't going no place... unless it was via the plank. And by the looks of the Rochdale Canal, all sorts of strange beasts might lurk within its murky waters — scaly scallies and beasties, and a fair few tortured souls upon the seabed of Uncle Tom's Cabin.

"Ales for my friends and six of your best wenches," I barked at the barkeep, already feeling part of the party.

"It's unconditional fun," said Mad Dog, who had once literally pulled a lass with his hook. Hook, line and sinker.

Truly they are saucy sea dogs. On their watery website (which also features streamed "pirate radio") is a naughty webcam broadcast in which they call the female star of the, erm, "show" — who will do or say anything the caller demands. They asked her to turn to the camera and say "*Arrr*".

Night fell, the party now in full steam and we seemed utterly stranded in the mists of the canal. "No one truly knows where this boat actually goes," said Fly Guy, although at one point we passed Old Trafford; that much I know, for I spat at it, but missed. Pimp my barge. "Top production for forty quid," Fly Guy remarked, pointing out the balloons and fairy lights; Mad Dog adding, somewhat aggrieved at my lack of excitement, "those fairy lights do go at different speeds, you know."

Tucked behind the booth with the DJs, we jigged to a 4/4 beat (does that makes it pieces of eight?), the sea shanty soundtrack courtesy of original lowlife riders Kriss James, Xander, Miguel... and Kriss Knight, a Disco Nutbag of the highest order. Never did such a salty sea dog sail the seas and many an adventure have we had together. I didn't expect to find him amongst such low slung company. "I was captured and smuggled upon a vintage comedy barge," he said, apparently now resident DJ at such seadog-esque shenanigans. All hands to the decks.

I pointed at the dark waters. "Has anyone ever gone over?"

"Not yet," he replied. "A few have gone under though."

Eventually the bonkers barge returned to shore, the revellers rounding off the night with a big beer swilling, tankard bashing, sea shanty singsong scrub down at the Sankeys Soap afterparty.

"*Rrrr*-ism, that's what we call it," said Fly Guy. "We turn up at the club, dribbling."

I, however, could no longer find my land legs and soon — legless and lagging — one-legged it home, my headful of tales of sea beasts and mermaids and creatures of such evil and slimy degeneracy that you wouldn't believe it to be true, even if you saw it with your own one good eye.

Arrrrr. | *August 2005*

3, Foo Foo's Palace

UNDERCOVER INVESTIGATIONS IN A TRANSVESTITE JOINT: LOST
AMONGST SCREECHING HENS; TRYING ON WIGS WITH
FOO FOO LAMAAR

"I... am what I am / And what I am... needs no excuses"

To misquote Dorothy Parker, I've been some things and done some places but this had to rate as one of the most ravishingly wrong of them all: trapped in the dressing room of Foo Foo's Palace, trying on wigs with the grande madame of this bordello herself, Foo Foo Lamaar. It was bananas, it was bonkers... it was banonkers, if you will.

The dressing room mirror was lined by lightbulbs that transformed the room into some kind of twisted Broadway Barbie fantasy — a makeup pile up across the table; used fingernails littering the table like dropped scabs; a rack of dresses hung along one wall, so garish they made Joseph's dreamcoat look like a potato sack. Some were really short... the kind of short you needed two haircuts to wear.

In the middle of it all was Foo Foo, conducting herself with a certain chutzpah, applying geological layers of makeup and at the same time talking, without creating a San Andreas fault in her skin. I tried to avert my eyes but couldn't ignore the fact that with bosoms like Foo Foo's, it was lucky I hadn't packed lunch. I was already full up from the eyes down. Ms Lamaar had spent the day at Old Trafford, entertaining the troops during the England vs Greece game: "It was a close shave between United and Greece, but my little golden balls did it for us at the end," she rasped, with a fabulously camp northern accent, raked over coals. Beckham had indeed sorted it out for us that day. I watched the match in a local bar with some mates, talking tactics, drinking too much, jumping up and running around when our goals went in. It was all good blokey stuff, which made it all the harder to comprehend how I had ended my testosterone fuelled day sitting in the dressing room of a transvestite's club, trying on wigs and talking football with Foo Foo.

The answer of course lies in the gloriously banonkers world of the Wrong Side: Foo Foo is the Wrong Side personified, she is the Queen of the Wrong Side and her palace lies at the bottom of my street in Manchester. I have walked past the place for years and wondered what chaos lay behind its doors; watched Foo Foo drive past in her purple Rolls Royce (with number plate Foo 1) and resolved to uncover her story; the face beneath the makeup. Bottom panty line? I am not the sort of guy who can have a club called Foo Foo's Palace at the end of his street and be satisfied having never been in.

So it was with some excitement that I stepped down the stairs that led into the club — all glass and glitter, the spot where Moulin Rouge meets Studio 54. On Qualudes and wine. Foo Foo's is so tacky as to be beautiful; like sitting inside a mirrorball which is then rolled down a hill headlong into the window of an Ann Summers' shop. And the place was packed, wall to wall — and in fact bursting at the seams — with screeching, drunken females. They seemed to be split into tribal, hen night groups. Some were wearing L-plates, others were dressed as nurses... nuns... all kinds of wrongness. I smiled a broad smile. I was built for this kind of nonsense, I live for nonsense and at Foo Foo's I was in nonsense nirvana. You can just knock yourself out with your Creams and Ministry of Sounds — just dip me in banana daiquiri and throw me to the trannies. After three years investigating the Wrong Side — everywhere from Moscow to Las Vegas — this was like finding the mothership, the ultimate wonky night out.

I turned my beatbox up to Rhumba and climbed in. Everywhere... everywhere women were shrieking and drinking, already climbing

Discombobulated

onto the chairs and tables to dance as if Golden Balls himself were on stage. The whole room was bathed in a rouge ebullience. The DJ mixed records with all the grace of a number 29 bus. If you want eclectic, you can forget about the 333 and the groovy clubs of Old Street — you want to get yourself to Foo Foo's Palace where they really know the meaning of the word. From Gabba to Abba, in one easy step. A stripper took to the stage. He abandoned his thong in front of the assembled throng, put it about and put me right off my pint.

I decided to find Foo Foo, and headed for her dressing room. Once inside, the door swung shut, muffling the screams of the women outside. I panted for my breath to come back. "Ms Lamaar... or may I call you Foo... why do you have such an effect on those women out there?"

She stopped, momentarily, from applying her mascara. "Because I am very beautiful and so pretty and those jealous bitches out there would love to get their fat bums in my frocks."

"Your frocks are indeed... so very special."

"They would love to go into Sainsbury's with one of my frocks on."

That I don't doubt. I put a wig on and sat down to listen to her story. Believe it or not, Foo Foo Lamaar wasn't christened thus. Nope, Mrs Lamaar didn't wake up one night and tell Mr Lamaar that she had the perfect name for their progeny — Foo Foo. In fact, there wasn't actually a Mr and Mrs Lamar at all. In a previous — much less fabulous — incarnation, Foo Foo was Frank Pearson, the son of a rag & bone man from Ancoats. One Christmas it was decided to hold a concert in the canteen of the cotton mill where Frank worked and he was persuaded to go in drag. As if by magic, a glorious peacock emerged from a field of grey pigeons, opening up her multicoloured tail and casting a wonderful sanguine light across the city of Manchester. And so it came to pass that Frank transmogrified into transvestite Foo Foo, discovering in the process that s/he was born to take to the stage, to contribute to the nefarious nocturnal world in her own, deliciously unique way — a leviathan in a frock.

"I used to do the little pubs and clubs," she recalled, "and I was that popular in them days I thought to myself — I'm packing these little pubs and clubs, why not do it for myself? So in 1971 I opened the Picador club, which was on Shudehill. It's been pulled down now. I kept that for four years and earned my money to buy this. In 1976, Foo Foo's Palace was born."

It must be the dream of every little girl, or indeed six-foot man, to one day own their very own palace. Of course Dale Street is no wonderland, and Foo Foo's Palace is no Versailles but it is, in its own camp way, a kind of fairyland that has attracted many princes to dare unlock its secrets. "I've been offered a lot more television if I go to London... but I won't go to London," Foo Foo fumed, with more front than a Woolie's window. "If they want me, they'll have to come here for me. Because I think this is the nicest city in the world."

Clubland is a strange, amorphous kind of place, with space for many weird and wonderful scenes and Foo Foo Lamaar has made her very own special contribution to clubland, through which she has met everyone from Take That to the ultimate queen, erm... The Queen.

"Throughout the years I've been very lucky — but I've worked very hard," she said, adding the finishing touches to her makeup. "People have said to me many times, with all this work why have I not been given an honour? But I say, probably because they wouldn't know whether to make me a Duchess or a Duke." As well as her magnificent work treading the boards, Foo Foo has helped raise £4 million for various causes, including cancer charities, which had a special resonance when the Grand Dame was herself diagnosed with cancer. "Only four months ago I had a kidney out. But the mere fact that I have to entertain — because it's in my blood — threw the illness to one side. I've no time to be ill and no time to grow old. That's the essence of showbusiness."

The show must go on. And when Foo Foo stepped out onto her stage, the roar that went up was enough to convince anyone she's carved herself out a little diamante corner of Manchester. Of course it's all fake, from the tits to the chandeliers, but clubland doesn't always have to be built on a bedrock of seriousness; there is equally room for boudoir and sillyness. Pretty soon I was standing on the tables and dancing with the brides-to-be. The fact that we were being entertained by a man in a frock seemed fairly irrelevant. Because when it comes to trying to figure stuff out — like what I was actually

Discombobulated

doing in a transvestite's dressing room — I guess the answer is simple: Everybody's got to be someplace. And for Foo Foo, it's her very own palace. | *October 2001*

Postscript: Foo Foo Lamaar lost her battle with cancer in 2003, stepping gracefully up to that great powder room in the sky. I hope she enjoys trying on wigs with Marilyn Monroe and Judy Garland as much as I enjoyed trying them on with her.

4
Snow
business

Wrong. Several shades of wrong. A deep, dark pit of wrongness. A dank puddle of wrongosity. If you were to look up the word "wrong" in the Oxford English Dictionary the definition would read: "British Snowboarding Championships" with a supplementary heading under "lost Cubans in loud shirts". But if we can tempt clubbers out of their dark disco burrows and onto Ibiza's beaches maybe, after all, we can catapult them up a mountain. Like yer man says, if the mountain won't come to Mohammed... maybe the answer is to provide Mohammed with a snowboard, clip him into a pair of dancing trousers and gently nudge him off a nearby Alp.

And so onwards, to the gorgeous village of Mayrhofen in the Austrian Tyrol where the Champs were to be held. I hadn't made it three feet inside reception of the Sporthotel Strass before bumping into Elliot from Manumission, working at the resort after the chaos of the last Ibizan summer. A couple of steps further and I collided with other people I knew from that wonky island, further confirming my view that for many people with ingloriously stained passports and psyches, life consists purely of mountains during the winter and beaches during the summer. The vista may change but the folk don't, surfing that hedonism highway right across Europe. Before I made it to the check-in I was plugged into the hotel bar. After dumping my bags and readying myself for the evening I was already tipsy, unsteady with the shift in altitude, falling straight down the stairs as we proceeded into the hotel's basement club. A couple of cold ones later and I slipped over again, trying to negotiate the toilets. The consequence of such tumbles was that, before I'd even climbed on a board I was hobbling, bruised and pathetic, back to the sanctuary of my room.

The profile of British snowboarders is rising sharply, with Lesley McKenna and Melanie Leando hoping to compete at the next Winter Olympics. "It's so detached from that Eddie The Eagle thing," said boarder Johnno "Back Flip" Verity, the next morning. "That was seen as a bit of a joke really, but people are now getting coverage in international magazines, so I do think we're taking it a step further." Taking it a step further seems to be the vibe of snowboarding and the après ski has a next-level, hedonistic incline as steep as a black run. "The Champs are a really good time for that," he smiled. "Personally I've been going out, partying quite a bit at this year's Brits but throughout the season I really take it quite easy. My first couple of seasons I drank quite a lot and stuff but now... you can become a professional snowboarder but you can't become a professional drinker."

Well... let's not be hasty here, Back Flip. I'm semi-professional at the best of times (and I'm still looking for sponsors to take the last branding space on my hipflask). Take the next night. I got embroiled in a session at some strange Twin Peaks shack up a hill (all stuffed animals and Fear) with Elliot, an old mate of mine Kirk, and Tim King, one of the Cuban Brothers. Back at the Strass we did in my bottle of scotch and... at some stage I guess I went to get something from my room...

... I woke the next morning fully clothed, passed out on the bed, with the door of the room wide open. I tried to get up and found someone had emptied the contents of the room out on top of me — the TV, chest of drawers, all my clothes, the chair, the whole kit and kaboodle. Quite evidently wrong.

"You have ruined my holiday," I barked at Cuban Tim, clearly the culprit, chuckling as he strolled back into the site of dereliction at some lost slice of the afternoon. I found myself quite unable to clamber my way from under the mess. It took four Nurofen and a pizza before I could even focus. "STAY OUT OF MY LIFE!"

The sentiment didn't last long and the evening continued in a Cuban fashion, as the Cuban Brothers took to the stage of the lobby bar of the Strass — and ripped the roof and all four walls off the place. It's difficult to put into words what transmogrified before my eyes, but it was a cheerful combo of singing, rapping, DJing, bad clothes, bad taste, big hair (as opposed to big air), bad Latin accents, sketches from the Cuban Rolf Harris and lots of breakdancing in underpants. I turned my beat box up to Rhumba and got involved, as the crowd's enthusiasm sparked a near riot.

On stage and off, the Cuban Brothers tore through Mayrhofen like a hurricane with a big furry moustache and after the gig I caught up with the front man, the hombre with the big cojones, Miguel, halfway up a mountain and a long way from home. "Si," he replied, in a drawl as slow as a Havana afternoon. "The thing is *El Simon*, for this one is to do a small show for the mountain, you know. And for me, is never seen the snow-surfing before. No snow for us in Cuba... is crazy! Is plenty snow you know but you do the surfing off your nose... the nostril surf. Let's go!"

Viva la révolution! I guess Fidel must have let these guys out on some kind of cultural exchange with the Manic Street Preachers. I can't help but feel we got the better deal. The Cuban Brothers have taken it upon themselves to distribute the message of Latin love across the globe, from Rob Da Bank's Sunday Social at Cargo in London, through to Manumission's 2001 opening party; from their homeland of Cuba to the British Snowboarding Champs, their mission apparently centred around "touching".

"We have touched a few chickas. It's been great, you know."

"Touched them emotionally?"

"Touched them internally. I am still the gentlemans so I cannot talk too much about who has been touched. Because the thing is *El Simon*, sometimes we fun other peoples' wives. You can't fun other peoples' wives. DON'T FUN MY WIFE!" I had no intention of funing Miguel's wife, especially with his random brother wandering the halls of the hotel packing a pistol under the sweated pit of one arm.

Discombobulated

The next day we went back upside the mountain, watching the boarders twang themselves through the air to a soundtrack from Normski, Paul Thomas from Radio 1 and Becky. Also amongst their number was Magnus from the Positive Sound System, a friend I had met at the last two Champs. Magnus embodied the full-on boarding/DJing crossover in that he boarded, he DJd and occasionally he combined both... by boarding on his record box. After about an hour boarding with Magnus I got my turns sorted, finally saved from the indignity of having to scale half the mountain backwards.

That night we headed for an overnight stay at a mountaintop cabin straight out of the video for Wham's Last Christmas. The evening was stuffed full of nonsense — more of Kirk's wrong games, Cuban Tim and Darren from Ninja Tune providing the soundtrack by spinning vinyl on a portable record deck — the twisted bi-product, it seemed, of a drunken liaison between Technics and Fisher-Price. Breakbeats may not seem the ideal thing when you've got four limbs to consider, but after the godawful *please-will-someone-just-put-a-bullet-in-my-skull* oompa lumpa music that was heard from the locals, it was a blessed relief. "Skiing is the mainstream, snowboarding is the underground," Darren explained, "and as a DJ you're going to want to try out the underground." I'm not sure about the underground, but when everyone began to nod off, Kirk made us take off our shoes, go outside into the cold, black night, dash 100 metres to "touch a hut" and then tonk it back down. I gave it a go — the freezing midnight snow burning my feet — and made it halfway, forced to turn back when confronted with the sight of two fully naked Cubans hightailing it back down the slope. Put me right off my schnapps, I can tell you — I'm not sure how you're supposed to drink that stuff, but after seven pints it was all kinds of bedtime.

Once again the Champs had been wonderfully wrong. The full wrongness of it all was palpable — emotionally, mentally, physically, spiritually, sexually wrong. And yet somehow so deliciously right. As I left the hotel I heard voices agreeing to bring it on once again for another Balearic summer. Sand during the summer, snow in the winter. It really just comes down to what you have to extract from your pants at the end of the day. | *April 2001*

5
Sharm el Sheikh

INTO THE SINAI DESERT; TRADING WITH BEDOIUN; AVOIDING
LANDMINES AND ATTEMPTING TO STAY UPRIGHT ON A CAMEL
WHILST INEBRIATED

Cairo. I have something approaching a half litre of scotch inside me
and I'm trying to ride a camel — for the purposes of this Dispatch we
shall call him Colin. Colin is doing his level best to keep me vertical
while he ferries me around the pyramids, the sight of which is enough
to knock anyone off their dromedary. Only it won't take that much
to separate me from Colin — duty free at Heathrow was enough to
do that all by itself. I haven't slept in a couple of days and I'm in the
same clothes as last night. I vaguely remember drinking in a hotel
bar, smoking hookahs, lying on a beach, looking up into the Arabian
night. But right now I'm on a camel.

What really makes the experience so deliciously wrong is that I'm
not supposed to be here at all. The press pack were staying in a resort
called Sharm El Sheikh on the southern tip of the Sinai Peninsular,
but since we were delayed in Cairo, someone suggested making a
break for the pyramids, catching me, and the luggage of my inebriation, somewhat off guard. The pyramids took like, a kigillion years to
build, and I've got ten minutes to take it all. Ten whisky soaked minutes. I'm laughing so hard I can barely keep a hold on Colin and by
the time we climb back onto the bus back to Cairo I can only vaguely
recall the experience at all. Wrong.

Discombobulated

Sharm was a whole different kettle of fish, or rather magic lantern of dreams. Sharm is where the Arabs go to play and will soon become another disco destination for this planet's wandering tribe of clubbers — playing that enormous game of join-the-dots between this planet's finest dancefloors.

This was my first time in the Middle East, or indeed Africa and I wanted to get out amongst it, get out in search of hookahs and the Truth. And there is no one better to show you around than Adly El Mestekawy, a man who ditched his nine to five life in Cairo some twenty years ago to become one of the first people to stake a claim in Sharm, building the Sanafir hotel where we stayed and played. "For me, living in a tie and a suit, being an employee... I wanted to feel free," he told me on our first day, as we boarded a boat and set sail onto the Red Sea. "And once I came to Sharm I felt that... this is freedom. The Bedouin philosophy is just great. It's the opposite of a consumption society — when you don't have to consume, you don't have to work for money, so life is reduced. But at the same time it gives space for your brain to think, for wisdom." I found a tub full of cold beers and a horizon full of warm possibilities, donning flippers and a snorkel to join the exotic fishes of the coral reef, my body floating on the surface of the Red Sea like the detritus of a shed-wreck. That night Renaissance set up in the Bus Stop nightclub, the focal point of the Sanafir hotel. The central dancefloor was out in the open air; the stars formed its ceiling, the rooms of the hotel its walls and Nigel Dawson provided the moonlit soundtrack.

The next day we assembled in the middle of the dancefloor — somewhat alien now it was harshly illuminated by the floodlight of the sun — and split into groups, all climbing into four-wheel drive jeeps. I found myself behind Rachel Photos, wearing a jacket with the words "the luxury of dirt" on the back — an extremely perplexing slogan or perhaps an ancient riddle just teasing to be unravelled. We followed Adly in convoy, until all at once he turned off the road and seemed randomly to blast off into the desert, the very desert where the Israelis left a million landmines when they pulled out from the Sinai, some twenty years ago.

The jeep did the bump and grind with the desert, sending us

bouncing around inside as an Arabian voice floated from a radio, chanting words from the Koran; beautiful, when set against an empty skyline — save for our convoy, spinning across the desert floor like a stone skipping across a pond. I did my best to chat to our driver, a DJ at the Sanafir called Graham. "Even though a lot of this music is brand new to the Egyptians," he explained, "they're very knowledgeable. The religious music that comes out of this area is very hypnotic; so while dance music is new to them, that hypnotic, progressive tribal sound — they already know it, it's in their blood."

Lunch was by the shores of a mangrove swamp, then we headed further into the desert, at one point stopping to trade with some Bedouin. The Bedouin have an amazing grace — the way they lead their camels has a wonderful fluidity, as does the loose clothing that hangs about them; it's all part of their philosophy, that they are part of the wind and will move only when it picks up. But all that space and freedom — it engenders a kind of creeping agoraphobia in a frightened city kid like me, a long way from the tight comfort of his apartment and the chaotic cuddle of an urban lifestyle. I contemplated trying to exchange Rachel Photos for some camels but concluded I'd be lucky to come away with a pack a Camel Lights.

Further, as darkness enveloped the desert, we came to the Echo Temple — an outdoor arena that gave new meaning to the art of disco al fresco, taking you back to the days when the desert itself was a dancefloor, the only boundaries the sky above and the walls of the valley, echoing music, reflecting light.

We ate at a nearby hotel and partied at the next door Mexican bar, which threw us all through strange geographical hoops. What was more disturbing however was Rachel Photos taking issue with a couple of tiny pinprick holes in the back of my T-shirt, persuading me she could remedy the situation with a couple of tears in the back, thus rendering it "trendy". So she ripped a little, then ripped a little more and before I knew what was happening hands were coming out of everywhere and a ferocious female scrum left me looking like a dodgy extra from a Tarzan movie. I know for a fact *Muzik* and *Ministry* magazines were implicated. I have my suspicions about other magazines and at one point even a random Egyptian lady took one

Discombobulated

of the sleeves clean off. It was horrendous, like being covered in fish food and dropped in a tank full of starved piranhas and I can see the experience making an appearance in a future counselling session. Back at the Sanafir I changed out of my ravaged T-shirt and headed for the bus stop, which had been transmogrified into a Ministry of Sound soiree, with Graham warming up for Dave Seaman, lifting the veil for the Arabian crowd.

There were some heavy heads the next day, as we sailed back out onto the Red Sea, mooring by an old shipwreck and jumping into the cool water — perhaps the only hangover cure to beat my favourite patented method, which is to not stop drinking. "Instead of nursing your hangover, you're nursing your soul," chuckled Bob Stamegna, who had cobbled this whole exercise together. His vision was to take clubbers out to places like Sharm, places a little off the beaten track, and then encourage them to stay in touch via Archangelas, a cyber-city he is in the process of constructing. It's quite a vision, especially when waking up with any kind of vision is an achievement in itself.

That evening we were the guests of a nearby hotel, our meal accompanied by belly dancers, who wiggled bits I never even knew existed. Eating pudding seemed tantamount to cannibalism. From there we made a brief stop at a casino (I came out with twice the money I went in with... though to be fair that was only five bucks) and trawled the bizarre bazaars, looking for last-minute presents to take home. That night John Kelly rocked the Bus Stop and the crowd loved the guy, but me, I was all partied out. I kicked back at a nearby bar, trying my best to smoke a hookah, which sounds disturbingly like American slang for murdering a prostitute but actually refers to those strange, wobbly pipe contraptions, filled with flavoured tobacco. Rachel chose to call them Hubbly Bubblys. With a headful of smoke and a permanent smile etched onto my face, I walked down onto the beach, lay back and stared up into the Arabian sky.

Did you ever have one of those "fuck me it's fun being alive" moments? Right then, on that beach, under those stars, I had a phat one of those; at the same time realising just what was meant by the phrase "the luxury of dirt." | *March 2002*

6
Fukdup

Goddamn it, those peskie Ruskies can drink. They down booze like it's water and then launch themselves on the nearest cutie. And the blokes are pretty wild as well. They nearly did for me with their endless vodka and irresistible good spirits — they've got good souls, they're incredibly warmhearted and, above all else, they are gorgeous. When I told my mother I was going to Moscow, she commented only that she'd seen a programme on the telly and I should watch out for the prostitutes. So I did. I watched out for them all over Moscow and spank me twice if they weren't more gorgeous than anyone else. And who better to share all this depravity than Mark Luvdup, a libertine of the highest order. If you're going to take anyone on a visit to the Wrong Side, Mark's your man — ever prepared to squeeze the juice out of life until the very last drop has been wrung out.

We touched down in Moscow to find it snowing like the cover of a perfect Christmas card — real chunky snow that makes you giddy like a child. Gregory, owner of The Park, the club where Mark was booked to play, appeared on the right side of Immigration. I went to shake his hand. He brushed it aside and grabbed me in a bear hug, with a bear's broad smile across his face. Back inside his apartment, he thrust bottles of Russian beer into our hands and we munched down on dried fish. Gregory's father won gold for the 10,000 metres at the 1960 Rome Olympics and is a famous figure in Russia. After his victory the Americans offered him $1 million to defect. As Gregory explained, his

Discombobulated

dad simply replied "*Niet*. I am a Russian." Proud bunch, the Ruskies.

We drove fast to the club. Gregory cranked up the car radio and if you think you can do eclectic, try listening to Moscow radio, which segueways from dance to folk to rock'n'roll with the grace of Pavorotti belly flopping into a bowl of profiteroles. Outside the venue the snow was balls deep and the deserted outdoor garden resembled a scene from the Rough Guide To Narnia. The club itself was a wing of a grand old theatre, so named because it lay nestled next to Gorky Park. "Business is booming right now," Gregory explained. "This club is basically the underground. I'm trying to move towards a less commercial sound, to incorporate some harder trance music, rather than pure house. And we try to change the interior and the design as well as the music that we play."

Although it was hard to imagine during this freak snowstorm, The Park rocks even more in the summer months, when Moscow is energised by the sun: "In the summer we have wild parties outside," Gregory continued, with an infectious chuckle, "with dancers, performers and freaks. And we have a boat for afterparties. Everybody is literally loading into the boat, with a PA system and lights and stuff, touring up and down Moscow River."

That day happened to be Women's Day — the Russian equivalent of Valentine's Day — celebrating a strike of female workers in New York in the 1800s. Even the male and female troops in Chechnya had stopped their trooping to have a disco together and at The Park, male strippers in soldier's uniforms danced on stage, a military take on Westlife. (Eastlife, perhaps?) And the women? Oh... my... God. "Give me a woman who loves beer and I will conquer the world," said Kaiser Wilhelm and even the club's manager Olga looked less like an Olga than you could possibly entertain. Pretty soon we were all shouting "vodka, vodka, vodka." Mark climbed up into the DJ pod to spin a spunky little set and I bounced around the dancefloor, unable to talk to anyone because of the language barrier, but able to communicate via the universal language of insobriety. I was (at least I thought I was) making progress with one blonde girl who seemed to be extremely friendly and who also turned out to be a stripper. And strip she proceeded to do... as, for some reason, did Mark. Never needs asking twice, that guy.

I was only in Moscow for a couple of days and wanted to fit in as much as possible so I was slightly irked when I woke at five the next afternoon. Mark was already up and about and so, together with Gregory, his girlfriend Anna, Olga (who turned out to be her sister) and Andrei (who was their brother), we walked into town. At Red Square I was hit by childhood memories of tanks and missiles and troops parading past various decrepit presidents during the Cold War, and that was hard to reconcile with this fairy tale view, with St Basil's Cathedral at one end and the tall imposing walls of the Kremlin to the side. But it was still Red Square... it was still Moscow... and it was still hard to escape those James Bond spy connotations.

"Do you have the microfilm?" I whispered.

"Not here," Mark replied. "London's getting jumpy."

Luvdup have previously featured on the cover of *DJmag*, standing in almost the same place but things have since changed, with Mark and Adrian Luvdup no longer working together... after the big Luvdup comes the big Cumdown. "We've just gone our separate ways really," Mark explained as we strolled back through the quiet evening streets. "It wasn't an amicable separation and I found myself with lots of problems because of it, but I'm forging ahead with the Luvdup name."

Luvdup were renowned for outrageous antics and unrepeatable behaviour but beyond the booze and bravado is a more sobering story. Mark is South African and his status in the UK is as political refugee — he refused to do national service in his home country. After thirteen years living in England, he was recently granted British citizenship: "I just fucking cried. I burst into tears for about ten minutes. I've been waiting so long, it was very emotional for me." He's now able to travel more freely, across a planet that really grew up in the last few years of the twentieth century. South Africa, Russia, even the UK... we've all gatecrashed the new millennium a little more clued up and chilled out.

"Russians like to party and they like to party hard," Mark smiled, "and there's no holes barred. People are very free, free to express themselves. They're throwing off the yolk of oppression and just lap-

Discombobulated

ping it up."

The streets were strangely quiet and devoid of cars which, through the snow, made Moscow timeless — as if we were a bunch of nineteenth century students, stumbling around with our heads full of Marx, vodka and Big Ideas. At a nearby restaurant, a live band tortured various Russian and western songs while we enjoyed a gorgeous meal, which started with caviar and got better from there. Mark for some reason felt it necessary to set fire to the hair on his chest: "I'm absolutely in love with this place," he declared, his torso erupting in flames.

"Mark, one last question... do you have the microfilm?"

Mark didn't have the microfilm.

Later in the evening we headed back out, ebullient and ready once again to lord it around Moscow, this time at a club called The Circus, not surprisingly on the site of the Moscow Circus. The queue at the door consisted exclusively of rudely attractive women in long fur coats. Through the doors lay an equally svelte club, packed with blokes who looked like Robbie Coltrane in the Bond movies surrounded by girls who looked like girls in the Bond movies (most of whom, I was informed, were prostitutes). It was the national holiday for Women's Day and so the club offered a little something for the ladies — a catwalk parade of blokes wearing what appeared to be elastic bands around their waists.

I was left with little to no time to get to the airport and get my ass out of there. The snow was still falling in a blizzard of dandruff. Andrei informed me that a plane had crashed that morning in Moscow, killing nine people, but that I shouldn't worry because it wasn't the snow... just sabotage. I just about made it to the plane — which was being de-iced so that it could actually take off — sat back, and cogitated. The more I travel the more it becomes obvious that electronic music is pulling the world together, a kind of funk coagulant. And I don't mean that in a hippy dippy way, it's more that when you're on a dancefloor and you're a little spangled, you sometimes forget whether you're in Moscow or Manchester, such is its connecting power. We've been close before, us and the Ruskies — through our royal families (before they executed theirs), through to the way we have fought together. After all the fuss and nonsense of the second half of the twentieth century, it's become obvious we were more likely to be bitten by daffodils than to indulge in a third world war. Now, we can get over to Moscow and party together again, in a funky city of fur coats and bear hugs.

I ordered a gin and tonic.

"Would you like anything else?" asked the stewardess.

"Yes," I replied. "Do you have the microfilm?"

She didn't have the microfilm. Nice G&T though. | *April 2000*

Barcelona 7

GAUDY GAUDI; HOW TO MAKE MCDONALD'S A GORMET BANQUET

easyLady

Flshhhhhhhhh. I zipped up and was about to unlock the cubicle door when I heard voices... female voices. Strange? Then it slowly dawned on me why there were no urinals in these toilets — they weren't designed with señors in mind. Holy Crapola. Just at that point more women walked into the toilets and began chatting, something to do with boys and their boy pieces. I was out of options. I unlocked the door, nodded to the ladies, and walked out.

easySpinback

The whole episode summed up the disjointed vibe of the weekend, on which note let's spin this story back to Friday, to the Right Side, to Liverpool John Lennon airport. A statue of the great man stands on the upper level, just by a poster of him, kindly printed by the good people at McDonald's. "I'm not entirely sure that Lennon had McDonald's in mind when he wrote Imagine," I said to Antony Photos, who had agreed to share my journey to the Wrong Side.

"Imagine there's no burgers..." he volleyed.

"Above us only fries..." I sliced.

We reached the departure lounge bar. "Not serving alcohol yet, lads," intoned the jobsworth scouser barman before I had even opened my mouth, looking me up and down like I'd just climbed out of a skip. It was 9am. I had no intention of drinking. It's only polite to leave it until the clock ticks to pm, be that a meagre 12.01pm.

easyGooner

And things went wrong from there. Me and Mr Photos boarded the plane and sat in front of Sunderland manager Peter Reid and footballer Niall Quinn. Being a head-to-toe Gooner, I wanted to shake Niall's hand, maybe sing him my favourite football song, *"Niall Quinn's disco pants are the best / they go up from his knees to his chest,"* for the entire two hour duration of the flight. I made do with humming it to myself.

The fact that the flight was a mere two hours is the crux of why I'm so proud to be European, a continent containing within its star-system a claustrophobic cuddle of cities: Paris, Amsterdam, Berlin, Moscow. What a place to call home. And with a pocketful of euros and a headful of dreams, we caught the Metro and headed down La Rambla, a street that formed the trunk of a fabulous magic tree, with branches shooting off either side, sprouting bars like liquid-laden leaves. Rather than make any superficial plans, we determined to get properly underneath the city and mooch about. So, rather than go *in* the Gaudí cathedral, we stood beside it, and over the course of the afternoon saw Barcelona through a barroom window, warped through the bottom of a glass.

easySpaniard

The cab was driven by a man I called Gay José, mainly because he seemed intent on pointing out Barcelona's gay clubs to me and Antony, getting something of the wrong end of the sexuality stick; and because he handed me a bit of paper containing his phone number and name, which was José.

easyBooze

I've got a question for you: Why do things taste better when they come out of a mini bar? It's the same arena of questioning as: Why do sandwiches taste better when they're cut diagonally, rather than perpendicularly? I pondered that very fact as I transferred the contents of the mini bar from their box to my belly, flicked on the telly and had a nice sit down with myself. In the spirit of this somewhat askew visit to the city, rather than go and see the outdoor show taking

Discombobulated

place at the Palau Nacional fountains nearby, we watched the tips of the fountains as they erupted behind buildings, just as a full, hidden orchestra launched into a muffled rendition of Freddie Mercury and Monserrat Caballe's Barcelona. It all sounded very special, although it was hard to tell when you're craning your neck like a giraffe after treetop product; when you have one hand on the window ledge and the other on a G&T.

easyCompany

In early June, Miss Moneypenny strolled into Barcelona like a model onto a catwalk. It was a clash of interlocking brands, a match made in glamour heaven. The club has a long standing association with Ibiza, but Barcelona was always the logical next step, especially when Ibiza promoter Lee Garrick began the relationship with his girlfriend Melanie Jebrai, herself a native of the city. And how do I know all this? I had a Jacuzzi with them both a few years ago... but that's an entirely different story.

"We've been seeing each other for about four years," Lee detailed, "so I've been taking trips over to Barcelona, visiting clubs, getting in with people over here and trying it that way. Obviously Barcelona's dance scene has really started to kickoff now, and it's a very artistic city — did you get to see any of the Gaudí buildings?"

"Kind of."

"There's fantastic clothes shopping as well, and then there's just the whole Mediterranean chill out vibe. All that's fantastic. And the nightlife starts out on a Thursday night and continues until Tuesday morning. It's absolutely manic — they definitely don't sleep."

And it seems the Spanish were going loco for our very own *señorita ingles* — Miss Moneypenny — with the party appealing to a local crowd, as well as the UK folk ready to save their moneypennys and join the party. The first party at the Torres de Villa nightspot with Danny Buddha Morales and Lee hosting was, by all accounts, rather splendid. But that was then, and this was now — this discombobulated, dented weekend — and there was a glitch in the programme. The grand dame of English house couture had been unable to join us for the evening; Miss Moneypenny was unwell. But Lee wished us a wonderful evening at their venue and promised she would be back to grace Barcelona soon.

easyEvening

In deference to 007 I clipped on cufflinks, and walked back out in the warmth of the night. Spaniards — with inbuilt thermostats set permanently to cool — spilt over their city like space dust, with a fondness for fiesta that is infectious, intoxicating. Take McDonald's. In the UK those golden arches of chaos are an icon of uncool, a signifier of sin. In Barcelona however, it's perfectly possible to stumble upon a line of girls huddled in a doorway munching McDonald's, and for each one to look like an angel. It's that kind of scruffy chic look — that urbane, thrown together vibe — that enables you to sling on some clothes, drift out into your city and ooze groove all the way.

easyDisco

I was looking forward to running full pelt at el weekendo diablo, banging my head viciously against its wall until its masonry came tumbling down around my ankles. After a few drinks in a bar we headed over to the venue, formed from the walls of a castle atop a hill, overlooking the city. Two turrets formed the twin towers of the club, with two dancefloors at their bottom, another two halfway up, joined via a gangplank, and a couple of DJs rocking the rooftop garden. Disco al fresco: The warm, musty scent in the air, the view over the pubic mane of the park and down, down into the gentleness of the city, the melody like an intoxicating scent carried on the warm, Mediterranean breeze.

easyTiger

People mooched, slumped into corners with girlfriends, nodding *ciao* to people as they left the roof, if not by the lift, then via the Escher-esque staircases that wrapped around one another and never met. Downstairs, at ground level, people swirled around the dancefloor with a real lust, a real desire to grab the night by its ears and kiss it on both cheeks, hard.

I danced my way through the night, through the doors and out

Discombobulated

of the club. Well perhaps not so much danced as stumbled, gripped by a sudden sense of injustice: that my stumbling was a product not so much of inebriation but evolution, in the sense that... it's hardly my fault we decided to stand up on two legs... if we'd only stayed quadrupeds this wouldn't even be an issue. But try explaining all that to a Spanish security guard at Fear o'clock — that he should blame Charles Darwin for the fact that I could barely stand up to stumble-mumble "*Donde esta el hotel?*" at which juncture he nodded to the building next to me which, indeed, was my hotel. Just as I had left it.

easySleep

I mooched out of next morning and into the elasticity of the sub-sequent afternoon — didn't go up in the cable car, didn't do much of anything. We did stand briefly in the queue for the Picasso museum before it dawned on us that to actually go inside would betray the wonky asymmetry of the weekend. Instead we took some time over lunch, cracking crustaceans and conversations, sinking slowly into terrace seats, staying perfectly still as the world walked past.

Never has it been so easy to get down with your bad self and become a member of the Euro jetset, the clubland glitterati, partying across this great continent like a plague in Patrick Cox. So if you are tiring some of your local McDisco, grab your passport and your euros, carjack your nearest easyJet and sink into the beauty of Europe's dancefloors. Gaudí himself couldn't have knocked up anything finer.
| *July 2002*

8
Gus Gus

REYKJAVIK: INTERVIEWING THE ESOTERIC ICELANDIC BAND GUS
GUS; BLUE LAGOON; A COACH CRASHES OFF A MOUNTAIN ROAD;
DEAD OR MERELY ASLEEP

"The concept is fairly easy to understand."

from the album sleeve, *Polydistortion*

Yeah right. Maybe it's easy to understand if you've got a belly full
of Icelandic firewater and a mouthful of dead sheep head... but that
was yet to come. Sitting in my apartment prior to the trip, listening
to fractious beats and skittish vocals, it was harder to get an angle on
what Gus Gus actually was. But if it was going to take a trip to Iceland to skate that angle then goddam it if I'm not gamer than a goose
who's game for a goosing. I've read some of the Icelandic sagas and
was more than prepared for a weekend saga of my own; preferably
of the ravaging, pillaging variety as opposed to the more recent 'Saga
holiday' version for coffin-dodging, incontinent old folk.

At the hotel just outside Reykjavik I ordered a beer and was introduced to the besuited Baldur Steffasson, Gus Gus manager, and the
Clooney-esque Magnus Jonsson, singer and guitarist. Baldur carried
with him a legendary reputation for fiscal prudence, with a wallet shut
tighter than Brooke Shields' legs. As such, he is the perfect manager.
He even danced his way out of a career in politics to immerse himself
in the politics of dancing: "It's marketing and selling," he revealed,
a little politician still in him (Robin Cook, perhaps). "It's qualitative
things instead of quantitative things, it's about selling things that you

33

Discombobulated

can't pinpoint, whether it's music or politics. It's about packaging, imaging, visual representation, philosophy."

Gus Gus are a modern take on Warhol's Factory: a nine piece production line with departments for music, production, visuals and business, and an end product that happens to be entertainment. If that sounds kooky, that may well be because Gus Gus were never meant to be a band in the first place. Filmmakers Stefan Arni and Siggi Kjartansson were casting for a short film called Pleasure. In producing the soundtrack for the movie, the members of the cast came together for ten days of madness and mischief which gave birth to the first album Polydistortion. That album made its way to the office of 4AD, who reeled them in like an Icelandic fisherman with a whale on the end of his line.

"Gus Gus is probably one of the few bands that were formed after they got offered a record deal," Baldur deadpanned.

With such a potent collection of wonderful weirdness, the outcome was bound to sound unshackled and original, as fresh as the fish they consume like packets of crisps (singer Hafdis later remarked that she eats dried fish at the cinema instead of popcorn). While *Polydistortion* sold 700 units in Iceland, it moved a couple of hundred thousand worldwide... and that's a lot of dried fish.

Gus Gus have spent more than a year on the second album, with the result that *This Is Normal* sounds more focused, homogenised. "I think it's probably a little bit more mature," said Baldur, "but I hope we haven't lost the soulful side, the playful elements. I think the beauty of it is that what totally keeps the band together is the philosophical interaction between us."

Without sounding drier than a cinema fish, there is certainly a political context to the group, a frisky intellect feeding the music and the way that music is constructed; a profoundly Utopian ideal that you can make music by committee, the very process of making music expanding outwards so you feel Baldur is ultimately going to implicate the whole of Iceland in what is fast becoming not so much a band as a conspiracy theory. "I've often said that it's the ultimate Socialist test," Baldur said, and while I'd be inclined to think Marx Lenin and Trotsky might have something to say about that, they would have to concede that in dealing with Imperialist Russia they had a easier beast to wrestle than the music industry.

In a typically bizarre Icelandic Friday night out, we started proceedings at a political 'party' (in both senses of the word) to launch the candidacy for one Jakob Magnusson, angling to become the MP for Reykjavik. Strange things were afoot indeed as I was introduced to Jakob, whose career included a spell in the band Ragga & The Jack Magic Orchestra, before a stint as the Icelandic Ambassador to London.

Suitably stranged-out we retired to Kaffi Barinn, the London Underground symbol indicating that this was the bar Blur's Damon Albarn bought into, after falling in love with Reykjavik. It was a comfortable, Hobbit-like hole, full of cold beer and warm company (the Icelandic people are descended from marauding Vikings who escaped Norway and the Irish slaves they took with them to fix drinks and trim the lawn... It's a rum concoction).

"It is a unique place," said Herb Legowitz, who along with Biggi Thorarinsson makes up the production/engineering arm of the Gus Gus Corporation. Herb has been DJing around Iceland for years, as well as remixing tracks with Biggi at the Gus Gus studios. The pair also enjoyed a previous incarnation as T-World and were brought into Gus Gus to add an electronic angle. True to the band's elasticity Biggi is also, wait for it... the accountant. Purple, the glorious floorquaker from *Polydistortion* was actually a T-World track from 93, many moons before Sasha remixed it.

"It must have been weird to have the track given the Sasha treatment?" I asked Herb.

"Everything is weird in Iceland," he replied, languidly. "And that's the reason why the band is so weird," Biggi added. "It's basically some cinema people with some actors who are singers, and then me and Herb Legowitz... because nobody else knew how to work any instruments."

"And this is normal?" I quizzed.

"But it is normal!" Herb replied.

The next day Rachel Photos disappeared to do her click-click thing with the band while I decided to walk through the snow into

Discombobulated

Reykjavik for a good mooch. Before we finished breakfast I asked Maggi what there was to do in Reykjavik.

"Do?" He looked befuddled, as if I'd suggested we go nude sledding.

Soon I began to understand. After arriving in a new city I like to get myself lost — wandering the streets and finding your way out is a great way of getting to know a place. But getting lost is impossible in Reykjavik — every few minutes you turn a corner and end up somewhere you recognise. And yet on another occasion you'd turn a different corner and there'd be a gargantuan glacier at the end of the street (where Jules Verne's heroes began their journey to the centre of the earth). The day was cold enough to crack the ice in a double scotch but I decided on advice that the thing to do was sit in a café and watch the world go by, which I proceeded to do, enjoying three big cups of the best mocha I've ever had, leaving the establishment so wired on caffeine that there and then I felt like donning a horned helmet and going on a Viking rampage of my own.

Fortunately it was Saturday night. At the hotel we were joined by a bunch of industry types just off the plane from the UK, among their number Rajesh Merchandani, a presenter for BBC's *O-Zone*, who I hadn't seen since our school days. And if seeing him walking into a hotel lobby outside Reykjavik wasn't weird enough, the ride out to the ski lodge was truly bizarre — driving through a white blizzard as if we were driving straight up the nose of Liam Gallagher.

At the lodge the band indulged us with a playback of *This Is Normal* — a visceral slice of melodic dance music and iced pop — while I munched on dead sheep head (the tongue and cheek are very appetising) and also shark, which apparently is buried in the ground for a year and urinated on, to keep it fresh. Like the saying goes: When in Rome... eat pizza.

By this point I was more than a little sozzled, with the profoundly pungent aroma of dead sheep and pissed-on shark mulling about my head. I made it back onto the bus — just — but then fell into a deep, wonderful slumber. My next memory still strikes me as a dream. I was stumbling through the snow, my feet sinking deep into the fluffy duvet covering the island. Through a blizzard of flakes that fell like cocaine dandruff from the nose of heaven, I saw two ethereal lights piercing the blackness. I thought I had died, that I was approaching the pearly gates only, the lights transmogrified into the headlights of another bus, which I clambered onto.

I slumped next to Rachel. "Just what the fuck is going on?" I said, angry at finding myself so rudely awakened.

"Simon, we just crashed."

I've since pieced together what happened via a patchwork of stories. Apparently the bus skidded off the road and ended up hanging over the edge, in a manoeuvre reminiscent of the last scene from *The Italian Job*, except we're talking about a few feet here, not a few hundred. Everyone was hurried from the bus; no one could wake me up. After half an hour of shouting and tugging, they left me there, perhaps the necessary ballast to keep the bus from tipping over and tumbling down the mountain.

On the way to the airport the following day we stopped off at the Blue Lagoon, a naturally formed hot pool in the middle of the Icelandic tundra like an ice blue swimming pool in the bleached backyard of one of Hockney's LA paintings. It's quite a vibe to step out of the changing rooms, as if in your local pool, only to emerge like Mr Ben into a brave new world — an exotic, preternatural moonscape formed, essentially, of lava with moss on top. Then, freezing, you step into the crystal blue lagoon and into water almost boiling — visibly boiling — so that you're sat there, trying to get your head round the incongruity of it all, meanwhile fast becoming an integral part of a human soup. And diving down to the bottom you can scoop up soft, grey mud and apply it to your face, which Rachel proceeded to do, emerging from the depths like the Creature from the Blue Lagoon.

Lying in the lagoon offered the opportunity to catch up with the other two singers with the band — Daniel Agust and Hafdis Huld. Daniel already had eight gold albums tucked under his belt by the time he joined Gus Gus. "At first I didn't think that you could make music through a machine," he said, floating back in the water. "I was affected by the former approach of making music, which was in a traditional rock band. Squeezing my songs into a computer was quite a task for me in the beginning."

Discombobulated

"And if you bring a song into Gus Gus then you have to be ready to hear it change," chirped Hafdis Huld, the elfin teenage singer who seemed to contain more potential energy within her frame than the national grid. Her heavy, pronounced accent was hypnotising, rolling over the vowels as though she were sledding down a hill. "You have to be able to communicate or else you can't be working in such a big group."

The waters of the Blue Lagoon had a certain toxicity that melted my neural spark plugs and I spent the rest of the day in a semi-hypnotic fug. As much as everyone in the band tried to persuade me otherwise, this could not be passed off as normal. It's not normal to have a singer who also plays the part of Benny in the Icelandic dubbed version of *Top Cat*; it's not normal for a teenage schoolgirl and occasional Sunday school teacher to be allowed time off school to tour the world with a band; it's not normal to have a singer who as a sideline performs as a drag queen; it's not normal to have one of the main music producers avoid playing live with the band, while people who have no input musically appear on stage; it's not normal to have a band member who catches fish as big as a man by punching their lights out; or goes to New York, is spotted by legendary photographer Herb Ritts and ends up working as a model; it's not normal that something this good comes out of an isolated island in the outer suburbs of Europe when, if you got the entire population of Switzerland in a barn for jam, they couldn't come up with a band half as good as Steps.

No, none of this if normal. And that's why it's wonderful. | *January 1999*

Ibiza Xbox 9

I'm a hard living, hard drinking writer at the Gates of Dawn. My pen is full to bursting with juice and I take no prisoners. I'm gonna come round your yard, drink your women and seduce your booze... something like that... anyway the point is I can outwrite Kerouac... I can outparty Jagger... I can... I can...

A knock on the door cracks the fabric of my reverie; my mother's voice shatters my dream. "Simon darling, I've been thinking — there's no point you messing around with tubes and trains — why don't I just drive you to the airport?"

It was five thirty in the a.m., I was stopping at Mrs M's en route to Ibiza, the world looked weird and I was in no mood to argue. It merely rendered it somewhat embarrassing to meet writers from the other magazines at Stansted at some rude hour, and field the question "so how did you get here?" with the reply "my mummy drove me to the front door." It was the media equivalent of being mollycoddled on your first day at the big school — she may as well have well wiped the corners of my mouth with a spittle dampened hankie.

But nothing could be certain in these gruesome, Godless times. Microsoft had invited a random gaggle of the media to spend a night in a villa up in the hills above Ibiza Town, playing some of the new games to be released in the run up to Christmas. I immediately threw something of a spanner in the well oiled works of the Microsoft PR machine by deciding to stick around after that night and remain on

Discombobulated

the island as long as everyone could deal with both myself and my increasingly fragile hold on reality. I needed to track down my best friend from the two summers I spent living on the island — Simon Drake. When I first met him I was the editor of a magazine in Ibiza and he was one of our distributors. By the end of that summer he had acquired a Porsche and a bar, whilst I had acquired a nervous twitch and a violent phobia of trees. I subsequently drunk so much from his bar, QPQ, that I ended up in contention for the role of best man at his wedding last year. In the end I couldn't even make it to the island and Lord alone knows what he'd made of that whole debacle, because we hadn't spoken since. I had no contact details for him at all, which freaked my mother out completely; she couldn't get her head around the concept of merely mooching about an island until you bump into someone you need to crash with. But I understand how Ibiza works... or rather, doesn't. It's coast to coast serendipity — you just kickback, take your mind off it all and relax. These things have a habit of working themselves out.

"Jesus, I didn't think you were allowed back on the island!"

Charmed, I'm sure. I had only just picked up my Imelda Marcos sized suitcase, walked out of Ibiza airport and climbed aboard the people carrier when the driver barked out his greeting.

"I'm terribly sorry, do I know you?"

"Sure, I did some distribution with Simon the first year you were here."

"You know Simon Drake?"

"Sure."

Bingo. Not half an hour on the island and the connection was made; the pieces of my fiendish puzzle were starting to fall into place.

At the villa I dived into the pool and did the aquatic mooch until the sun slipped behind the hills. By the time I climbed out, the barbecue had been fired up and guests were turning up for the evening — Mike and Claire Manumission, with their son Stanley and their new progeny; Lenny Ibizarre, who DJd with someone I can only describe as a better looking Yoko Ono; Rui da Silva, Darren Hughes. A rum blend. By the time we'd finished dinner the darkness had formed a blue curtain behind plasma screens that had been set up on the terrace, and jousting commenced on the various Xbox games. Mike and Stanley Manumission did battle on the game version of *Buffy The Vampire Slayer*; I played *Splinter Cell*, which involved a lot of stealth and cunning and steadier finger than mine; Rachel Photos played a game that seemed to involve bashing dinosaurs over the head with a big stick.

After satiating the desire to kick the heavenly doo-dah out of one another in any bountiful number of ways, we headed into town — to a couple of bars on the port and then to Pacha, possibly the most wonderful place to spend an evening this planet has to offer. I managed to round off my embarrassment by giving it the Extra Large One with the other journalists, in a kind of "yeah I used to live here actually, let me show you round the club" and then promptly leading everyone straight into a dead end on the VIP balcony. After that it got a little hazy — *uno poco disco loco* — and I woke up at some stage late the following afternoon to discover I'd lost all my credit and debit cards (it transpired someone had used one to buy a round of drinks that came to £200... actually quite impressive) and I was left with nothing but a burning desire to spend the afternoon in the pool with a bottle of rosé.

Everyone else was heading back to the UK that evening and I also had to vacate the premises; some bigwigs from Microsoft were coming in for a meeting and everyone had to be out of the villa. I went up to my room to start packing, start figuring my next move. OK, so I had Simon's number but no means of getting there, or any idea where there might be. It was sometime around 7pm. Pack man, at least pack. With arcade games occupying the frontal lobe of my imagination I put two shirts into the chasm of my case (pacman, at least pac) and was already tired. I lay down a while on one of the twin beds in the room; let my eyelids slowly, slowly drift down over my eyes, like freshly washed sheets on a summer lawn. Nice...

...My eyes snapped open. It was dark; really, impenetrably dark. And quiet — a deafening quietness that overwhelmed the small room. This... this was not good. Checked watch. 3am. All the other journal-

Discombobulated

ists had left hours ago and I was now alone, home alone, save for the dudes from Microsoft who had flown in for their meeting. I locked my door from the inside and tried to think... for the love of God man, THINK! I looked around the room for ways out of this perilous predicament but every which way I shaped it I came back to the same conclusion — I was goosed. I could hear voices; someone tried the handle from the outside. Gadzooks this was a bad scene. It could be anyone. It could be Bill Gates, ferchrisakkes. I'VE UPSET BILL GATES! One word from him and my life would unravel like a ball of string tied to a Microsoft mouse.

Sweat oozed from my pores as I lay back on the bed. Strange images played upon the plasma screen at the back of my eyes. Bill Gates crawling around the villa complex, using all the stealth tactics he had learned from *Splinter Cell*, finding the combination to my room and...

... when my eyes opened again it was morning and a bright light cut through the fabric of the curtains. I had been asleep, or thereabouts, for fifteen straight hours and I needed to get out. I'd pushed the good people of Microsoft too far this time. But I should at least shower first and put a brave and fresh face to it. As I dried off I noticed something written on the towel. "Can Simon". Just two words. "Can"... "Simon". What in the name of Satan's paisley pyjamas does that mean? Can Simon what, exactly? Can Simon get the hell outta here before the full force of Microsoft's foot is planted squarely upon his behind, sending him spiralling into the outer reaches of cyberspace? Had Bill Gates already been informed of my overstay? Already sent people into my room to contact me via cryptic messages on my towel? Jeepers this was clearly getting out of hand.

I unlocked the door cagily and stepped out onto the terrace.

"Simon, you're still here!"

It was Barbara, the PR lady who had been looking after us for the weekend.

"Yeah... I kind of overslept back there."

"Everyone thought you'd left without saying goodbye. They've taken your flight tickets back to England."

"Oh."

"Would you like some scrambled eggs?"

"Sure."

And so, to quote Austin Powers, that plane had sailed. I was stranded in Ibiza. Nowhere to sleep, my credit cards in someone else's pocket, my flight home flown home. I caught a lift into Ibiza Town with Barbara. As we pulled out of the drive I noticed our villa was called Can Simon, which at least unravelled that particular puzzle. In Ibiza Town I found a bar on the port and ordered a beer. I noticed I'd started smoking again. | *September 2002*

10
Naples

"Braaaccceee!" Marco barked in his rotund English accent, gripping hard onto the car seat in front of him.

I half opened one eye. Oh, you have got to be kidding me... not again. The girl in the front passenger seat screamed. Antonio struggled to control the car but it was already aquaplaning on the shiny street, skidding fast towards a post.

"Brace," Marco repeated, readying himself for impact. I was still half asleep — unsure of how to distinguish landscape from dreamscape — enveloped in the warm blanket of a post-club slumber. *Crunch*.

It was always going to be a bumpy ride, I knew that soon as I touched down on the Friday evening. Naples with the Manchester DJ Jimmy Bell. Our mission: to hook up with our friend, the DJ and promoter Marco di Marzo. Our objective: to spend a weekend partying and playing records and living *la dolce vita*. Marco is one of those people you meet at the other end of a random handshake, who become fast friends. Marco is Good People. And there he was, at the arrivals gate, helping carry our bags to the car, driving to his mum's apartment, in a seaside resort called Villago di Coppolla.

"Napoli is a good place for house music in the world," Marco explained, as we sat down to eat at the Trattoria Medina, "Neapolitan people are really, really hot. They like the good music."

A couple of bars later and we wound up in this jazz club, watching the band tear it up on the stage, talking to American soldiers and getting tanked. I don't recall what time we left the place; it was closing, I think. Jimmy had been asleep on a couch for hours; the staff putting the chairs up on the tables around him. Marco's friend Tony di Matteo DJd, keeping the dying embers of the night alight. Outside we wound up at the Piazza Municipio, a square where the cognoscenti of the city gather to talk and eat ice cream as nighttime melts into morning. It was a strange cultural gear shift — in the UK the weather engenders that post-club ritual of nuclear "back-to-mine" meltdowns full of tea and biscuits, of left over chemicals and radiators ramped up to 11. In Naples it's different for two reasons: The weather means you can disco al fresco, and most of the people I partied with live with their parents — even the most liberal of mamas Italiano wouldn't appreciate a bunch of rave gibbons pitching camp in their livingroom come six in the morning.

So they do a lot of standing around in Naples — people revving up on scooters; humans coming and going; arguments and romance unfolding in the empty piazzas of the city. But eventually, as the first chink of dawn penetrated the fabric of our evening, we climbed into this guy Antonio's car and I fell asleep in the back. Then... *Crunch.* And that's how I started my first morning — wrapped around a pole in an empty backstreet in an industrial part of Naples. Marco called Tony to come pick us up; when he arrived it transpired that, on the way, he had crashed his car as well. "Please," I implored, "will everyone... just... please... stop... crashing... their cars."

I didn't wake up until five the next afternoon. Me and Jimmy were on camp beds in Marco's bedroom and we lay there a while, nursing our injuries and talking, like kids on a school trip. Being in a car wreck with someone immediately puts your relationship on a completely different footing and I could now understand what military veterans are on about — this was another skirmish in the Disco Wars — we survived it together.

Jimmy, apart from being an absolutely hilarious kook, is also part of the Garage Council, formed of three guys from the northwest of England and one from Chicago. "We've been going for about three years," Jimmy explained, rubbing his wounded knee. "We became friends and started working together, remixing records and DJing in Chicago and all over the place. We all play different, though. Sony Miguel plays soulful, Alex West plays vocal house, I play deeper and Swank is deeper than me. When we play together, as four, we play all the way through house."

The first Garage Council tracks have been monster monster Funkzilla grooves, generating interest from the likes of Music For Freaks. Believe. This scene may be getting tired for some hacks and jocks; for others, the adventure is just beginning: "This time last year I'd just played in Manchester, I'd never travelled," Jimmy grinned. He's now played the States three times and along with Marco has created a kind of Bermuda Triangle linking Manchester, Naples and the Supperclub in Amsterdam — a kind of pan-European game of disco swapsies.

A couple of cups of Marco's chewy Neapolitan coffee fired up the funk furnace and I was all set for Saturday night, to be spent at the club History. History is a disco bellisimo. A balcony hugs a large central dancefloor, with another room behind a huge glass window, allowing the VIPs to survey what's going on, like Caesar giving the thumbs up to the gladiators on the dancefloor. The club soon swelled with humans — of the extremely attractive, olive skinned Italian variety. Goddamn this anaemic north European skin, I bemoaned, as Jimmy plugged in his headphones and pressed play, fusing Garage Council tracks with deep US and UK cuts. The dancefloor lapped it up, whatever language it was in. An MC called Malk got on the mic to add a somewhat camp commentary to the proceedings, asking the crowd to give it up for "Jeemee Belle" and "*Sighmon* from the *deejay margarzeene*". On the stage, dancers writhed to the music — impossibly gorgeous creatures in catwalk couture — at times difficult to define from the denizens of the dancefloor.

I detected another cultural difference: that Italians don't seem to fully comprehend the subtle nuances and simple pleasures to be had from the excessive consumption of liquor. I couldn't even work out how to get a drink — quite aside from the linguistic hoops through which I had to jump, people weren't paying with euros, but tokens.

Stumbling about the place, trying to find out where one might acquire some of these mythical tokens I took a wrong turn and ended up outside the whole bastard building. Discombobulated, I turned to get back in, only to be confronted by this slab of a doorman who thought I was trying it on. Eventually he took pity — as much, I'm sure, to get me out of his sight as anything else. I partied through the night with random and very friendly Italians and eventually it was just me and the dancefloor, as Marco smoothed off the edges of the night with his trademark deep down and dirty music.

As we piled back into a car (all thoughts of the morning's crash but a vague and distant memory) I sat in the middle of the backseat and mithered Marco like some belligerent brat.

"Where's the afterparty?"

Marco chuckled. "*Sighmon*, for this question — there is no party now, we go home."

"Home? Home is not an option." At that moment we passed the airport.

"Kindly drop me right here. I want to catch a plane to Wigan. They have nice pies in Wigan. I want to fly to Wigan to eat a pie."

Next morning. I awoke, surprisingly clearheaded, and grabbed my book, taking a stroll down to the harbour — past the yachts gently resting on the water's crust; past the derelict promenade of cafés and bars that hinted of past glories for this city by the sea; onto the beach, finding some rocks to nestle into like a literary limpet.

I had been there maybe twenty minutes when I heard the words "Hey, *deejay margarzeene*" carried on a coastal breeze. I looked up to see Jeemee and Marco clambering over the rocks, big grins on their faces, calling me in for lunch. Marco's mum cooked up an amazing lasagne (ahhh just-a like-a mama used to make), washed down with some vino rosso, and after it had settled we drove back into Naples for one last evening. From high up in the hills above the city, the bay curved gracefully like a shawl across a woman's shoulders. Naples is an extremely beautiful city and I realised at that moment that conventional medicine has let me down on two counts: I remain an incurable alcoholic, and an incurable romantic. As such, Naples is

Discombobulated

a good place for me to be and I will be back, I have no doubt about that. The music is too good... the people are too beautiful... Marco is too important a friend... and his mum's lasagne is too perfect to even contemplate a future without the city of Naples.

But if I were writing a travel guide I would heartily counsel against getting into a car, post-club, with a half cut Italian with delusional notions of driving like Giancarlo Fisichella. Be warned: in this part of Italy there are secret dangers beyond the belching boil of Vesuvius. | *January 2004*

11
Stockholm

We stepped off the plane and I massaged my lungs with Swedish air. *Ahhhh*, come to daddy — that's the good stuff. I love the smell of Europe in the morning. I love being European, period. You can keep your Down Under down under... give me the cramped claustrophobia of my comfy continent anytime.

Just take a look around — whichever suburb of Europe you're in — and tell me this isn't the most deliciously wrong continent on the planet. We're all kicking about the same piece of land, no one knows what the chicken scratch anyone else is on about, and we're all mad as a box of incontinent badgers. From a city like Seville in the south to Stockholm in Scandinavia we've got it all, us Europeans, in buckets and spades.

I guess at this juncture it is beholden upon me to explain what the Volvo-Eriksson-Abba-Ljungberg we were doing in Stockholm... and it wasn't because they'd run out of tablelamps in my local Ikea. No, we were guests of Absolut vodka which, I presumed, would involve the good people of that most venerated of companies pouring copious quantities of the booze down this bozo's neck.

Absolut had accompanied us on the journey to Sweden; thus and therefore I didn't feel it appropriate to tell them... well... shucks I don't actually drink vodka. Despite being a self-confessed lush, I pretty much skate a merry dance betwixt beer, red wine, scotch and gin (and that's before brunch) and for some reason never really liked the spud stuff. But free is my favourite price and I'll drink lighter fluid when it costs that much.

OK, brace yourself for the PR bit: Absolut have always been a funky kind of a brand, with a groovy Scandinavian bent. Appreciating the pervasive role electronic music plays in contemporary culture, they commissioned three producers to create three tracks that in some way reflected the distinctive stout, square necked bottle that encases their lovely boozes.

Now, the less generous amongst you might be thinking... corporate art wank. But hold onto your Hoegaarden, folks, because these things have to be worth investigating...

The three producers were Rollercone from Switzerland, Aril Brikha from Stockholm and Taxi from, erm, Norwich. Nowt wrong with Norwich, but I chose to chat to Brikha because out of the three I thought he may be able to give me the lowdown on the locals.

We shuffled into a top floor room of the Bern Hotel (when I first saw that on my itinerary I wasn't sure if that was its name or yet another instruction from the voices... I can't, Master... please don't ask me that... I told you last time... get out of my head... exit swiftly via the ear to your left.) Brikha chose to take the brief literally, downloading the image of the bottle from the website, running it through a programme and converting the image into sound (if you really need to know, the Absolut bottle sounds a little like a cyber fax machine), using it as the intro and outro to the piece. If you run the music through an oscilloscope you'll see the bottle, composed of pretty green lines like a cardiovascular Absolut heartbeat.

Of course, one might be tempted to say '...*and?*', but that would be a little ungracious and I don't get like that until much later in the evening. Plus, the music was good, Brikha was a personable kind of chap and seemed to share the same reservations: "I took some convincing because at first I thought it would be like a jingle sort of thing. I didn't want to have an obvious vocal in it, saying Absolut... or vodka... or whatever. I wanted to give it a futuristic twist." Brikha studied keyboard from the age of seven, getting into UK synth-pop and buying an Atari "because Martin Gore had one" He began to make music himself, a kind of electronic lone ranger until his friends began buying imported records and told him what he was making was Detroit techno.

"I basically love everything from there," he eulogised. "It's something that appeals to me more. It feels like it has more soul, or something behind it, rather than just being made for the dancefloor."

Brikha tried for three years to get tracks released in Sweden. It took him three days once he'd sent stuff to Detroit, and he's played there live three times this year — not once in his native Sweden.

"I don't know what the problem is," he quipped, "but that pretty much says it all about clubland in Sweden." Apparently it's not exactly kicking in downtown Stockholm. "Sometimes you miss going out," he conceded, "and, as I would say in Swedish, getting raped by a kickdrum."

Ah yes, what the Scandinavians were once famous for, in the days when men were real men, with long blonde hair and beards... and I'm not talking about Benny and Björn — I'm talking about the Vikings and their obsession with the incessant raping and pillaging. You don't see much of it about these days — the former has been boxed off by premiership footballers and anyway, it's more the pillaging I'm interested in. How might a young gentlemen such as myself get into a bit of pillaging? Is there, perhaps, some nightclass I might attend? "An Introduction to Pillaging," with Mr Binding, straight down the corridor, third door on the left...

With that thought heavy on my mind, I took an afternoon stroll, over the bridge to the Old Town, almost impossibly cute: quiet cobbled streets leading down narrow lanes fronted by boutiques and bars, connecting old higgledy-piggledy squares where serene Swedes sat out on terraces and drank from large cups of coffee. The place was beautiful, the people were beautiful — it gave me the Fear. No wonder they don't want the rude throb of dance music shattering their delightful tranquillity. If I lived there I wouldn't be doing no disco dancing, no siree — I'd be shacked up some place with a bottle of schnapps and a couple of the local lasses and you wouldn't see me for a month of Sundays.

That night we strolled along the harbour to a boat that was to take us to a distant, deserted factory where the evening's action was to un-

Discombobulated

fold — so neo-industrial, so overtly postmodern I thought I'd walked into a Derek Jarman film. It was, like, cool and everything, but there was a press conference moment that was pure nonsense and left me thinking: Life is far too short and trivial to get bogged down in the academic minutiae of music... better to crank it up to 11 and start breaking furniture.

On the one hand, I could enter into a philosophical discourse re: the absolute versus the relative; about how, at least in epistemological terms, absolute denotes the certain or indubitable as opposed to probable or hypothetical; about the progression of concept from the Greeks through to the idealism of GM Hegel. On the other, I could head for the bar, fix myself a drink, gorge myself giddy and make like a one-armed circus freak at a bachelor party.

In the end it was a little bit of both — they led us into a huge white cube construction, each of us told to don a set of white headphones while, in the centre of the room the producers of the three tracks played them live and the accompanying videos were projected onto the sides of the cubes. The scene was surreal: Everyone in white headphones like cybermen, nodding their heads to invisible music. It was a DJ dalek convention.

Back on the boat the choppiness of the water made me aware for the first time of how damned drunk I'd gotten myself (one blames the overdose of culture, not vodka). I vaguely remember the walk back to the hotel and I can just about recall the afterparty, dancing around a bit, failing fast, being put to bed by a helpful Viking lady who raped and pillaged me for a bit before we fell asleep.

The next morning I awoke, amused and bemused to note two presents had been left in my room: a bottle of Absolut and an umbrella. Kind of a strange combination, don't you think? Maybe I was supposed to open the umbrella and then have someone pour the vodka onto it from an upper storey window. Who knows? These are tit-twisted times in which we live, disco amigos, and almost anything is possible, especially in a place like Sweden, which is unhinged in a way you can't quite put your finger on. And I like that. A flat packed approach to reality — you think you know where you are with the thing, but then there's always that one screw missing. | *October 2003*

12
The Politics of Dancing

WHY DO HUMANS LIKE TO GATHER TOGETHER IN CERTAIN
BUILDINGS AND BOUNCE AROUND TILL DAWN? AND WHY DOES
AUTHORITY HAVE SUCH A PROBLEM WITH IT? HERE'S WHY...

"... the politics of oo-oo-oo-oo... feeling good."

"Oh do shut your neck, Morrison — just rack 'em and stack 'em, why don't you." He looked at me with daggers, as though I had not the singing voice of an angel but had enquired instead whether he would like to have loud sex with several small farmyard animals.

I looked around me. Disco detritus. The nuclear fallout from New Year's Eve; the whole planet locked into one shared slump. Bodies slumped over the couch; couch slumped on the floor; floor slumped in my apartment; my apartment slumped in a corner of a city; cities slumped all over the planet. A livingroom of human bodies — post-millennial explorers, sliding down life's slip road into the outer suburbs of experience.

"Sorry, who's getting married?"

"For the love of God, man, no one's getting married!"

Jeepers. I was sure someone was getting married... perhaps the thought was only a remnant from a conversation long since lapsed into obscurity. I do enjoy these post-club meltdowns — imaginations snapping free from all moorings; conversations moving so fast your brain is like a computer running Windows — one conversation opened on top of another not yet finished, parallel programs, tracking

53

back to ideas already deleted. I was messed up, no doubt about that. I had done a real good job on myself, my brains splattered to the four corners of the universe. Or at least the four corners of the livingroom. I wanted to verbalise what I was thinking, but I'd forgotten what that was. I do remember thinking that with all this talk of marriage I was the kind of fella who would suit having an ex-wife; and whether that was technically possible without first having had a wife...

...And I was thinking how strange it was that the whole planet had collectively joined in a round-the-clock ding dong of a disco the night before. I mean, let's break it down here: What exactly were we doing... really? Rounding off the year with a few hours of physical exuberance; collecting with a number of like minded individuals in certain quarantined zones to move our bodies in a rhythmic way before going home to discombobulate on the livingroom carpet. I mean, what's up with that?

Picture this scene, and see whether it means anything to you: It's New Year's Eve and you've been in the bath so long your toes are webbed. Then you're in front of the mirror, with enough CFCs in your hair to blow a hole in the Ozone layer the size of Lisa Riley's fat arse and enough perfume on your person to floor a rhino at fifty paces. You take your favourite shirt from its sacred hanger in the alter of your wardrobe and all of a sudden you get that tingly sensation, as if Hannah from S Club were blowing softly onto the nape of your neck, a sensation born from the thought of the pleasures that lie ahead... or the beach load of Persians that have found their way up your hooter. Either way, there's a dancefloor with your name on it and no one's getting in your way. The dancefloor. The magic carpet ride that carries you out of reality through a blur of tunes and twitching bodies.

I know I got into dance music for what it did to my legs as well as my head and it stands to reason that — unless you're a DJ in a large anorak — you may well agree. You see life most clearly through the bottom of a glass, from the epicentre of a dancefloor, not by standing next to a DJ with a notebook in hand, trying to work out the last time Pete Tong took a crap. Dancing. What a strange way to get around. It is, of course, a pure form of communication; it's a non verbal language all of its own that connects people, through an expression of mood and feeling. Dancing is, at the same time, the greatest abstraction while also a way of expressing something that can't be expressed in other ways. The dancefloor is a great parliament of feet and voices — everyone has equal access to both observe and engage in its performance.

Wow. Try thinking of all of that when you can't even lie on your livingroom floor without holding on. But I like to connect the dots at times like this; make that visual connection between ravers pogo-ing in circles around the dancefloor, and Native Americans pogo-ing in circles around a fire, all of them patting their mouth with the palm of one hand. Similarly, cast your minds back to the heady days of breakdancing — the collection of peers encircling two people in the middle, in an act of sublimated fighting that mimics dance forms like Capoeria.

Our dance music revolution makes Russia, 1917, look like a garden party. It's taken us back to our primal instincts — a concrete jungle sprouting grass roots — we've just invented different machines to beat out the same rhythms. I dance... you dance... he/she dances. Put that in your crack pipe and conjugate it. But still, the thought remained: Why? It's all very well going down to Liverpool's Chibuku Shake Shake because we want to shake shake with other souls, but what's driving us there?

The rusted cogwheels in my brain continued to turn. There's a pseudosexual aspect — sublimated copulation. Think back to your session in front of the mirror on New Year's Eve — singing into your hairbrush, dancing around in your pants — tarting yourself up. Is that not at least partly about modes of display and attraction? It's the peacock's feathers syndrome; it's about showing yourself on the dancefloor, displaying yourself in a conspicuous way... trying to attract a mate, perchance? From Dome to Dominion I challenge you to find a New Year party where that wasn't a factor. You're selling your genes, aren't you? Or rather you're selling what's inside your jeans. And there you have it — the dancefloor is the H&M of humanity.

And then again, the sensation of moving itself, whether you're on a rollercoaster or a seesaw, a rocking chair or a dancefloor, is something people seem to find pleasurable. Why? Grab a nearby scientist

Discombobulated

and he'll tell you the vibrations caused by music in the ear activates other organs, triggers reflexes in muscles, such as tapping your foot in time to the music, or pogo-ing round a dancefloor like a goonball. Loud sound also opens up the pathway to the hypothalamus, the pleasure centre in the brain, and seratonin is your transport to the ultimate destination. Conclusion? Music causes movement causes pleasure. In other words, we wouldn't dance unless there was a reason for doing it, and mother nature has made dancing a pleasurable experience because it's a way of bringing people together for community, celebration and procreation.

Dancing is as central to human experience as eating, breathing and supporting Arsenal. Central to everyone... and yet terrifying to some. For instance, why were Puritans so scared of us dancing around maypoles? Why were Americans so shocked by Elvis and his pelvis? Hold on to your sombreros, *mi disco amigos*, I'm fast aquaplaning towards a conclusion here because, while at first glance politics and dancing may seem mutually exclusive activities ("politics" and "dancing" are not words that sit together well — sort of like "Fame", "Academy" and "talent"), there is more than meets the eye to these unlikely bedfellows. For instance, politics is something you can indulge in individually to affect the wider world; similarly dancing is an individual activity that transcendentally affects the feel of the dancefloor. And if there's a right wing to politics, then it stands to reason there's got to be a Wrong Wing, right?

So, if you'll allow me the space for a Party Political Broadcast from the Wrong Party, on that new morning it dawned on me we are collectively staring down the barrel of a fucking frightening year. I may see the planet as one big dancefloor, but it seems some other folks don't want to dance. I think it was the Specials who sang: *"This town / is coming like a ghost town / bands don't play no more / Too much fighting on the dancefloor."* Well, to paraphrase Michael Jackson, another well known American psycho, I'm a writer not a fighter so politicians, let's cut a deal here. I won't come down to Westminster and tell you off for fiddling the books while London burns; and I won't gatecrash the White House and accuse Bush of being a warmongering oil baron dude. I won't do all this, and in return all you

56

have to do is drop the bravado not the bomb. C'mon it's so old... so 1990s. Instead, let's get Bush and Saddam into a disco and settle this like men... with a dance off. Get those two out of their pinstripe suits and encourage them to bust some shapes on destiny's dancefloor, indulge in a little line dance of the chemical variety.

When it comes down to a choice between dancefloor and battlefield, if you're asking... then I'm dancing. | *January 2003*

13
Oh, Vienna

ON GUARD AGAINST THE AVANT-GARDE. WORLD WAR III BREAKS
OUT AROUND THE DINNERTABLE BETWEEN THE YANKS AND THE
LIMIES

Silence. Sometimes the most incredible noise in the world. I'm not entirely sure what four minutes and thirty three seconds of the stuff is supposed to represent, but I was tickled to the gills by a story in the *Herald Tribune*, ingested on the flight to Vienna. The avant-garde composer John Cage's "composition" for the piano, the track 4'33" — consisting of four minutes and thirty three seconds of brilliant silence — was the subject of a court case regarding plagiarism. The publisher of 4'33" took one Mike Batt to court, accusing his track A Minute's Silence of plagiarising Cage's silence, principally because Batt credited his track to Batt/Cage; a situation made more surreal by the fact we're talking about Mike Batt... of The Wombles. And you know what? Cage won. I was struck dumb, if you'll excuse the phrase, by the whole concept of the ownership of silence, but inspired to further garrulous chuckles by the *Tribune*'s final line: "The parties had tried to prove their points with performances of both pieces. The results were inconclusive."

The story seemed nothing but gentle amusement at first, but the silence eventually became deafening, the soundtrack to my time in Vienna; white noise against which I could sketch my thoughts. For Vienna is undergoing something of a cultural renaissance. And we're not talking the drapes and Digweed kind of Renaissance here but a real seismic shift in musical ideas, based around what I can only

58

describe as neoclassical electronica. Vienna has always been one of the most culturally important cities in Europe — Mozart, Beethoven, Strauss, all dancefloor denizens of their day, even if the chosen delivery of the 4/4 in the mid nineteenth century was operatic rather than ravetastic. Beethoven lived in sixty seven homes in the thirty five years he lived in Vienna. Why he felt compelled to move twice a year is hard to fathom. It could hardly be because of the neighbours' noise — a thought that led me to conclude Beethoven would have approved of 4′33″. And he would have undoubtedly liked the Wombles' version best. Elsewhere, the home of Johan Strauss is now a McDonald's.

Vienna remains a beautiful city; a grand dame amongst European cities, its history locked into the curves of Baroque architecture. On the first day we were shown both the old city and newer developments over the Danube; new music evolving within the envelope of a new city. Lunch was at the Restaurant Palmenhaus, a huge conservatory structure with a butterfly house on one side, a palmery on the other and us in the middle, drinking schtum — a semi-distilled wine that is only in season for two weeks, after which time it explodes if you don't uncork the bottle. I sat with the American press contingent, from *Wire* magazine amongst others; nice enough folks, if a little earnest. We got to talking war and *Rolling Stone*, and the fact it's now edited by an Englishman.

"He'll probably start putting naked ladies on the cover," smirked one of the Americans.

Snap. I placed my knife and fork calmly on the table. "Instead of turning Johan Strauss' house into a fucking McDonald's, giving us Billy Ray fucking Cyrus, killing John Lennon and DRAGGING THE WORLD INTO A FUCKING WAR THAT NO ONE UNDERSTANDS?"

OK, so maybe I didn't say that but, again, silence is louder than bombs. Regrettably, I have this terribly oily cod and chip on my shoulder when it comes to flippant remarks and casual assumptions about culture. And that edginess carried into evening, when we were taken to a well formed building housing MICA, the Music Information Center Austria. MICA is a resource centre dedicated to assisting Austrian musicians evolve their electronic sound. A commendable

Discombobulated

idea for sure, but as we sat politely and were played snatches of electronic music, I couldn't get over the feeling that I was in a lecture; that the overwhelming seriousness with which this was being treated was all a bit of a joke. When people start to intellectualise music you suck the juice out of the thing; leave it withered, desiccated, sterile. It's an anarchic animal — you can't tame it with the whips of academia or the cage of intellect — you can't have conference calls about it, or make it by committee. And isn't music supposed to be musical? Did I sleep through that meeting? I could accept this stuff as art maybe but music should move the heart or the feet... I'm not sure what happens when it hits the brain. The Americans took notes. I felt like standing up and saying, "Hi, I am a conceptual artist known only as Crust. I wear a plant pot on my head and make music using my arse." I'm sure I would have received a standing ovation.

I was twitchy and on edge. After a superb meal in the Chrinor, with the guys from the Viennese label Couch, we headed out into the city — to the Guertel — the Red Light District — where the best booze and sleaze is always to be found. At some stage I was in the Rhiz, a club formed from the Stadtban arches. A kid sat on stage, producing music using a Gameboy. I don't recall how I got home.

The next morning I awoke a little discombobulated, with a half-finished scotch on my bedside cabinet and the TV still on. I leant up and switched over to CNN to see if the war was on. Apparently not. Slightly let down, I headed to the museum quarter and the newly opened Quartier21 — an arts complex housed in the old Imperial stables. Much of Quartier21 is devoted to the evolution of electronic music — a positive thing, even if some of the means of production of that music are questionable. One funky guy made music using sounds created by squashing insects, and he also showed us how to make music by hitting the outside walls of the Modern Art museum. After lunch I spent a couple of hours within its bruised walls, mooching modern.

Our hotel, the Conran designed Triest, was in a good part of town: the Freihausviertel is a bustling, funky district, perfect for whiling away a soft Saturday morning. I excavated an extremely funky pair of trousers from a vintage shop; we had a terrific lunch in Babette's, a place that combines a restaurant with a cookbook shop; and gorged on gorgeous fresh roasted coffee in Alt Wien. You could smell the beans roasting halfway down the street. We also checked out the contemporary art of the Generali Foundation but the excess of culture and lack of sleep were fast becoming irreconcilable. I longed for squalor, reminded of Dr Johnson's famous line: "He who makes a beast of himself gets rid of the pain of being a man." An intellectual equal to Dr Johnson, Shaun Ryder once said of the Happy Mondays: "We turned arsing about into an art form." It was for the likes of Mssrs Johnson and Ryder that I got involved with the sleazy world of nocturnal culture in the first place. It certainly wasn't for the health care and pension, that much I know. And that's the sociological justification for why I spent the beginning of the afternoon in a sports bar watching the football, and the rest in a strip joint, instead of the museums where the septics went. A more practical, superficial reason was that my friend and fellow Gooner, Acid Ted from *Loaded* magazine has remarkable talents of persuasion. Now that afternoon was a real work of art. Just remember — never confuse behaving stupidly with being stupid.

In the evening we headed over to Porgy & Bess — a swanky downstairs kind of a club, with a good sized main room, a stage at one end and a balcony running around the perimeter. The place was filled with human beings for the launch of the second album from Viennese producers Dzihan & Kamien, *Gran Riserva*, out on Couch. At last, the real vintage deal — no random abstraction here — every note serving a tantric, tannic purpose, every instrument contributing to the warm, full bodied, roundness of the sound. The cover of the album featured the pair's fathers, also musicians, who were also on the dancefloor of Porgy & Bess. Their influence could certainly be felt in the seventies vibe within some of the music — score-core music for the kind of porn that had occupied the afternoon. Mix in a string section that Dzihan & Kamien found in Istanbul, a horn section, a vocalist, and the percussionist Sammy Fugueroa, and by the time they stepped onto the stage there were about twenty of them. I nudged my way to the front. The energy of the music crackled about the room, the excitement of live musicianship and the energy of the

Discombobulated

playing drove peoples' feet as they played through the album, their final notes signalling the end of my time in the city.

Oh Vienna. The city is pretty, the wine divine, and some of the music is good, good stuff. But when it comes to the avant-garde, my only advice is to... always... remember you're a Womble. | *October 2002*

14.
Exit, Serbia

SERBIA'S EXIT FROM REPRESSION IS CELEBRATED WITH ONE
ALMIGHTY PARTY ON THE DANUBE; BUST BRIDGES, NEW
FRIENDSHIPS AND SKYDIVING TURTLES

Situation. Sitting at the rickety desk in my hotel room with a glass of warm scotch, writing by the flickering LCD light of a laptop screen because the electricity is down. I need to have a shower but the water is off again. I'm hot and sweaty and I can't see straight for a whole bunch of different reasons. And I'm having a ball.

Location. The window's wide open, revealing a panoramic view over the river Danube, down to the bombed out bridge and the city of Novisad. It's a warm evening — the chirruping of the crickets merges with the rhythmic whistles of the revellers, their whoops carried on a velvet breeze, muffled by distance. I can see them crossing the bridge from the campsite on the other side of the river, gathering numbers, mounting their assault on the fort.

Summation. Switch tense. I've always talked about the Disco Wars. Now I truly was a discorrespondent, dropped on the Wrong Side of the lines.

Question. Whose line is it anyway? The fort was built during the years of the Austro-Hungarian Empire and was the largest of its kind in Europe, now converted into what, effectively, was a disco — a disco for 150,000 to celebrate Serbia's exit from the repression of the Milosevic regime.

Lesson. The country Yugoslavia (translation, roughly, is Southern Slav Nations) ripped itself apart through several brutal wars. It's the

Discombobulated

year 2000 and Milosevic is desperately trying to keep hold of power from Belgrade. Further down the Danube a group of students are hosting a cultural festival on a beach. It goes on for 100 days, is called Exit and the authorities don't have a scooby about its real intent.

Today. "Nobody knew what we were doing," grinned one of those students, Dushan, sipping a beer on the terrace of the fort in July 2003. "It was a natural response of the youth of Novisad. They wanted to change something and bring something to the city. We used culture to motivate young people."

Exit really is way out. It's already provided the most powerful platform of all: the dancefloor. On the dancefloors of the main stage, reggae stage, DJ stage, Asian stage, Balkan Fusion stage and others, the peoples of the former Yugoslavia were trying to get on and get on down. "That's one other aspect that's really important." Dushan continued. "Because of the wars of the last ten years nobody travelled from Serbia to Croatia and Croatia to Serbia but now Exit is really helping that movement around the region. You couldn't imagine that happening three years ago."

The festival takes a year to plan and involves hundreds of people. In the UK they have found a partner in Paxton Talbot and Lily Event Management, the guy who brought *DJmag* to the party, along with the likes of Danny Rampling, Layo & Bushwacka, Christian Smith, Darren Emerson, Lexicon Avenue, Pete Tong and Jeff Mills. Not bad. Add to that the likes of Tricky, Stereo MCs, Henry Rollins, Dirty Vegas and Roni Size on the main stage and you've got yourself a party. Only, I was in trouble the moment I stepped up to first base, first night. My legs went to jelly halfway through Rampling's set and I had to carve a stumbling path through thousands of rambunctious revellers to my bed, whereupon I collapsed, fully clothed. It was the same the next night; same jelly legs. In my self-reflective moments I like to think of myself as a bit of a bruiser when it comes to booze, constructed with a titanium constitution when called upon to sample the liquid pleasures of foreign lands, but this... I could hardly stand up and was talking absolute gak to anyone unfortunate enough to stand within reach of my conversation, principally two local DJs who had adopted me for the festival — DJ Z and DJ Fakir.

The next morning my eyelids peeled back like theatre curtains and the first thing I saw, stage left, was a half empty bottle of beer and the number twelve. I blinked a couple of times and brought the morning's drama to the forefront of the stage. 12%. "Twelve per cent? TWELVE FUCKING PER CENT! No wonder I'm so flaming fandango'd."

Jeepers. I checked my watch. Two in the afternoon and I had arranged to meet Z and Fakir in town at three. My legs swung into some jeans and walked me down from the fort and over the bridge, getting lost in Novisad's varicose lanes, waiting outside Martha's pub beneath a sign that read "God save the pumpkins," swinging low in the slow wind as they arrived. Z and Fakir led me round and down some stairs into the only DJ shop in Novisad, called, helpfully, DJ Shop. It was a cute and cuddly place, a bit like the store's proprietor — the Godfather of the dance scene in Novisad — named Slow Hand for bringing the same silky skills to Technics that Eric Clapton did to Stratocasters. "I know this man," said Slow Hand, hugging me. "This man is a crazy man." It was then I noticed the slipmats on the shop's turntables were from *DJmag*. He put a fatherly arm around my shoulder and led me to a corner of the shop, to a stack of *DJ* magazines half as tall as me. He had every copy going back years — travelling to Budapest in Hungary to buy every one of them — and my heart climbed straight into my throat when I saw it. The missing *DJ*. My Holy Grail.

I have written ninety of these Dispatches thus far, this being the ninetieth visit to the Wrong Side and I have every copy except one — the one that got away. How weird it is, then, to travel to Serbia to finally find it, sitting in a pile of magazines in a downstairs store in downtown Novisad. Slow Hand bagged it up for me, and after lunch we caught a cab to Z's apartment, where he lived with his girlfriend and his studio and his turtle. Z and Fakir have been making music and throwing parties as Noise Destruction since 92; hosting a dance music programme for five straight years, and releasing records on a continental label.

"The music scene has always been here," Fakir was keen to explain, as Z cued up some of the stuff they'd been working on recently. "It's not that it happened after Milosevic. We got into house and tech-

Discombobulated

no in the late eighties — our first sources were tapes from friends who were living in England."

Guys in Serbia absorb music with the zeal of people who, in the grooves of each record, divine a little slice of heaven... and a 12″ kick in the nuts of authority. "They didn't understand what it was so they didn't bother us," Z chuckled. "Drugs was not a problem because in a way it was good for Milosevic that people are busy with drugs; when you give to the crowd drugs and amusement and everything... they are not interested in politics."

Is opium the religion of the masses? Was Marx dyslexic?

Full of such thoughts we headed down to the beach. Just downstream was a modern looking motorway suspension bridge, except where the middle bit should have been there was a distinct lack of a middle bit — just two dead stumps, reaching out to touch one another. You want to find out more but feel awkward; maybe as awkward as your new friends feel that the country responsible is your country. By that I mean the Yanks and Limies, best fucking buddies when it comes to a barroom brawl — a regular Butch Cassidy and the Sundance Kid. In 1999 the Allies bombed Belgrade and Novisad for ninety days and it all went wrong for the producers, known achingly, as Noise Destruction. Everyone agrees that Milosevic needed a slap — some utterly inhuman things were done at his behest — it just bugged me that the Americans seem so slaphappy in their new age. We... they... the Allies... bombed the TV station where Z and Fakir worked. And the bridge to get to it. Life stopped. When the bombardment ended they tried to re-start their career but inevitably things had changed at the label and they couldn't reconnect: "We are Serbs," Z shrugged. "We have war and bombardment and all kinds of shit stuff. So they don't want to bring someone from Serbia to play music."

We kicked sand along the beach as the sound of a thousand stereos drifted from the campsite, forming an organic wall of sound that carried us back to the fort and everyone else, wrestling and giggling and drinking on the slope behind the DJ booth, drifting into a warm and chemical morning as the sun rose over Novisad and Fakir played us into daylight.

Coda. I have exchanged one memory for each and every party I have attended; swapped one coherent thought for each pill I have swallowed. What is left is a kind of cerebral sludge — sludge and these stories — which will always be there for Slow Hand and me. | *July 2003*

15
Fairies across the Mersey

A DISCO ON THE MERSEY FERRY; PITCHING UP WITH THE
GARLANDS CAMP; ADVENTURES AND INDULGENCE WITH BARRY
MAC; A DESPERATE BID FOR FREEDOM AT MANCHESTER AIRPORT

"Life, goes on day after day / Hearts, torn in every way / So..."

OK so let me write you a little picture here:

I'm in a restaurant, but I can't eat anything; in an airport, but I'm
not going anywhere. And wait, because it gets worse: I'm waiting for
a heavily delayed flight to Ibiza that I'm not even booked on. It was
supposed to take off at 8.15am but ain't going no place 'til gone three.
But in any case that doesn't matter because I was never on it. And yet
I wait. The person I am with *is* supposed to be on the flight, but can't
find his ticket. But at least there is a point to his procrastination. I
haven't got a scooby why I'm still here.

And I'm getting the Fear. I haven't slept, my clothes are sweated
through, my hair looks like a cactus plant and people in the restaurant are looking at me funny. The place is full of civilians; real people.
I simply must get out, make my escape. I don't belong here. Never
before have I tried so hard to squeeze all the juice from a night. When
you're still out from the night before, waiting at an airport for a de-

layed flight you were never even on, you know it's time to give it up... accept that the night's run its course... that it's time to go home now. *Jesus, I'm supposed to be at my office in an hour.* I make a call, try my best to explain what's happened, go home, hide under the covers and curl up into a ball. As I close my eyes a slogan is projected onto the cinema screen behind my eyelids. It's the answer to this airport riddle. Like the sticker says: "Garlands made me do it"...

Flashback to the previous night. I had wanted, innocently enough, to unlock this Pandora's box — to find out the secrets of Garlands. I knew that Garlands was a venue and a Saturday night of scouse house in Liverpool, and I also knew that three times through the summer these buccaneers take a boat to the water and spank the plank — or whatever swashbuckling pirates do these days — for *Fairies Across The Mersey*. The gag derives from Garlands' positioning as a gay/mixed club, which in itself is quite an achievement. As a straight man I find the concept of segregated clubbing offensive in the twenty first century. Of course I understand the historical justification for this, but the idea of a sexually apartheid clubland just strikes me as sooo eighties — surely we've all grown up a bit since then and can party together? At least Garlands had got it right: Just because you're heterosexual it doesn't mean you're going to get trolleyed, trash the gaff and start punching people.

"We don't try to be mixed," said Huey, promoter and resident DJ, as we drove out of Manc Land and towards Scouse Land, "the crowd just do it themselves. We don't go out and say, this is a mixed crowd come and join in, because that's the way not to do it."

Also in the car were our respective partners in crime, Rachel Photos and Dave Booth. Dave & Huey DJ together all over the north and play my kind of music — hip-swinging, sweat-dripping house music and I was looking forward to partying with them. Only we were late, and as we swung the car into the port, a mad array of Garlands punters lent over the boat singing Hang The DJ. The psychedelic, multicoloured gaggle of people hanging off the ferry reminded me of a warship leaving for battle, with all the dashing young sailors waving to their loved ones on land. Only, when I stepped off the comfortable shore of reality and walked up the gangplank, this lot looked more

Discombobulated

like escapees from the Yellow Submarine.

The gangplank was raised and we set sail on a sea of memory bliss, messing about on the river. The boat was immediately port-to-starboard wrongness — trannies, heteros, homos and don't knows. The theme was Torremolinos and Tacky Tourists but people seemed to have given that a broad reading. There were schoolgirls, aquatic creatures, sailors and groups of friends dressed alike, just to confuse the bejees out of you. It was waterborne anarchy — wacky and utterly wonderful. The ferry was called *The Royal Daffodil* — the actual, real life Mersey ferry that Gerry Marsden crooned about when he cranked his pacemaker up to 11 and sang *"Ferree, crass de Meerzee."* The upstairs main room hosted the party proper, already rocking as much as the boat itself. Dave and Huey massaged their decks and I manoeuvred around the ship's, bumping into the strangest assemblage of human beings I think I have ever encountered, the boat like a human zoo, a Noah's Ark of weird and wonky party animals.

On the outside decks people chilled out two by two as a summer breeze blew across the Mersey and it was there that I caught up with the other promoters, Barry Mac and Marky J, the guy who added the tinsel to proceedings. "It all started about seven years ago when Garlands was in its infancy," said Marky, "and we thought... what's Liverpool got that's really special... oh God, yeah! Then the title Fairies Across The Mersey came along."

Of course the gay community isn't averse to a little cruise every now and then, except this cruise was flying the skull and crossbones — according to Marky, the first time that had been done on an official vessel in some 300 years, a crime which is still considered treason. "There's been 300 years without piracy and that's what Garlands is all about. What we've done is say, hang on, Mark's gay but he doesn't go to gay clubs, which are abysmal in Liverpool. And I've gone: these guys are straight but they don't go to the straight, coppy-offy places. So what I think we've managed to do with Garlands is create a podium for the black, the white, the gay, the straight. I don't really like that ghettoization."

People staggered about the boat looking like they'd already been out for a lifetime of Saturday nights — the fluorescent detritus of a normal, grey society, finding their own society in the company of one another. "If you try too hard to be bonkers you end up looking shit," Huey remarked. "We want people to make their own entertainment and have a laugh." Garlands is just that: a club where they don't have to book a performer as the dancefloor is already a ready-made Moulin Rouge, a chiaroscuro of hugs and sunshine. "These are all unpaid performers," Marky added. "And they like to sweat."

For many, Liverpool is still synonymous with the sixties — for the Fab Four, Gerry and the Pacemakers; everyone rocking to a Mersey-rather than a 4/4 beat. It's the role of clubs like Garlands and Cream to break that down: "The thing about Liverpool and the north," Marky said, "is that we're not secondary to the south anymore, we really are our own contenders. What we've got is equal if not better than what the south's got to offer."

Clubland has been around since Jimmy Saville sparked up his first cigar, and any ideas that put a twist and a couple of kinks in the whole sordid affair have to be welcomed. In leaving the safe, solid shores of reality and taking to the water, people seemed to have metaphorically unshackled themselves, letting themselves float away on the choppy seas of insanity. Huey smirked: "I think one thing about this stretch of water is that people think it's lawless. They think, oh you can't get arrested here." Indeed when the party was once buzzed by a police helicopter it merely encouraged the punters to strip down to the nud and flash their choppers to the coppers.

Our laps around the Mersey continued. I took in the view and walked back inside, finding myself in front of the makeshift decks, dancing and going disco overboard. I tried to accommodate the nautical sway of the boat into my dancing and managed, just about, to stay vertical. When the boat docked back into Liverpool, Barry informed everyone that Garlands (the club) was open. Many of the revellers attempted to find their land legs and swagger on over there. Rachel Photos bailed, explaining she was catching a lift back to the sanctuary of Manchester with Dave and Huey. But I felt a certain tingle of adventure, of danger — a tingle I hadn't felt in a while — that I thought had been snuffed out long ago by the overwhelming weight of the bothersome business of growing up.

Discombobulated

"Listen I've got to get to Manchester airport for 6am anyway," said Barry, "there's a party on after the club and I can give you a lift back after that."

Did you ever have one of those fork in the road moments, fork in the night decisions, that put you on a magic travellator towards your disco destiny?

"You will look after me, won't you?" I asked Barry.

"No," he replied.

"Good. Then let's go." | *August 2001*

16
Berlin

HOW TO UPSET BOTH THE GERMAN GOVERNMENT AND SPECIAL
FORCES BY THE SIMPLE USE OF ONE GASMASK

The look of abject disgust on the woman's face beat any that has been aimed in my direction in the thirty five years I have been on your planet.

Then again, try to consider it from her point of view: The doors swoosh open to the plush, glass lift of the Berlin Radisson, within which she finds a man in shabby attire, moist with the booze sweats, hair greasy and unkempt, attempting to put on what looks like a rubberised gasmask and which turns out to be, on closer inspection, a rubberised gasmask.

Not a good look. Hurriedly, I pushed the thing back into a plastic bag and tried to persuade her through bloodshot eyes that everything was OK. No really, fraulein, it is. It was Berlin and I couldn't help but be reminded of that song by the band of the same name... something about taking one's breath away? Well, the look on her face, as she shielded her children and looked up at her husband protector, I will take it with me to the grave; the combination of terror, loathing and utter apoplexy. I can imagine her even now at polite dinnerparties trying, for the benefit of her grey-dull friends, to decipher what strange and brutal evil she had witnessed that day.

We live in difficult times and maybe I should have known better. The innocence of bygone days has now left us, like childhood itself. Even at Manchester airport that first morning, a man had gone bonk-

Discombobulated

ers on the runway and legged it towards a plane armed with a brief-case. The cops Taser-ed his ass, and conducted a controlled explosion on the briefcase, no doubt blowing the guy's tuna sandwiches into a thousand tiny shards of bread and fish.

We were met at Berlin Flughafen and driven to the aforementioned Radisson — a modern, elegant hotel on the East Side of the city, next to the famous TV tower on Alexanderplatz. The main feature of the central atrium of the hotel is a magnificent multistorey aquarium, all manner of marine life within.

"Gee whiz," whistled ace photographer Jimmy the Hat. "That's quite a fish tank."

Dinner was at Bar 25, a wooden hut construction on the banks of the River Spree, journalists from around the world grouped on tables according to nationality (perhaps to prevent any explosion of xenophobia between courses). If dinner was strange, dancing was stranger: several storeys up inside an office block on Alexanderplatz, one floor had transmogrified into "Club Weekend" — a central bar area, windows overlooking the city and über-trendy Berliners slouching to some low slung bar grooves. It was essentially an open plan office minus the desks and photocopier. You felt at any moment David Brent might appear from behind a pot plant and buy you a Babysham.

My phone woke me the next morning. Everyone was already on a bus waiting for me. I swung my legs out of bed, rearranged my groin and pulled open the curtains to be confronted by the strange sight of a frogman swimming in the aquarium with the fishes, perhaps picking out that evening's menu. I got my sorry ass downstairs and subsequently sat on it as it was transported to a champagne reception on the outdoor terrace of the Akademie der Kunste (try saying that with a straight face), overlooking the Brandenburg Gate. I was in Berlin in 1991, not long after the wall came down, when crossing the Brandenburg Gate was like stepping into another dimension; swapping Western prosperity for eastern poverty, BMWs for Trabants. Such has been the passing of time that it took me a while to figure out whether we were now on the east or west side.

The afternoon unwound gently with a boat cruise along the Spree. For some reason a Lebanese-based, pan-Arabic TV station wanted to interview me about music and Manchester. I had planned to tell them the problem with Manchester was the recent infestation of midget monkeys, but bailed at the last moment and instead talked about the year 1989, interesting to me because it was the year I started university in Manchester, same as Tom and Ed, aka The Chemical Brothers.

"It was just a brilliant place to be," said Tom later that evening, deep within the bowels of the Velodrom, the venue for the gig. "Before that, making records or going into the studio seemed a very distant thing, that other people did. And there, you went to the clubs and you met the person who made that record. It just felt like you could make something happen."

"We did a degree while at the same time being pretty much immersed in dance culture," Ed continued. "We were on the same course and started going to clubs together. Haçienda, every Friday."

Ah the Haçienda. Warped, shapeless, misty watercoloured memories of the Halluçienda.

"Did you play there?" Jimmy the Hat butted in, rather unprofessionally.

"No," said Ed.

"We played the Haçienda!" Tom contradicted.

"Oh yeah we played the Haçienda."

I know they did because I was there. At least I think I was. No, I *know* I was because it was one of the first pieces I wrote, back in 1995, for a magazine called *Metropolis*. The magazine printed their name as "The Chemical Brother", somehow sidelining one of them.

"It was a fucking mad night!" said Tom.

It was probably was, Disco Amigo, it probably was — that enormous cathedral swollen with electric eccentricism, melding guitar noise and dance beats in a freeform baggy aesthetic so removed from the monotone vibration of certain DJs now.

"A lot of electronic music is made to be utility music that blends into a set and is almost indistinguishable," Tom detailed. "We take a different approach to making records. We want to make records that stop the club."

Achtung Disco! First up was Mylo, strapped to a guitar as part of a full band. Then the boys stepped up behind their banks of synths and sequencers, two lone humans almost overwhelmed by technology and the impact of the massive screens behind them that carried powerful visuals to illustrate the music. They slam dunked their way through all their big tracks, the Velodrom's race circuit creating a curvaceous cuddle that enclosed the dancefloor, the press encamped on beds in the VIP.

Sunday. We had big ideas about being tourists but in the end made it only as far as the terrace bar of the hotel, kicking back in the warmth of autumn sunshine as the Berlin marathon ran past. Over the other side of the river I noted the bustle of a market, selling East German war memorabilia and bits of the wall.

"Check out that gasmask," said Jimmy the Hat, pointing at one stall. Perfect. I have a friend who runs a club called 2Kinky, the logo for which (for reasons I have never got to grips with) is a pink gasmask. He recently bought himself a club in Burnley and I was thinking... buy it, paint it pink, and, hey presto, the perfect club-warming present. Back at the hotel Jimmy suggested I get the lift up to my room, put it on and then leer out so he could take a picture. I was edgy and twitchy and forgot you needed to put your swipe card in to get the lift started; instead it went down a level, the doors opened and... you know the rest.

But worse was yet to come. Such was my fragile mental condition that the concept of buying a gasmask had seemed the eminently — nay *only* — sensible thing to do. I hadn't, however, quite worked out how I was going to get it back to the UK; or considered that in this day and age smuggling a gasmask onto a plane might be, well, somewhat frowned upon.

That worry niggled like a pebble in my mind's plimsoll as I waited for my bag to appear at Manchester Airport. I opened her up to check the gasmask was safely stowed. Instead, at the top, was some official looking documentation, with the eagle crest stamp of German authority. The wording was in German and English. "Dear passenger," it started, "your baggage was inspected by security agents authorized by the German government." Gadzooko, this was a rum do. I looked about me nervously, expecting at any minute to see besuited men whispering into their lapels before heading towards me. How would I explain that I had only wanted to paint it pink for 2Kinky? I scanned down further. A box had been ticked, which read "because it gave reasons for a further inspection according to EU-Regulation 2320/2002".

What in the name of Satan's five arses was EU-Regulation 2320/2002? What in the hell had I got myself into now? I placed everything back, and stuffed the documents deep inside my pocket. Terrific. In another anonymous city suburb, in another anodyne office block; in another anomie filing cabinet, another fresh case had undoubtedly been opened, and placed back in the drawer for M, just alongside Machiavelli and Moriarty. | *October 2005*

17
Tribal
Sessions

GETTING DEEP DOWN AND TRIBAL; ASSIMILATING WITH THE
RAVE NATIVES IN THEIR URBAN JUNGLE; THE MULTIPLE USE OF
HAWAIIAN SHIRTS; SOBERING UP FOR LUNCH WITH TAKE THAT

A warm bass throbbed from the warehouse ahead as though the brick
building were a heart pumping music around the arteries of Manchester like mainlined junk. I walked through a metal gate, jingling
the chemical change in my pocket and became aware — via my rozzer
radar — of the group of maybe six or seven policemen following in,
directly behind me.

The first copper talked down into his walkie-talkie, attached like
a limpet to the plastic of his luminous jacket. "We're in," he said, the
speaker crackling a distant reply. He turned to look back at his colleagues and broke into a smile. "Hey, they'll let you in anywhere wearing these jackets!" His colleagues erupted into giggles and I loosened
the grip on my change. Comedy coppers — Christ, what next — Spurs
winning something... dogs and cats living together? It's anarchy I tell
you... ANARCHY! Where's God's Cop when you need some new order restored to the universe?

Once through the large, open access to the warehouse, the space
opened up like the kind of secret hangar where Area 51 meets Studio 54, a hangar full of wide-eyed disco aliens trying to climb the
walls and swing upside down from the steel rafters. I was still in that
sort of disco limbo faze of an evening — when you're in the build-

ing but you're not quite yet a part of the party. But I was starting to get a fix on things. This was the tenth anniversary of Tribal Gathering and, rather than celebrate in a field somewhere, they decided to take it back to those rambunctious rave dayz. Like a hermit crab, they crawled into one of the uninhabited warehouse shells scattered across the urban seabed of Ancoats, adding a phat PA, a bunch of the planet's best jocks and 14,000 sweaty bodies.

The place was heaving with humans, and as soon as I was welcomed into the cuddle of the dancefloor I lost about fifteen friends to the crowd. But I'd come prepared, armed with the relevant disco accessories to cope with this madness, including a high calibre glo-stick and a maximum strength tequila lolly — the worm still in it (both presents from my recent trip to Ibiza). There was no way I was going down without a fight.

Already alone, it was hard to make anything out through the gathering mists that enveloped the room and the sweat that hung like dirty raindrops on the windscreens of my eyes. I moved onwards, into the heart of the disco darkness, switching between the two cavernous warehouses that lay side by side, and the smaller Chibuku room, finding something to engage my attention around every corner, some person, some song. The night was full of Manchester moments: Sneak dropped Blue Monday and the whole room lifted their arms to the heavens, in a kind of communal prayer to that record and the Haçienda; A Guy Called Gerald sat quietly at the front of the stage and played Voodoo Ray and the room erupted; Laurent Garnier played Man With A Red Face — one of my all time favourite tracks (maybe not exactly a Manchester moment, but then Laurent was once chef at the Haçienda... it all leads back to those doors eventually).

In the other room lasers bounced around the walls and Jeff Mills filled the room with sound. My legs seemed set to *"permanent wander"*, occasionally letting me stop to talk to familiar faces. As I stopped to catch my breath I felt a pair of eyes boring into me. A guy approached. "Are you that daft cunt from the magazine?"

Hmmm, that all depends, I pondered. Are you that daft cunt from over there? I hazarded a response. "I'm not sure about the whole cunt bit but I do write for a magazine, yes."

Discombobulated

"I know all about you — you just hang around in clubs and get paid for it, don't you? Some of us have real jobs to do, you know."

My dear, dear boy, I interior monologued. I *am* working, even as we speak. It may look like I'm doing nothing but looning around and sweating, but therein lies the skill, you see. It's so subtle that to the untrained eye it may indeed look like I'm doing fuck all, when really *this* is my nine to five, *this* is my office. He returned to his friends and began pointing at me, which did nothing for my slowly enveloping paranoia.

The hours passed by like the *Generation Game*'s conveyor belt, carrying people and prizes past my eyes. I found myself talking to this one girl and was totally mid conversation before it dawned on me I had no idea how or why I had started talking to her, or indeed who she was. I think maybe I'd asked if she wanted a go on my tequila lolly. She pretty much adopted me for the night. She had a nice smile and made me laugh. A wide-eyed Rave Bunny, she seemed hell bent on challenging me to chemical contortions of almost gymnastic dexterity, and when you're something of an old warhorse there's one thing you relish more than anything and that's challenges from young whippersnapper Rave Bunnies. So we held hands and hit hedonism hard — elbows out — steaming through the walls of the night like the couple in that ad, crashing through walls in a race to who knows where — Sunday morning, perhaps... the other side. It was wrong. And just when I thought it could be no wronger she came up with the notion of going on the fairground rides and so, with a headful of ugly chaos, we climbed on, brutally thrown around like booze in a cocktail shaker, shaken and stirred and spun right into the morning.

It was six a.m., the sun was shining and I was on my own (Rave Bunny had gone to Sankeys for the afterparty). I spilled out of the warehouse with all the other factory funkers, dispersing through the streets of Ancoats like Lowry's matchstick men and matchstick bats and frogs — the grand old mills mostly empty, their windowpanes smashed in as though someone had kicked out their front teeth; no pride left now, just a toothless smile and the memories. I walked amongst them, humming that Lowry song (*He painted Salford's smoky tops / On cardboard boxes from the shops / And parts of An-*

coats / Where I used to play) before phoning one of the friends I had supposedly gone to the party with — a person I had last seen some eight or nine hours previously — to find out where the hell everyone had got to. They were outside my apartment building, waiting for me to come back to open up so they could have a party (the very least one should expect of one's best friends.)

So I opened up and we had a party. Pretty soon my buzzer buzzed. Rave Bunny had abandoned the afterparty and decided to come over. She wore a tribal feather in her hair and set about my fridge and cupboards in a whirl of activity, managing to assemble sangria when I swore all I had in there was cornflakes. I mixed drinks for the assembled company: a vodka & platonic for the lady, ales for my friends and gin & tonic for the lucky ones (the reputation of my G & T stretches all the way from Bradford to Bingley).

As the morning elevated into day I determined to take things to the next level, without entirely knowing how, or indeed where the next level might be. I challenged the livingroom to a game of Who Can Throw Themselves Out Of The Window The Best. I suggested we discover how spangled we could get using only household products (always a favourite), before settling on next level clothing. My usual means of achieving this is by the multiple donning of hats (my best is seven on the one head), but as this was a special occasion I raided the depths of my wardrobe, never daring to believe that man could cope with such a level of tropical wrong behaviour but, as God is my witness, I achieved it, people — six Hawaiian shirts, of varying degrees of vulgarity, all worn at the same time. And that, my disco amigos, is how you next level it when the spangle juice has run dry and you need to lift things a little. I stripped off each layer like a Russian doll with a surfboard, passing them around until everyone had a shirt. And that seemed to do just nicely, everyone bouncing on my couches until all concerned, including the couches, were all worn out.

I waved them bye-bye about midday and tried to retreat from the Wrong Side to reconnect with reality. I had a lunch appointment to keep with Howard Donald from Take That and the day wasn't about to get any less surreal. *September 2003*

18
Leaving
Las Vegas

WEIRD SCENES INSIDE THE MANDALAY; PARTYING WITH
SUPERSTAR DJ PAUL OAKENFOLD; DOWN THE STRIP

Vegas, baby... yeah!

So giddy was I about the trip to Las Vegas that I especially commissioned and cultivated a set of Elvis Presley Memorial Sideburns. They reached right down to my chin, looked absolutely ridiculous and made me immensely proud, like a father in his local boozer after the birth of hirsute twins. But it was important to make an impression; we were promised a charter jet which would fly the media and the VIPs over for an Oscars party, a red carpet list that included the Spice Girls, All Saints and, for some reason, Ronnie Wood.

Kindly catapult me into a confined space with those females and I can really cause some damage (I'd even have a pop at Ronnie, given enough gin) but I soon twigged the PR spiel was going way off the bullshit radar. Why do PR companies have to be so lubricious and starfucky about everything? You could just as easily got me on that plane if you told me John Craven was a passenger. Vegas is sexy enough on its own, so absolutely grotesque it's beautiful, as plastic as it is fantastic, a Pamela Anderson amongst cities.

The whole premise was that Vegas is this year's "new Ibiza". Virgin are the first airline to fly direct from the UK on supposedly cheap flights (at the moment you have to go via LA and it takes, like, a trillion years) and the best of British DJs have been booked at Club Ra, the nightclub of the Luxor casino. Now there is a slight problem with this ingenious theory, and that is the cupboard under my kitchen sink looks more like Ibiza than Las Vegas. But peel back the layers of PR hyperbole and they may just have something going here...

How Virgin can get their planes so right, baby, and their trains so wrong is quite beyond me, but the flight over was hugely enjoyable: you watch some movies, get a little squiffy and before anyone can say, "Sir, I think you have had enough gin, and Mr Wood has requested that you stop goosing him," you've touched down in Vegas and are ensconced at the Mandalay Bay, a brand spanking new hotel at the end of the Strip: 3,000 rooms, acres of swimming pools that curl around the hotel's grounds like a loopy lagoon, man-made beach, tropical theme throughout and the obligatory casino on the ground floor, full of weird and wonderful people feeding quarters into coin hungry poker machines. *Ka-ching*!

My room was on twenty fifth floor and was the size of my apartment. I pulled open the curtains and choked at the panoramic view over Vegas, and the sheer drop to the lagoon pools below. The bed alone was the size of a football pitch — big enough for all kinds of gymnastics — well, at least for forward rolls. How do I know? I climbed on up and proceeded to do a couple, which woke me up enough to get downstairs and sink a few beers with Rachel Photos and some of the other members of the UK press corp. In the early hours I crawled back into my room and knocked myself out with a couple of hefty measures of scotch, leaving the curtains drawn back so I could watch the lights of Vegas sparkle like fallen stardust as I fell asleep.

The next morning I woke with the TV on and, disoriented, what I thought was a man outside my window. I slid-snuggled back into sub-duvet unconsciousness, thinking I was back in Istanbul. Then I thought it was evening time. Then I thought the phone was ringing. The phone WAS ringing. Rachel. She wanted to know if I could make it down for breakfast. Breakfast? Hm, I could do with some breakfast. Put down the phone and watched the news. America was suffering a chronic shortage of Twinkies. I shook my head until the fear fell from

Discombobulated

my ears and flicked through the channels, settling on *Tellytubbies*, which had been dubbed into American and subsequently lost all of its political edge. At the sign of movement my eyes trailed back over to the window. *There was a man outside.* He was risking life and limb — twenty five floors up — to wash the outside glass, so I waved good morning and went downstairs for breakfast, weaving through a casino full of strange cardboard people, still gambling.

I've been around the block a few times and know most cracks in the pavement but out in the sunshine of the Strip, Vegas has to be the ultimate: a glistening leviathan residing like a lost UFO in the middle of the desert. It's like being on acid... only with fewer leprechauns. Each of the casinos was pure plastic eye candy: Excalibur, the Vegas take on ye olde worlde England; the theme of New York, New York was easy enough to fathom (a rollercoaster of New York cabs curling through the Manhattan skyline kind of gave it away); then there's the Paris one; Venice; Treasure Island (with a full on battle enacted out front to encourage people to come inside and relieve themselves of their pieces of eight); and of course, Caesar's Palace, perhaps the last word in decadent excess.

And tonight it was the turn of Paul Oakenfold to "do" Vegas. After dinner I caught the monorail from the Mandalay Bay to the Luxor, a casino shaped like a plastic pyramid, and walked through the Sphinx entrance into Ra, which bulged with more Egyptian décor than the Cairo branch of B&Q, enough to make Tutankhamun blush. The press core was slowly discombobulating with jetlag fatigue but luckily promoter Joe Abdullah had the energy to lift us, an ex-pro football player for the Denver Broncos. "I would compare this to a football game," Joe barked. "I've been playing football since I was five years old and there's nothing like preparing and practising and running all summer and then, when it's showtime your adrenaline is pumping like crazy. And it's kind of like that when we do concerts. It's time to play the game. It's a good feeling."

The US and UK have long been playing a transatlantic game of ping-pong with dance music. Even trance has managed to go trance-atlantic. "And check this out," Joe continued, "it's Wednesday today and this place is nuts! Wait till Friday — it's off the hinges! And when there's a holiday — oh man, forget about it!" So it was a Wednesday, at least I could cling onto that certainty, even if I lacked Joe's soul-sapping energy. A queue formed outside of people who had travelled from Arizona, California, Utah, Washington... all to get that slice of Oakie. Between the cheap flights and clubnights, it seemed Vegas might now have more to offer than financial bankruptcy, insobriety and a neat collection of STDs.

Time for a pick-me-up... a pick-up truck sized pick-me-up. I asked about in the VIP room and was pointed in the direction of a chemical consultant, some guy who was supposedly a millionaire playboy. I spotted Oakie heading through some doors so I presumed there was some kind of VVIP room back there, somewhere offering some solitude for such furtive inculcation. I led the guy through the same doors and....

...we were in the casino kitchens. One of the chefs looked up at me, with a kind of "hello buddy, can I help you?" look across his physiognomy. I returned a well formed look that said "I know precisely what I'm doing" and headed past him, pushed through some more doors and...

...then I was out back of the kitchens, outside the casino. "OK, let's get this over quick," I said.

"So you've got some stuff," he replied.

I looked back at him. "Erm... no. You do."

"No I don't," he said, quizzically. "I thought you did?"

"But... but that's the whole point... I thought... oh, Christ..."

This conversational seesaw carried on rocking for a while, the fear crawling up my legs like lascivious lice. This was not good. A glance back through the doors and two bouncers were approaching, quickly pursued by the same chef, dramatically gesticulating towards the doors with a ladle. It dawned on me that I was with a stranger in the kitchens of the Luxor casino in Las Vegas, in the midst of a deal in which neither participant had anything to sell — and that it was all about to go very wrong. Security looked ready to bust my head with the nearest pots and pans they could lay their hands on and then do a prompt and thorough internal investigation. With plastic gloves. Fuck spanners.

Discombobulated

I pushed open the doors.

The security guy reached me first. "What you doing?"

"I'm lost.... I'm looking for the rest rooms... I'm English," I replied, all at once and in the plummiest voice I could muster, then walked straight past him without making eye contact. It's amazing how far you can get with an English accent and a well placed smile. They looked flummoxed. By the time they turned to follow I had already ducked back into the VIP, and quickly slugged back a couple of beers to get my BP back under control.

OK, so that didn't work. I needed cover. Oakenfold was still backstage. "Erm, hello," I said, gathering my thoughts. "I'm a journalist and I'm here to interview you, oh yes, siree!" (Disguised as the very person I was supposed to be, the perfect ruse.) "So, you been up to much lately?"

"I was fortunate enough to be invited over to do the *Vanity Fair* Oscars party."

"Nice," I said, calming a little. "I was under the misapprehension that this was an Oscars party, but anyways how was it?"

"It was... different."

And relax. The gig at Club Ra was the start of Paul's Perfecto tour of America, a punishing three week schedule for a DJ who was determined to crack the States. "All sounds very rock'n'roll... "

"It's not really. I don't want to be blasé but it can be difficult for people to understand. I arrived here at 7 o'clock, went straight to bed, woke up, came straight here. I haven't seen anything. And then I have to stay up all night to catch the 6.30 flight to Boston. It's not glamorous, like a lot of people think, but hey, listen, I ain't complaining, I'm just explaining and I'm very, very lucky to be in the situation that I am."

Paul was to be everywhere from New York to Miami, from Seattle to San Francisco, pushing the Perfecto sound out to an American crowd who are finally bang up for what he's doing. "For sure. When I was playing four or five years ago at Twilo, they really didn't get the sound, they really didn't want it in America, so I thought well, it's a waste of time, I'll wait until they catch up with what's going on." The gig at Ra was close to Paul's 180th show in two years... they've caught up. "The only way to truly break America is to tour it like a band," he detailed. "I was actually told that when I toured with U2 — Paul McGuinness told me how they broke America and I've just adopted that approach."

Oakenfold is as big a name in other fields of music as he is in club land, credited with joining the dots between indie and dance with acts like the Happy Mondays. "Why can't you take rock and give it a dance feel?" he asked. "Why can't you take reggae and make it more mainstream? And I've not done it for anyone other than myself really. I've grown up on all kinds of music, I'm not just into dance and I'm very lucky to be offered the chance to work with these kinds of bands — U2, The Smashing Pumpkins..."

Paul was dressed immaculately but it was still Vegas and it still conjured images of ageing rock'n'rollers in sequin jumpsuits. Is Vegas, then, the new Ibiza... or the old Butlins? Are we soon to see the great and the good of the UK dance scene at Caesar's Palace... dinner and dance... ten dollars a head?

Paul seemed unimpressed. "I've played here a few times before so I kind of know what to expect. It's a fun place... in short doses. Last time I came here I played, then took a few days off. We drove out into the desert, we went gambling, we went to a couple of shows. Yeah, it's a good fun city."

"So would you say you've 'done Vegas'?"

He grinned. "I have actually. In more ways than one."

Towards the end of the night I returned to my room, through an underground series of passages that linked the Luxor with the Mandalay Bay; the subterranean air con air deliberately keeping the air fresh and scented, blown through the hotel to keep gamblers awake enough to keep feeding the ravenous slot monsters their metal meat. I smoothed off the edges of the night with a drink, and Vegas through my TV window. I slept well.

The next day I stayed by the pool to recover from the excesses of the previous night; occasionally falling into the lazy stream that automatically carried you around in a loop; occasionally lazily flicking the switch on the lounger that alerted a passing waitress to your alcoholic desires; mostly just chuckling at how close I had been to get-

Discombobulated

ting busted and charged with First Degree Nothing. In the evening we caught a cab downtown, the original gambling area before the Strip took over. Each side of the street was walled with neon. One street had a roof of lightbulbs, a screen for an overhead lightshow. I sat down at the bar of a nearby casino, took off the jacket and stetson I had just bought and ordered a bottle of Bud, pondering the sum total of my trip... beer and clothing in Las Vegas. | *April 2000*

19
Big Day Out
Val d'Isere

HERNIAS A GO GO; HOW TO SLIDE DOWN A VERY TALL
MOUNTAIN, ATTACHED ONLY TO A THIN PIECE OF WOOD WHEN
DRUNK

See more

My eyes creaked open and began to feel their way around the room. OK, so where the trouser jazz was I? The room was of a wooden construction; ski apparel hung in an open wardrobe; beside my bed was a chair, on which lay the usual wrong paraphernalia — my inhalers, my journal and an unfamiliar hipflask next to a bottle of scotch. An X was etched into its side.

I leant up on one arm. My head hurt like a landslide; my hangover an avalanche tumbling down my cranium, carrying with it the loose debris of uneasy recollection... that during the previous night, artificially buoyed by altitude and attitude, I had challenged someone to a dance off, tonight, in some random Alpine discotheque. The memories overtook one another as, with rigid horror, I remembered it was a girl called Jo... and that chick's got moves. James Brown would run a mile.

Christ on a snowboard, this was a bad scene. I blame Bill Gates. Again. This time Microsoft had arranged a press trip to Val d'Isere, to test out some of the new Xbox games, whilst at the same time putting at risk the lives of those very souls who would be writing the

89

Discombobulated

reviews; sending them up an Alp for the express purpose of watching them stand on a bit of wood and then slide back down it again. World's gone mad. Quite why these snowboarding types can't derive the same adrenalin rush from lying on a couch and reading the paper, is quite beyond me. Extreme lounging — that's where it's at.

Hear more

I have always had an ill defined, death or glory approach to life and flinging myself off mountains seems to dovetail nicely with my love of flinging myself around discos. Especially when both involve tunes from hip hop DJ Shorty Blitz, brought over to create a sonic backdrop to the Alpine scene. His tunes instilled in me a reckless bravado. Up the mountain I took myself off on a little adventure. How wrong could it go? After all I had my hip Xbox hip flask with me, a latter day St Bernard's box of booze, if I got really stranded.

Turns out it can go real wrong.

So I'm there giving it all the fly moves on the board of joy, when I lose it big style. Now I don't mind taking a tumble now and then — I go ass over tit most Fridays on the walk home from the battle cruiser — but this... this was one of those occasions when you just know it's going to hurt. All of a sudden the sky's not where it should be and you're waiting for the thump, thinking... here... comes... the... PAIN.

Feel more

BANG. I came down hard on my coccyx; so hard it sent a shiver-splint sprinting up my spine, crunching the bones in my neck. I even felt the fucker in my forehead. Needing a quiet sit down with myself, I steadied my nerves with a few scoops from the flask; taking in the fact that I was sitting on top of the planet, the sorbet crust of the planet, watching a valley curl away towards a huge Hooveresque dam. Then I climbed up again, resumed my descent and went straight back over, breaking my fall with the same piece of ass. Lucky for me I have a firm tush, but still I'd had enough — I had bust myself up real good — my bottle had gone, my bindings had gone and I unstrapped myself and limped back into port like Ellen

McArthur with a broken mast.

Back at the ranch everyone was playing one another at the various Xbox games — everything from *Xtreme Beach Volleyball* to *Transworld Snowboarding*, featuring some of the boarders we had been partying with the night before. I limped over to Jo, trying my best to conceal the ignominy of having busted my bum.

"Jo," I coughed, attempting to interrupt her gaming, "regarding our dance off."

"Yes?"

"I have to inform you that I must respectively withdraw. I have broken my backside and would be unable to perform to my usual standards."

Before she could protest I backed away, climbing up the stairs and into the shower, discovering to my horror that I had a bruise on my bootie which was basically... well, the size of my bootie. I wish you could have seen it, although even as I write those words I'm brutally aware of the moral and ethical issues that raises. Not to mention the lawsuits that would result from such media mooning.

Play more

We were due to leave at seven the next morning, not an appealing prospect when that night's party at Dick's Tea Bar didn't finish 'til four. Me and Rachel Photos concocted a plan, asking the Xbox dudes if we could switch flights to later in the afternoon (not for nothing is her nickname Luxury Bitch — the lady don't do 7am starts). I pleaded comprehensive professionalism, that I needed time to get fully tucked into the action, time to play more. All sorted with new flights and with more room for disco manoeuvres, we walked up the hill to where the main competition was taking place. The Big Day Out began when an Australian known only as Gumby invented... wait for it... Gumby's Big Day Out, involving (a) a Big Air competition during which boarders (and increasingly skiers) threw themselves at Heaven itself and (b) when they returned to earth, a party for them to go get arseholed. Sweet deal.

I truly was seeing, hearing and feeling a great deal, and when we moved onto Dick's I planned to play a helluva lot more — a few shots

Discombobulated

in me, some stripper in front and music all around, from Shorty and Brandon Block; as at home in the Alps as the beaches of the Med. But I was hurting all over and despite my earlier bellicose belligerence, swerved off the piste and into bed. And to sleep. Face down.

I woke early the next day, and climbed out of bed to discover I had started walking like Ozzy Osborne. I checked the bruise. It was on the same cheek as my tattoo of Charlie Brown and now the black and blue bruise had swollen like some kind of fifties B-movie blob, threatening to consume Chuck in its all-conquering wake. I packed. My new flight had only bought me a couple of hours and, as well as the three hour cab ride to Geneva airport, now involved a transfer at Basle which meant, agonizingly, that almost the entirety of the day would involve sitting down. But there were definite advantages: I got to say goodbye to everyone and I got to share that cab ride down from the mountain with Shorty Blitz and his manager Suzanne, who regularly stopped the cab to leave a little of last night by the Alpine roadside.

Shorty has a show on Kiss Radio and spins hip hop from the Zap in Brighton to Bed in Sheffield. My kind of hip hop — funky. "It has to be funky," he smiled, an attitude to life that no doubt endears him to the snowboarding community, themselves dedicated to the ethic of a freestyle lifestyle. Music is an integral part of the snowboarding culture — phat beats for phat Alps — music for people to fling themselves off mountains to. "Yeah definitely," Shorty agreed, filming our descent with a camcorder. "As long as they can connect with the music, it's kind of like magic, really. If you can feel that music then people can relate and that's wicked — that's what it's about — people jamming together. Why can't it be like that all the time?"

As our path down the mountain continued I became increasingly aware that I was leaving the pristine beauty of the Alps and returning to the soporific sludge of sea level society. My ears popped as if to mark the point where I returned to greyality — a world defined by fear and paranoia, by big bullies ganging up on the weakest kids in the planet's playground. I hadn't missed it one bit.

Shorty and Suzanne went to sleep. I put my headphones on and looked out the window, left with one abiding memory of my time in

Val d'Isere. I was sitting in the chalet playing *Kung Fu Chaos*, trying my best to fuck up my compadres, when one of the girls on the trip sat down behind me and gave me a hug. It was utterly random, without ulterior motive and ultra sweet. | *March 2003*

20
Kuala
Lumpur
Loony

HOW DOES ONE EXPLAIN THE PRESENCE OF A GUN IN A BAG AT
KUALA LUMPUR AIRPORT?

Kuala Lumpur airport. Just have to get past this dude at customs and
I can vacate this country before they mess with my head anymore. I
hurt all over. Never before have I been wronged by so many people, in
such a variety of ways, in such a short space of time. Utterly wonderful. I've packed more funky fun into the last five days than I've had in
five years and if I don't get out now I'm either gonna explode or move
in. Rest. Must rest. But first I must explain to this customs chap why
there's a gun in my bag.

I look back and wave weakly at the grinning guys who have
wronged me throughout the last few days: Colin, Matt and Rodney
from a company called Fuse. For some reason they've taken to calling
me Susan Fishnets; their fresh rack of smiles making me nervous.
I approach the customs goon. He's a big brute of a man — his arms
like Technics turntables — and he's already eyeing me suspiciously.
Jesus, what have they done to me.

"Hi," I offer hesitantly, "I know this sounds kind of kooky but I
feel compelled to point out that there's a gun in my bag."

Kualar Lumpar Looney

Southeast Asia is my kind of town. I've been in Kuala Lumpur before (or KL, if you're an LA kind of guy) on an Asia jaunt and let's just see if I can get the chronology right: utterly arseholed from Gatwick to Bangkok; caught sunstroke looking for somewhere to stay; straight into a drinking contest with some Thai bloke over shots of maekong (Thai whiskey) in random strip joint in Pat Phong; passed out drunk in the middle of Khao San Road, knocking out one of my front teeth and nearly losing an eye; called girlfriend feeling sorry for myself; she flies out; travel together down through Asia; argue constantly for two months and break up on top of an active volcano in Sumatra.

Yep, it's all good in Asia, but that was some ten years back and as soon as I touched down it was obvious things had changed. All I remember of KL back then was going to a mosque for eastern prayer and McDonald's for western trash. This time I was heading out with superduper club Golden, the shimmering jewel of the north, as a guest of residents Dean Wilson and James Camm, hosting a Golden night at a KL club called Movement. Myself and James were room-mates, with a view straight over to the twin Petronas towers, the tallest buildings in the world and worth seeing. (If you can't be arsed, watch the movie *Entrapment*, they're in there. And if that pair of architectural inspirations don't turn you on, then maybe those of Catherine Zeta Jones will.) As we unpacked I noticed the slogan on James' T-shirt read "Golden — even better than an oatcake."

"James," I said, "care to explain what an oatcake is?"

"Basically it's a Stoke delicacy," he replied, with a Jamie Oliver lick of the lips. "You can have it any time of the day and night; it goes with cheese, bacon, sausages..."

"Yeah but that being said, how can you possibly calibrate that a disco is better than a biscuit?"

"It's been scientifically tested," he said without expression, and returned to his unpacking.

We nailed breakfast at 7am, battling the fact that it was something like midnight back home — and battling the greater evil that Westlife were staying in the same hotel — then slept all day. I awoke with what felt like a sumo wrestler sitting on my chest, as ex-pat Matt arrived and took charge of showing us around, a guy doing the geographical splits with one foot in the UK, one in KL, and a very tight pain in his groin. "The dance scene is a good way for Asian talent to get marketed outside Asia," he explained. "There's a stigma attached to being a Malaysian or Singapore artist but in the dance scene it's less about the personalities. People are more interested in the music. It's more anonymous — you get into the music first and find out who it is second."

Together with Colin and Rodney from Fuse, we slipped silkily into several bars: a rather flash new joint called Flux, some tropical bar full of ex-pats soaking up the nighttime warmth, and from there into a pit of carnal excess, which politeness prevents me from detailing (there is something about Asia and debauchery that blends like gin & tonic). All I recall is that when I fell back into the hotel at some wretched hour of the morning I had completely lost touch with what room I was in. Stumbling around entirely the wrong floor I was collared by security, who seemed to think I was trying to gatecrash Westlife's room, which, in retrospect, I very probably was.

The next day I found Dean and James draped elegantly by the hotel's pool and we were joined on the veranda by Matt, Colin and the Malaysian DJ Groovedoctor, chatting through the late afternoon under a colonial fan that swept around in cool, hypnotic rotations. Colin and Dean had met before, but this was the first adventure for Golden to KL, the exploratory mission that will lead to greater links in the future, between one of the UK's strongest brands and Fuse, who seemed to run things in this particular corner of the planet. "The dance scene is fairly new here," said Colin, "probably about six years old. It started in warehouse raves in airport hangars and photo studios where only local DJs would perform. It was illegal at the time but it soon built a following."

"It's that global market," Dean detailed, cementing my own belief that planet Earth is one big disco under a glitterball moon. "Countries that started five or six years later than the UK are expanding in the same way, and look to the UK and clubs like Golden as market leaders. So it's an ideal way of keeping the scene alive and fresh."

The colonial link between the UK and Malaysia is obvious and in a wholly funkier way, UK club brands are now returning to former colonies like Malaysia, Hong Kong and Singapore in a new wave of disco imperialism... by the ingenious use of club banners instead of national flags. "You book a UK DJ here and you've got a full club," Colin explained. "A US DJ... maybe not. It's all about the UK."

After dinner we headed to Movement for the Golden event, a real buzz bouncing between us all. Movement holds 3,500 people and as soon as I walked in I felt the energy crackle. James played a solid warm up set and when he handed the disco baton over, Dean had a fully fucked up funky dancefloor to play to. And he rocked it, combining a tight progressive sound with some of his own tracks on CD. "It's very emotional here," Colin smiled, as we hugged and bounced around in the DJ booth. "Because Malaysians are generally very emotional people, really touchy feely. It's as if they feel the music."

Being more of a punter than a pro, I joined the family hug on the dancefloor, Golden shining bright in the heart of Asia. Dean and James went back to the hotel and I was peeled off the dancefloor at some hazy stage in the morning, then poured into the back of a car and driven to an afterparty. As we pulled up to a tower block in an anonymous suburb, someone opened the door for me and I fell out, rolled into a bush and fell asleep.

Dean flew back for a gig the next morning but I had one thing on my mind. Shopping. KL is great for shopping. Caught up in a whirlwind of naked consumerism and rampant purchasing I gave my credit card a damned good rogering. Shopping list: a bunch of fake DVDs (I don't possess a DVD player); about twenty fake PlayStation games (which I can't play because my PlayStation isn't chipped); a new wardrobe of fake clothes (if you ever see me out in Evisu jeans, please don't think I've got the money for the real thing); and a gun, an extremely realistic plastic gun to use with my Playstation, which I bought without the first thought as to the potential chaos it might cause when trying to get it on the plane home.

That night more of KL revealed itself. They've got it all, from the purest evil Euro cheese to a Chinese hard house scene called "feng tao" — a loose translation of which is "head fuck". But I know what I like and I liked what I'd seen, so it was back to Movement for seconds, a night for the local scene called Mass. Groovedoctor and another lo-

Discombobulated

cal DJ, Gabriel, played back to back. One of the last tunes played was Daft Punk's Around The World and that summed the whole trip up for me — from the beaches of Ibiza to the jungles of Malaysia, the unifying power of dance music really is joining up the world in a network of disco dots.

The Wrong Side gets closer all the time. | *June 2001*

21
Croatia, put your mask on

SLAPPED INTO CONSCIOUSNESS BY A MEMBER HER MAJESTY'S
SPECIAL FORCES; STRUGGLING DOWN THE ADRIATIC COAST;
A USER'S GUIDE TO EASTERN EUROPE ON A HANGOVER

Someone slapped me. *Schlapqk.* Square across the chops. My eyes
creaked opened and felt their way around the room. It was gone 7am,
the latest time I could wake up and make the plane to Croatia. My
head hurt like a snapped limb. The last thing I remember was saying
something like, "for Christ sake, soldier, don't let me miss my plane."
And there he was at the business end of the slap, the soldier in question, a Major in the British Army.

Me and the Major, we met as trainee adults: same class, first day
at secondary school. These days he fires guns and I write about discos; he is special forces and I am special needs, with one night to
spend in Manchester before he shipped out to Iraq. So we kicked the
guts out of just about every bar in my neighbourhood. Who knows
what time we poured back into my apartment. Felt like only minutes had passed. I leant up on one arm and the room swam about
me then settled, like a wave retreating from a beach, leaving a trail
of broken reality driftwood. The Major had made me a cup of tea,
packed a weekend bag (meticulously of course) and was now clap-

99

Discombobulated

ping his hands, in a "get a grip, soldier" kind of way; every clap like a church bell going off in the steeple of my head. But it was all worth it. We had to have that night on the town before he went over there... to build sandcastles or whatever they have them do. Regular readers of Dispatches will know I don't care for that particular project. Doesn't mean I don't care for the people involved.

So that was the state I was in when they parachuted me into the Wrong Side, landing a mere two countries short of the drop zone. Clearly I was still drunk. Two funky Croats met me in Trieste, Italy and drove me over the boarder into Slovenia, then through two border patrols and into Croatia itself.

The Major and I studied the Balkans in history class, but nothing beats watching the pages of history books pop up into 3D reality. This area of Europe was once part of the Austro-Hungarian Empire. They built ornate resorts along the Adriatic coast for their aristocracy to come play. One such place was Opatija, on the other side of the bay from Rijeka, and it was there that I checked into a suite at the Hotel Imperial — a grand but fading palace — and uncovered what the Major had packed: Six pairs of socks for a two night stay; a little book of text message coding; speakers for my iPod but no plug adaptor. And no jumper (of course), just those six pairs of socks. Bastard. I texted him, blaming him for my mental fragility and just about every other loose concern I had kicking about in my head. Then I went out to dinner.

At the restaurant I caught up with the camera crew from MTV and Zelijko Vukovic, part of the Marabunti team charged with the task of pulling the ancient Rijeka Carnival kicking and screaming, spitting and biting, into the twenty first century. "The tradition of the carnival is really big," Zelijko explained, knocking back limoncellos. "But the younger generation need something more spectacular to make them put their mask on."

The tradition of the Rijeka Carnival goes back so far no one seems entirely sure what it's actually about. One common theory is that people put on scary masks, and dress up in crazy costumes to scare off winter and its associated evil spirits. Now the authorities want the young generation to connect with that tradition, which is where

Marabunti comes in, drawing them in like bats attracted to the sonar pulse of electronic music.

First, and for reasons I could never quite get to grips with, we had been invited to a masquerade ball in the palace of a local dignitary. A nod to the footman and we were through the ornate doors, to the top of a gracefully curving stairway where, within the baroque refinery of the ballroom, people danced to a live orchestra, behind masks of such magnificence, in costumes of such complexity, I felt like a right disco hobo in my flat cap and scarf. It was a total Ferrero Roche moment. I never met the Ambassador, but truly he was spoiling us.

Later, we headed into the centre of Rijeka and into the gaping jaws of the carnival itself. The electronic element of proceedings took place within the four walls of Kobla Square, under the open canopy of the sky. A succession of local and regional DJs took to the stage, spinning techno and more out-there electronica. I nestled into the VIP to one side, friendly Croats passing me beers like buckets of water along a fire chain. Tiring fast from the goings on of the previous twenty five hours, I could barely connect with the evening when... an angel appeared — literally, an angel — from the very fringes of reality, who woke me up with some heavenly trickery. Soon, the evening took me by the scruff of the neck. I hugged it up with the people I knew from last year — DJs like Renato, Amor and Darian. A band called Underground Sky took to the stage. A cross between Kraftwerk and Kiss, they stood behind laptops and brightly painted faces. The lead singer looked like Marilyn Manson. He came down from the stage and gave me a beer. A lady interviewed me for Croatian TV. I have no idea what I said.

My phone woke me the following afternoon. Neven. The same photographer as last year. He once won a basketball scholarship to the University of Hawaii and now lives in Zagreb with twenty seven snakes. He's Good People. Good People presently sat on the terrace of a café over the road. I climbed into some jeans and joined him, chasing the demons from my head on a river of strong, chewy coffee. It was a gentle, quiet morning. The quiet before the storm.

How best to describe the carnal brutality of the Rijeka carnival? Well, I was wearing a jacket, Zelijko's girlfriend's scarf and a cap. In

Discombobulated

the street next to me however, was a guy with no trousers, and his old chap in a sock. Next to him a man dressed in a wetsuit and flippers was doing the breaststroke along the street. The parade carved a carnivorous path through the city centre, one surreal float pursued by another: Romans trailed a huge wooden horse; an operation took place in a hospital ward, the nurses pushing equipment along, their fake boobs exposed to the heavens; there were dragons; clansmen in kilts. It was enough to drive any sentient man under. I held my nose, set my dial to *mucho dementio*, and dived in. Disney couldn't touch this shit.

"I'm going to have nightmares about this," I whispered to myself, sitting down for steak tartar that evening in a restaurant made of wood, in the hills above Opatija.

"... for years," Renato's girlfriend Marija nodded, knowingly.

"How drunk must you be to cope?" I asked.

"Very," she said in a sultry, Russian Countess kind of a voice, rolling the R as if it were a Havana cigar. "But for us it is normal."

Well that's precisely why I want to be here: Wherever reality prevails... wherever formality reigns... there you will find me — up to my gills in booze and potions, on a lifelong quest to bring surreality and malformality to the world. Praise the Lord and pass the ammunition.

"Everybody is waiting for this time of the year," said Zelijko, scooping tartar onto some bread, "because it's completely crazy. It's a release for everybody — you can hide behind the mask and do really stupid things. And people here love to do stupid things. Really, they love it. You're allowed to be crazy. The crazier you are, the better it is for the carnival."

After dinner we drove to the weekend's wind down party at a Rijeka club called Tocka — a stripped-down, bare-knuckle disco, set within a post-industrial space, with graffiti all over the walls and people all over the dancefloor, music filling the space like gas, from Amor, Renato and Arszenik; the kind of sleazy, dirty dance music that makes your hips twitch and your mind snap clean in two.

The innocent energy made me homesick for a time in the nineties when clubbing had a finer point; when brands were toothpaste and discos scared people. Maybe the action is in this part of Europe — the new Europe — the Wild East on the very edge of our continent. There is fun to be had in these parts, believe me, for those who like things on the edge. I think maybe that's why I like these Balkan badlands. Here, the edge is close. | *March 2005*

22
Skazi in Brazil

A CHA A CHA; NARROWLY EVADING KIDNAP FROM THE STREETS
OF SAO PAOLO; HOW TO RHUMBA TO THE MUSIC OF AN ISRAELI
THRASH-METAL-TRANCE-DANCE BAND IN THE RAINFORESTS OF
BRAZIL

The words had been hastily scribbled onto a compliment slip. It arrived in the post one morning and read simply: "Simon, do you want to go to Brazil?"

I turned the piece of paper over a couple of times, but that's all there was. So I grabbed a pen wrote "yes" beneath the question, and put it back in the post.

A couple of weeks later my phone rang: Tom from Cypher Press, author of said cryptic note.

It was a Tuesday, I think. "So you're up for going to Brazil?" he asked.

"Sure," I replied. "I'm in need of a Brazilian anyways. When were you thinking?"

"Saturday."

I fair spat my morning coffee all over my desk. Several issues loomed large: (1) I had writing assignments to tie up; (2) I had no idea what I needed in terms of jabs and inoculations; (3) what are you, crazy?... that's THREE GODDAMN DAYS AWAY! And (4) there was the small matter of the FA Cup final that Saturday. Tickets were rarer than rocking horse poop and I had my grubby little hands on one. Face value was £65 but they were already going on t'internet for £750. It was the game to end all games between my hometown's Arsenal and my adopted town's Manchester Utd (sorry, Tampa Bay Utd). Both teams had nothing to play for but that trophy.

"Can't do Saturday, amigo."

I paused, as the hamster started frantically turning the wheel in my head.

"How about Sunday?"

The next few days were a blur of writing and drinking. The doc said he could squeeze me in at late notice on Friday afternoon for more jabs than Mike Tyson could muster, but I went out for a long boozy lunch, then shopping, and forgot all about it. That meant I was now going full bore, headfirst into the very bowels of Brazil with no protection against any nasty, winged beasties; just the fact that my blood is pretty much pure tequila anyways and no good to anyone or anything on God's good Earth. On the flip side, I did find a rather splendid shirt in Diesel.

I always look for patterns in things — shapes in the sand — it's the only way I can make sense of the chaos inherent in this whole cumbersome business of being alive. And there I was in Cardiff (of all places) — watching Arsenal's two Brazilian players, Edu and Gilberto, running around the pitch with the cup and the green-and-gold Brazilian flag — thinking: That's where I'm headed, just as soon as I can get out of this stadium and into a dry martini.

It was something like a twelve hour overnight flight into Sao Paulo, which gave me some time to read over the press pack for Skazi and get a handle on what was taking me tora tora tora Kamis*kazi* style into deepest darkest Brazil. Even then it was hard to get my head around it all. From what I could glean, Skazi are an Israeli, genetically modified, rock trance act, with crow black rockers' hair down to their backsides and guitars ramped up to 11, thrashing it out over beats nudging 150 bpm. Brazil and Israel; rock and trance. It was a molotov cocktail no doubt, to be downed in one and then detonated in the stomach.

My first sight of Skazi frontman Asher Swissa came as we arrived at our downtown hotel, in rather polite time for breakfast. I couldn't figure out whether he had actually been to bed or just walked straight into the restaurant, dressed as he was in regulation black fatigues, with a wonderful glaze across his eyes that spoke of late nights and an ungodly lifestyle, self inflicted.

The Skazi management had already filled our heads with scare stories about Sao Paulo and these were backed up by others in the hotel. There are twenty five million people in the city and a lot of them have fuck all. De nada. Diddly squat. And when people have nothing, they have no fear because they have nothing to lose. In certain areas of town, I was quietly told, they would take one look at my blue eyes and blonde (well, yellow) hair — clock my watch — and, because they have no English, merely shoot rather than troubling themselves with explanations. In any case, I don't think English/Portuguese phrasebooks include chapters on heists and street robberies.

The conversation put me a little on edge. It's not the nicest thing to talk about over a breakfast of orange juice, croissants and jetlag. But we headed out anyway: through the smooth sliding doors of the hotel, and out from the sterility of the air con reception into the muggy wet warmth of a morning in Sao Paulo. In a nearby park, tropical birds cackled in the trees as a number of schoolchildren formed a circle beneath a concrete canopy and began carving capoeira shapes around one another — swerving and curving as their classmates cheered and clapped and beat out rhythms on drums.

"Do you like meat?" barked the Skazi tour manager Bijou, back at the hotel, as though there were an animal called "meat". As it happens I am a teeth gnashing carnivore, so we cabbed it to a Brazilian restaurant, where it is traditional to bring out various cuts of various beasts and carve them for you at the table. And they keep bringing it on until you are fit to burst, at which point you flick a sign on the table from green to red, which denotes: "For the love of god man, no more. I am spent."

Skazi were shaping up to be jolly good company. Asher had been a guitarist in an Israeli army band; his amigo Assaf had been a tank commander in the Lebanon. Everyone in Israel has to do a month in the army each year but these cats took a journalist on tour to show just how demented they are, and a subsequent military tribunal decided the Israeli army would be a safer place without them. Now they are a kind of cross between Derrick May and The Darkness. I was starting to like them. "Right," said Asher, banging down his glass on the table. "Now for the Holocaust jokes." I spat my drink out all over again, trying to figure out where Blair's anti-bigotry legislation might come into play when an Israeli is telling the jokes?

Emboldened by our positive experience of the park, the following day myself and other veterans of the UK press corp headed deep into Sao Paulo for a mooch; past the massive cathedral on the Parca de Se and through the many squares that connect the centre of this rambling, seemingly impregnable city. We did not pass one other foreign face all day.

As we walked back to the hotel, torrential rain came down as though the canopy of the sky had caved in, driving us into the nearest bar, one side completely open to the street as a rickety TV flickered with the Champions League final. It was half time and Liverpool were three down. Before long we were drunk, it was dark and we seemed to have become the centre of attention, possibly because there were cameras worth several thousand pounds sitting on the table next to our drinks. The situation began to gently rotate out of focus, the room rocking away from any sharp sense of reality. There was talk of getting a lift with a random guy who said it was too dangerous for us to go out into the night; that the cab drivers would rob us and worse. He made throat-slitting gestures. Something about what he said didn't hang right for me; the cab drivers had been fine. In a scene reminiscent of the movie 12 Angry Men, I had to persuade each of the others that it was a bad idea to go with him and, already drunk myself and thereby muggy-of-thought, managed to turn them one by one. Back at the hotel I was violently sick and became convinced someone had slipped me a mickey. When I got back to the UK I read in FHM that Sao Paulo is the kidnap capital of the world.

The next morning I woke with my head aching bad, as though Assaf had been joyriding in my cranium with his tank. I couldn't stomach anything for breakfast except a comfort cuddle. The flight across Brazil to Goiânia seemed to take an age. At the other end a bus picked us up and drove us straight to the site of the festival where Skazi was

Discombobulated

to play. Set in shaded woodland, strange creatures crawled between the trees; people were flaked out on mats, like the corpses from some medieval battleground; human detritus set against a dayglo backdrop; bronzed bodies and butterfly smiles fluttered through the trees.

People plied me with potions. A reveller stumbled into view — the only person I had seen in an English football top. Arsenal. I approached and started blathering incoherently about Gooners and Highbury... Brazilian flags in Cardiff and Arsenal tops in Brazil... shapes in the sand. He smiled, weakly. | *June 2005*

23
Singapore Sling

CLINT DAGGER, AND HIS FAITHFUL COMPANION KELVIN
RODRIGUEZ GO HARD UNDERCOVER IN THE STRIP-JOINTS AND
DANCEHALLS OF SOUTHEAST ASIA

In one corner of the bar, a man in a pink T-shirt sang slow songs to another man. Our table was covered with beers and ashtrays and it was so warm my shirt clung to me like skin. I was surrounded by hookers and for some reason had taken to introducing myself as Clint Dagger. Clones to the left of me; karaoke to the right; stuck in the middle with booze. This must be the Wrong Side of the tracks; this must be my kind of town; this must be Asia.

"Ah, Cwint, your name so nice," said one girl, giving my thigh a squeeze.

I turned slowly to my photographer Jimmy the Hat, who now wanted to be known as Kelvin Rodriguez. "Hi, I'm Kevin," he said to another girl, not even getting that right. He had the look of a kid who had fallen from the tree of innocence and landed in a pile of crack candy. The other two had stayed in the hotel, not daring to the sample the late night treats of downtown Singapore, but I was in a mood for mischief, for snuffling out troubles.

We downed our beers and walked out into the wet warmth of Singapore; the air sweet and soupy. The street was in the Colonial style, a little ghost echo of the good old days when we ran the world. Victorian balconies looked over the street, beneath which women (at least

Discombobulated

I hoped they were women) tempted us to step inside their bars and bodies with a seductive wink and curling finger.

But I'm getting ahead of myself. Our story starts in Amsterdam, where a firm friendship was founded over cold beers and handshakes. Myself and Jimmy the Hat had flown in from Manchester to rendezvous with a DJ called Solace and his manager, Sam Lambert from Mean Dream. I had no idea what either of them looked like, so I phoned when we touched down.

"We're the two good looking guys," Sam chuckled.

"Strange," I replied, scanning the airport bar. "I thought that was us."

We stole onto the red eye to Singapore — stealing wine, stealing sleep until — over the other side of the planet, we were met by Godwin, DJ and promoter of a new club called DXO. I don't rightly recall what time we reached the hotel. My watch is a GMT Master II, designed for pilots to exist in different time zones, but none of that really matters when the only time you exist in is the Twilight Zone.

I tried to wake myself from my jetlag by getting cuddly with the hotel's rooftop pool, which overlooked the lights of Singapore. At dinner, this silky cat of a waiter demonstrated the traditional art of dispensing tea — over the shoulder, under the arm, all manner of what can only be described as kung fu tea pouring. Then Godwin took us to DXO and ordered drinks. And you just know you're in trouble when your drink's on fire. I knocked back Flaming Lamborghinis; lay my head under a beer tower and let cold lager cascade down my gullet; dunked my head into pitchers of vodka Red Bull as though dipping for apples. All of it on the house. My kind of price.

"It's a huge structure," said Godwin, walking us around the club, "funded and guided by the Singapore government. The club is done for a social purpose. Music brings everyone together."

Singapore can seem a rather sanitised environment, but the government understands that as well as the more genteel traditional clubs they operate, they needed to get with the programme and build one for the kids. And that's DXO, which stands for Disco Extraordinaire (man, I would have loved to have sat in on that meeting — despite the harsh penalties, someone was obviously high as a hoot owl).

Only four months old, the place looked the business: the bridge of the Starship Enterprise for a DJ booth; a wooden terrace overlooking downtown and the river; a VIP area; even a cigar room, with bottles of vintage scotch older than dinosaurs.

"We're situated amongst all the theatres and we're still only a baby," Godwin grinned. "It's obviously appealing to the younger kids in Singapore, you know, trying to keep it fresh. Because Singapore is really opening up its doors to the world right now. We want to get a whole global perception going on. We don't want to be contained anymore." That process of opening up has created a hungry dance-floor, eager for music. "And it's not normal, mainstream Britney Spears right now. People are starting to listen — they're starting to read more and open up their ears here and that's brilliant, mate."

It was only the warm up night, but long ago I lost the ability to set my disco dial to "moderate lunacy" or even "slight mayhem"; long ago that switch snapped and now I'm stuck permanently on "disco bonkers". Now there's no messing, no prisoners — I'm going down in Flaming Lamborghinis and taking everyone with me. Outside the club I wrestled with Jimmy the Hat until the two of us ended up bruised and in bushes. Back at the hotel I couldn't even make it to my room, and fell asleep in the corridor, an outstretched hand reaching in vain for my door, key card in hand.

If there's one thing you need to do in Singapore, it's have a Singapore Sling at the famous Raffles hotel. It never happened. Our days were spent shopping in Singapore's maze of malls; strolling down the Singapore River, past the Merlion (the half mermaid, half lion symbol of Singapore... obviously that same someone from the DXO Naming Committee has been licking frogs again); checking the grandeur of the Fullerton hotel; drinking in the ramshackle bars of Boat Quay, beneath the skyscrapers of downtown penetrating the soft tissues of the sky; eating amazing food; travelling along the water on a river taxi; shooting pool in a bar on the banks of the river (I beat everyone, so long as I had a toothpick in my mouth; when I dropped it, everyone caned my candy ass). We watched the sun go down over the beaches of Sentosa Island, the huge hulls of oil frigates bobbing gently on the surface of the South China Sea.

Discombobulated

The evenings we spent in DXO, kicking back on couches and watching live premiership football (kind of kooky in a club at night-time); relaxing with G&Ts in the open air of the terrace. Dream Team is a real international affair: Sam is a Frenchman who lives in Holland, Solace is a Scot who lives in Ireland and they have DJs on their books located everywhere from Rio to Chicago. By the end of the weekend even Jimmy the Hat wound up on their books. I offered my services as DJ Wrong. I have DJd as such and trust me I'm not kidding with the name — I'm awful. But that's my gimmick, see? I'm a shit DJ. Here's my sales pitch: *Is your club too successful? Is your dancefloor too packed? Call DJ Wrong... I'll come round your place and fuck it right up.*

Dream Team is essentially a progressive agency, but consists of DJs who play across the genres. "With all the records I've bought," Solace detailed, "I've tried to develop a sound which is me, you know. Hopefully I've got something in the music there that people like, something universal."

Solace has played everywhere from Estonia to Mexico to Brazil, where the dancefloor can be a tough (Brazil) nut to crack. "Even if it's progressive or really selective, his music keeps people dancing," Sam added, "which in Brazil is really important. You have to make them dance — that's all they want — they need to move."

I hear that, brother. Godwin played first, followed by Solace who did indeed spin a chunky set of progressive electronic music, music that didn't flatline but built upon healthy sine waves that crashed out across the beach of the dancefloor. "It's one of the best places I've ever worked in," he said, stepping down from the booth after his set. "Without a shadow of a doubt. My hair was moving with the bass, man. I don't have much left but... "

The mean Dream Team back together, we sank a few and then headed out into the night, to a club called Attica where Greg Vickers was playing, where it nearly went really wrong with some Bangkok chick boys. What's that line about a night in Bangkok making a hard man humble? That's true right across Asia.

I consider myself a hardened professional but that night nearly did it for me. Because you just know you're drunk when you catch a cab home alone from a club... to entirely the *wrong hotel*... and then proceed to get into an argument with the bellboy as to why the lift's in the wrong place... | *August 2005*

24
Poland

"There's something wrong with the brakes."

The driver tore through the intestines of the Polish countryside at, I was amused to note, exactly twice the speed limit.

"Really," I replied from the co-pilot seat.

He turned to me and grinned manically. "Yeah!"

We had already put in some klicks that weekend, floating through Poland all somnambulant and snoozy, whilst our driver, guide and soul brother Polish Panti (a nickname derived from a Pantera heavy metal T-shirt he always wore) drove like Colin McRae on crystal meth.

"Don't worry, dogs," said Panti, dropping a gear to get the revs up and overtake another lugubrious lorry. "It's going to be OK."

It was a ramshackle journey that resembled *The Great Escape*. In the back seat was Antony Photos and two members of the band, Rare Unit. More were in another car, others on a train. If you looked really closely out across the fields you could see Steve McQueen vaulting fences on a motorbike. I love the Wrong Side when it's like this — for almost the entirety of the weekend I had no idea where we were or what was going on and that's how things should be. So the brakes were fucked. Plenty of time to slow down when you're dead.

One of the backseat passengers was Jafar. The first time we met was at the Southport Weekender. He approached me when I was particularly discombobulated and asked if I would go to Poland with him and, too disorientated to refuse, here we were — on tour together, ripping through the Polish countryside in a Honda with no brakes.

Another random collision brought Jafar and Panti together at Jafar's residency at Neighbourhood. Panti was in London working, and seized on the familial fact that Jafar is a quarter Polish. "For me that is very important," Panti said. "He's got Polish roots so I wanted to bring him back to the homeland. I can feel it in my heart that he is Polish."

Rare Unit, and its umbrella record label Kwaito, is a rather loose collection of individuals who all bring something a little different to the party, whether it be Andy Touchfinger's classical music training, Jafar's club background or Paul Madgwick's label experience at Ministry of Sound. What brought them together was London's deep house scene and a desire to make and release good house music — so far three 12s by Rare Unit, with tracks to follow from Rithma and one of Andy's protégés, a fifteen year old called Tim Split. The name Kwaito was bestowed upon them by South Africans who told Jafar it was a word meaning street beats. "It's just a voice for indigenous peoples over there who are sick of oppression," said Jafar, "and have created their own music by fusing house, socca, reggae, rap and hip hop."

"We are completely new," explained Panti (née Marcin Korgól) of his own promotions company Garlic Sausages (don't ask). "We are just big heart men, that's all." For this tour Panti wanted to weld Rare Unit with a rhythm section and trumpeter from the Polish jazz scene. "It was just an idea, dog," Panti said, his head seemingly full of such madcap schemes. "But it was not so easy to match together the house music with the jazz."

I have always felt that, rather like cocktails and chemistry sets, fabulous things happen when you try to mix it up some, say the smokey, muted trumpet of Antoni Ziut Gralak with the turntabalism of Jafar. Sometimes the cocktail is delicious; sometimes the test tube explodes. The first such sonic experiment took place in a club called Balsam, an ex-WWI munitions dump just outside the centre of Warsaw (although I soon found myself slurring my words and calling it a musician's dump). This collection of connected arches filled with a funk fertilization of house grooves and jazz melodies, the bass and beats laying the bedding on which trumpet, guitar and decks could grow.

"I am the Polish Paul McCartney."

"Yeah you are!" I replied to the burly Polish man who had grabbed me in a big hug. He turned out to be Jafar's uncle, a Polish recording artist who very probably *was* the Polish Macca. Band on the run; audience in the rum; the two slowly merged and melted into one and, together, danced their way into morning.

Ding dong.

I woke from my slumbers and reached for that first cig of consciousness, when you try to suck up the smoke of reality, the first high of the day. "Come in!"

Nothing. Then I remembered I have a new phone and had set the text alert sound to a doorbell. Blow me if it wasn't realistic. As far as I know you don't have to say "come in" to text messages, although, as an aside, Antony Photos does often say "thank you" to cash machines when they pay out.

I took myself for a mooch around Warsaw's old town, through the old square, reconstructed after the centre of town was completely destroyed in WWII, before our car convoy snaked out of Warsaw, leaving our own destruction behind. Saturday's gig took place in another city called Chorzow, in a club called Szuflada15; much more of a beaten up jazz joint. The band were tight as twins, the rhythm smooth, solid and dependable enough for the other instruments to take off on their own abstract, digressive journeys; the gorgeous diva Hannah out front, shaking the walls with her vocals.

Marcin had other devious plans for me and Antony and, whilst the band wound things up, we climbed back into the goosed Honda and drove through the night to Krakow, to a club I had been to earlier in the year called Prozak (where, bizarrely the same English guys were DJing: Manchester's 3am Recordings). We took in another club called RDZA and then it was time for bed, which was an apartment hired for us next to a door with a red light that looked suspiciously like a brothel. Feeling bored and drunk and mischievous we knocked on the door. "Come back in twenty minutes" a voice gruffled, in English. I have no idea how he knew we were English but in any case it was enough to scare us boys back to our beds.

Top tip, disco amigos: If you've had a big night out on the razzle-dazzle, best not to follow it up in the midst of a Sunday morning comedown with a trip to Auschwitz. It was truly one of the most harrowing experiences of my life, compounded by the oppressive, grey atmosphere that hung both in the sky and in my head. Antony didn't want to take photographs and likewise I don't really know what to say about it all. Which is something of a first.

In need of cheering up, the weekend — and indeed the tour — rounded off with a shindig at a bar called Flash Pub in Panti's hometown of Czestochowa (the literal translation of which is "many times hiding", referring to the Catholic cathedral which, despite its size, apparently keeps disappearing below the hills as you approach). Jafar and Andy Touchfingers DJd with some of the local guys and soon had the place jumping. Everyone was in the mood for a party and collectively put a big boot into the booze.

As we took a break and sat outside, beneath the sky, Jafar attempted the job of cheering me up by recounting the story of his clubnight, the Hasslehof Scandal. Week before opening and who should be in town but the Hoff himself. David *Knight Rider*, *Baywatch* "Oh-Do-Put-That-Chest-Rug-Away" Hasslehof. The guys couldn't let that opportunity pass and stalked and sweet talked him into submission... until he said he would maybe make an appearance. And blow me he did, turning up at the Telegraph in Brixton to sing the house track he's recorded (no shit, amigos, I'm sober and everyfink; he's done a house track) before taking off his jacket to reveal a T-shirt that read "I'm not dead yet".

It was enough to put a smile on my face and give me the energy to return to the party and to the dancefloor, hugging goodbyes to everyone in the band. It had been a long weekend. Six clubs and Auschwitz is a lot to fit into one body and soul. When I got back home and to my own bed, the first night's sleep was broken by a ferocious fear and a loose, amorphous dread. I continually woke up feeling someone

Discombobulated

was in the room, or that I was somewhere else. I hardly slept. The next day I mentioned it to Antony and he said he'd had exactly the same experience. Auschwitz has subsequently formed the location for dreams. | *October 2005*

25
Whistler

BUMS UP TREES; DRUNKS UP MOUNTAINS; SLOPING OFF ON THE
WEST COAST OF CANADA AND UPSETTING THE POPULATION OF
THAT GREAT COMMONWEALTH NATION. THERE'LL BE LETTERS...
BELIEVE ME THERE'LL BE LETTERS. AND THERE ARE

"Dude, you want to see me climb a tree?"

The voice appeared from deep within a beard, matted like bird-snest soup, sprinkled liberally with croutons. A passer-by shouted, "Don't bother man. The guy does it all day long. He'll want money from you." I was sitting outside a bar in Vancouver with a few hours to kill and a few bucks to burn before the night flight back to the UK. I had a glass of cold beer in front of me and the company of good people. There wasn't a single thing in the entire world I could think of spending my last few dollars on that could come close to the simple pleasure of watching a downtown bum monkey-up a sidewalk tree.

"Sure, why not."

You know you're in trouble when you wake up on your first morning in a ski resort, your muscles aching like bad memories, and then re-call that you haven't actually been on the slopes yet. When we finally got in to Whistler it was 7am according to my body clock, but 11pm according to the bartender's, and I much preferred to trust his chro-nometer. If he's open for business, then I'm open to suggestions. Now it was 6am, Canada time, and I couldn't sleep. I ran a deep bath and switched on the percolator, turning my coffee Irish with last night's leftover bedside scotch.

Discombobulated

No phone signal — literally cut off from the world. No bad thing, though kind of ironic considering it was phones that brought me here to the World Snowboarding Championships. My phone is an N-Gage and Nokia were using the Champs to launch a new snowboarding game, *SSX*. We know that the way to a journalist's heart is through his passport so what better than to assemble a bunch in Whistler, get them drunk as wild moose and nudge them off the nearest mountain, loosely strapped onto a piece of wood. Fine by me. Journalists had come from all over the States and the UK, some to cover the ski and some, I guess, like me, to cover the après-ski.

The UK press scrum congregated for breakfast, sorted out boards and boots and headed up the mountain. Go go gondola. I clicked into my bindings and took off down the mountain, stopping at intervals to take in the beauty of my surroundings and the fiery contents of my hip flask. The weather was all shades of shabby; quite worrying to be honest. Whistler is one of the most famous ski resorts on the planet but even they don't have the resource to fight this enemy: climate change. I don't mean to be dramatic, but I saw it. It's here. It was peak season and the mountains should have been perfect, snow falling like cotton candy dandruff from the shaggy hair of heaven, but it was too warm and instead was falling as rain. Now rain I get at home — I live in Manchester ferchrissakes. What I wanted was fairytale snow and red-cheeked girls. But this? I needed to take an umbrella up the mountain with me. The people in the resort tried to put a brave face on it but you could tell they were spooked; no one had seen the like of it. My advice would be to have a word with the drunken doughnut who runs next door. Just one word actually. Kyoto.

Nokia's motto is "connecting people" and I'm all for that. In fact, back down the mountain we connected with the Nokia people themselves, discussing some of their latest developments in a seminar. The way phones are going now: combining PDAs, MP3 players and games consoles is a natural and welcome evolution. These days you can download music direct to the hard drive on your phone, and use it like an iPod. Such digital distribution of music has put John Holmes sized willies up the backsides of the music industry and that's a good thing. Fuck 'em. The offices of record companies are, on the

(top) Perhaps inspired by such a well-brewed cuppa, Howard got the band back together soon after.
(bottom) A eulogy to Hunter S. Thompson, during a night of Fear & Loathing in StalyVegas.

..AND ON THE SIXTH DAY, GOD CREATED MANchester

THE HAÇIENDA

(previous page, top) Feeding metal pellets to
the ravenously hungry poker machines, Las Vegas,
and (bottom) Simon and his kid brother, 'aving it
large for 24 Hour Party People in MADchester.

(this page, top) Simon and Jonny Bing Bang in
an ungodly shoot out with vampires at the Titty
Twister, and (bottom) Trying on wigs with Ms
Lamaar in the dressing room of Foo Foo's.

(previous page, top) Hard at work in Ibiza. Pouring your own drinks is so last century, and (bottom) With Comrade Mark Luvdup, during one trip when Simon didn't get deported from Moscow.

(this page, top) Multiple murderer and celebrity gangster Dave Courtney shows Simon the cold, steel edge of the Wrong Side, and (bottom) With Jimmy the Hat, sailing back to the Right Side under the Golden Gate Bridge, San FranDisco.

(previous page, top) At Gatecrasher with some
of the fabulous random individuals you meet on
the dancefloor, all fellow veterans of the Disco
Wars, and (bottom) Photographic evidence that
the bum really did monkey up a sidewalk tree in
Gastown, Vancouver.

(this page, top) Antony Crook's shot of Nick Fry,
early morning Manhattan, after his cross-town
ride in the boot of a cab, and (bottom) Writing
New York Stories in the suite at The Chelsea,
NYC, with Lester Bangs and a single malt for
company.

(top) Colin and Simon became somewhat detached soon after this photo was taken.

(bottom) Before realising the beers were 12 per cent at the Petrovaradin Fortress in Novisad, Serbia... perfectly and blissfully unconscious and happy.

whole, the very orifices of Beelzebub, populated by A & R farts who wouldn't know a good tune if it snuck up behind them, undid their belt, whipped down their pants and bit them hard on their hairy tush.

The synergy between games and their soundtrack is, however, a more beautiful thing. EA Sports have started their own music company, EA Trax, to handle such stuff, sourcing music just like a regular record label and trying to break new artists via their games. For instance, there is an exclusive track on the *SSX* game by the band Swollen Member, alongside such avalanche inducing grooves as the Jason Nevin's remix of N.E.R.D's Rockstar. It was pretty interesting hearing about it all. I took notes. Christ, at one point I even asked a question. It was easily the most work I've ever done on a press trip. I was exhausted. Spent. Truly I had earned my next drink.

And what a drink it was. The après-ski took the form of an ice party in a club near the hotel. The Brits assumed their usual position, hanging off the bar, slamming shots of tequila, as three ice maiden dancers took to the stage, an artist painted onto a canvas and a DJ who looked like Rose West rocked the dancefloor. It was, all in all, a very strange evening.

Next day on the slopes, my confidence was growing and that spelt trouble. I labour under the misapprehension that I'm bulletproof, bombproof and generally immortal... get me drunk and put me on a mountain and things will go all kinds of wrong. And they did. Boarding fast, I wiped out, went down hard and felt my ankle twist, the pain reverberating through my leg and resonating out across the mountain. Not good. When Martin, my boarding buddy from Nokia, suggested we stop for beers I replied all kinds of yes. It was still morning.

The barroom conversation that evening switched between two subjects: (1) whether the Rose West DJ, who we decided was called Dr Sauce, was a man or a woman, and (2) whether it was worth heading out to the main gig that night, a hip hop guy called K-Os. To go or not to go, that is the question. As it turns out I ended up hobbling to the venue on what felt like a broken ankle. In the rain. To a gig I wasn't sure I wanted to see. Of — *it was starting to dawn on me* — someone I had never heard of. And then, when we arrived after all the procrastination, it was for the very last dr-dr-dr-drum beat of the

Discombobulated

night. "Thank you and good night, Whistler," said K-Os. You needed a little cloakroom type ticket to buy a beer. They had beer but had run out of the tickets. All the above is concrete proof of why there is no God.

We decanted to a local bar and within moments had managed to upset pretty much everyone there. I'm not sure how we did it; quite an achievement, actually. The TV was showing what could only be described as a sheep rodeo with dwarves riding bareback, or maybe they were children? I couldn't kick a random image in my head of trampolining monkeys... everyone had started to refer to the country as Canadia, perhaps in deference to Peter Andre's land of Insania... we had taken to reciting bits from the *South Park* movie... I don't know what all the fuss was abooot.

"You guys are always in the wrong place," said the waitress, pushing past us. We'd been there mere minutes. Besides, what did she mean by "wrong place"? Canada? Sweet cheeks, I was *born* in the wrong place.

Things were turning weird. Shiraz, a guy from the *Daily Mirror*, stopped the waitress and asked if Dr Sauce was a man or a woman. She looked at him as though he'd climbed out of a time machine and barked "What year is this?" I looked to Rich, my friend from *Nuts*, for support but he was too tired and (as he put it) going back to Club Duvet. One in, one out. He was right of course; the only escape from such viscous levels of peculiarity is the sanctuary of unconsciousness. I limped into sleep.

On the last day I decided, along with Shiraz and Ian (from the snowboarding magazine *Document*), to ignore the slopes and slope off to the city of Vancouver and some sense of sea level normality. Only, the cab driver who took us back down the mountain was quite the most mentally unhinged man I have ever met, and pushed me over the edge. I was suffering from the same kind of bends that hit divers coming up too fast from the deep — ears popping, mind consumed by visions of goddamn trampolining monkeys. The driver dropped us near a bar. We sat out on the terrace. I clung to my beer like a drowning man clinging to a lifebelt. A tramp approached our table. | *February 2005*

26
Kylie party

HAP-PY BIRTH-DAY DEAR KYYYYYLIE... FAST LESSONS IN HOW TO
GATECRASH A POP DIVA'S PARTY

I had a late night this morning.

Carried out from the West End of London in the back of a black
cab; an English Psycho. My suit was Armani (Collezioni). My shirt
was Armani. Even my boxers. Head to toe Giorgio. The taxi rolled
through the streets like a black ball bearing; London was nothing
but a big game of bagatelle. I smoothed the trousers of my suit and
popped the cork on the half bottle of Moët I'd swiped from The Sanderson, concealed amongst the folds of my jacket. The cork ricocheted
around the back of the cab, prompting the driver to turn his head, a
scientist peering through the safety screen of a glass divide.

The Sanderson hotel looked beautiful tonight, like something
built from the words of F. Scott Fitzgerald, full of light and laughter
and... her, floating above it all, like Tinkerbell sprinkling magic over
the Moulin Rouge. Kylie Minogue. Was it not a dream? Was I really
singing "hap-py birth-day dear Ky-lie" not two hours past? Be still my
beating heart. I clung to the curves of the bottle for comfort because
it was all true, I was indeed on my way back from a party celebrating
the end of Kylie's tour and her thirty fourth birthday.

Armani. Moët. Kylie. Sweet Jesus himself just dropkicked me
through the goalposts of life. It was all so dreamy, so sophisticated —
a Cinderella night with me as the cleaning girl, sneaking in for a few,
delicious moments under the shimmering chandelier of celebrity. All
I needed do now was go spuds deep with Tara Palmer-Doo-Dah and

Discombobulated

check in for a spell at the Priory and surely I was a shoe-in at the Met Bar. It must be only a matter of days before my portrait takes its rightful place in the hallowed hall of fame that is *Heat* magazine.

Of course ordinarily they wouldn't let a random, stumbling, halfcut journalist within a thousand arseholes of a party like that but I had a contact on the inside; and if you've got one of those, you can party your way into Osama's cave rave, should you so wish. The plan? Even the most celebrated of celebrity parties needs music, and if you need music, well then you need DJs and that's just a whole different kettle of collagen. So this was my route into Kylie Minogue's birthday party: the DJs invited to provide the soundtrack were the MYNC Project; the MYNC Project are involved with the label Credence; Credence is under the umbrella of Kylie's label EMI; bada-bing bada-boom, ka-ching ka-ching... and that's why ducks have feathers.

And that's why I found myself, earlier that evening, trying to find the Sanderson. Which I failed to do. Instead, I hailed a black cab, which drove around two corners and twenty seconds later dropped me at the door of the hotel — in itself an extravagance but a splendid bit of manoeuvring because, as I climbed out, the paparazzi leapt to sudden attention, holding aloft their cameras for an optimistic moment before it dawned on them I wasn't actually Chris Moyles. I waited outside for the DJs — my route in — the music industry equivalent of sneaking in the back door. Eventually the cognoscenti congregated. Our party consisting of the MYNC Project, the MYNC PR (if that's too acrobatic an acronym, it stands for Mark Younghead and Nick Corelli's Public Relation's manager, Tania) and Mark's girlfriend Charlotte. I bunched in with the group to make sure I was carried through the bottleneck of the hotel doors with the tidal flow of this entourage; to make like I belonged in this hotel as much as the piano in the corner, as the pictures on the wall, as the bar full of... SWEET MARY MOTHER OF GOD WOULD YOU LOOK AT ALL THAT BOOZE!

I strolled around celebrity Shangri-la, finding my way into a self-contained vodka bar; a dark, soft, velvet kind of a room that felt like sitting inside a cat. Putting on a suit somehow propels one into the realms of the raconteur and *bon viveur* — or perhaps voyeur — and to unusual choices of drink. I ordered a vanilla Martini — which I discovered to my delight was the booze equivalent of a grown-up milkshake — and chatted to the boys, as they got ready to play. The MYNC Project may sound like a housing estate in New York, but Mark and Nick actually came together via the Red Room at Passion, the renowned club in Coalville. Since then, music has taken them all over the world: Poland, the US, Malaysia, building a reputation as fine purveyors of funky house, played over four decks, two mixers and plenty of effects to really mash it up some. But you can't really crank it up too much, or spin nasty, dirty house music when one of the most patently delicious people on the planet is wiggling what has to be the planet's most famous behind on your dancefloor.

"It's more of a party night," Nick surmised. "I don't think the music is as important as some of the other clubs we play at but it's all good fun. We get to play stuff that we wouldn't normally play."

I took an ungentlemanly gulp from my Martini. "But what in blue blazes goes through your mind when you're packing a record box and trying to figure what might go down well at Kylie Minogue's birthday party?"

"We decided there would be no Kylie records in our set. That's one thing we did say," said Nick, Mark adding: "It is difficult because the crowd that go to these sort of parties aren't clued-up clubbers. They want to hear big records, whether that be a house record or a hip hop record."

Of course, with no disrespect to Coalville I was guessing Mark and Nick could never have imagined that playing records would lead them to step out with the glitterati at such showbiz shenanigans but then that's the weird and wonderful world of dance music. It's no accident, it's their involvement with Parlophone that has allowed them to get involved with Kylie and her remix packages...

"... we all want to get involved with her packages," Nick imparted, and ain't that the truth. It was big news that she'd split with her boyfriend, James Wotsisname, and when you hear something like that, there's always that tiny, tiny moment when wild thoughts storm the Bastille of your imagination and declare that, if only you were to be put in the same room, Kylie might suddenly see the light and realise

Discombobulated

that what she's been looking for all these years is actually a dented, mangled car crash of a writer, corpulent of frame and fierce of appetite. Perhaps this was that room?

There was enough free juice to keep us all fat and crazy, all paid for by Ms Minogue herself (I would guess few people can say Kylie Minogue got them pissed). We danced around a little and hovered, as media are wont to do, near the safe sanctuary of the decks, as Nick and Mark took turns spinning their party soundtrack, playing around with tracks like Van Helden's Chocolate Covered Cherry and Sneak's Fix My Sink.

Then a wave of excitement broke across the room, carrying Kylie into her party. She was indeed Tinkerbell-tiny, and beautiful, dressed in an ivory coloured Christian Dior dress; a pocket icon for the twenty first century, standing out against a pink neon sign that simply said "Kylie". Yep, when you are known to the world by a single name you really have made it. A couple of hundred people — many of whom, I guessed, she had never met — gathered around her to sing happy birthday (note to self: chalk that one down on life's list of surreal scenarios) as she received her presents and blew out the candles on her cake.

She looked happy, content, with a smile all out of proportion with her frame, as though its edges might break out beyond the physical realms of her face. I was naturally perturbed to note that her supposedly ex-boyfriend James Wotsisname was there, but I'll leave speculation on that subject to the tabloids; I just wanted to get squiffy as all hell and cause a scene. Naturally when you blag your way into Kylie Minogue's birthday party the first thing you do is tell all your pals. I had promised them I would engineer some chaos, at the very least cause some kind of inter-antipodean, international incident, thereby shoe-horning my way into the morning papers. I contemplated going up to Kylie to tell her my Australian ex-girlfriend named our goldfish after her, but was put off by the bouncers who formed a human shield around her; I contemplated getting sloshed with Mick Jagger, who was supposed to be turning up later; I was really pinning my hopes on Jay Kay showing up because he's always a sure bet for some fisticuffs.

But ultimately, inevitably, the machismo and bravado wore off with the booze and I conceded it was time for Cinderella to abandon the ball. With my suit mischievously loose and bulging about my body, I left the Sanderson and hailed a cab. As it pulled away I did my level best to get her out of my head. | *May 2002*

27
Ibiza and le Bon

MEETING SIMON LEBON, POOLSIDE; AS SMOOTH AS YOU LIKE

Without inferring any medical negligence on the good people of Microsoft corp and its affiliated companies, and without suggesting any aggressive, homosexual wrong doings, but it must be more than mere coincidence that whenever I party with the guys from Xbox, something always happens to my backside.

When we went snowboarding in Val d'Isere a bad tumble nearly broke my bum for good. This time I was goosed before I'd even started. They'd kindly invited me back to Ibiza (whats I gotta do to get myself barred from that place... sleep with someone's wife?) and I felt it only prudent to get some rays in prior to departure. So I booked my bootie in for a serious session on the electric beach, stripped down to a smile, and stepped in for a full-on nuclear blast. The net result was a red raw rump and an inability to sit down for any great length of time, which made the train journey to Stansted all the more painful: buckling tracks, burning tush, I was walking like John Wayne by the time I caught up with the rest of them.

Cherry ice cream smile I suppose it's very nice

On the first afternoon the swashbuckling reprobates of the English press transmogrified into pirates of the Mediterranean, climbing aboard a Spanish galleon. Arrr, mo 'artics, aiii. Us salty sea dogs set sail on them rough seas, making ready to storm the Radio 1 festivities, cutlasses held tight between our clenched teeth. Arrr.

At the front of the boat we discovered the same sort of wooden boon that Simon le Bon clung to so fabulously while filming the video to Rio. This sparked an inventive round of speculation as to why Duran Duran broke up, throwing a million teenage girls into the welcoming arms of those brutes from the Ballet. We settled upon the theory that Simon le Bon's pecs-out machismo when filming that video must have made him so seasick he threw up over Nick Rhode's chest. But how could it ever be proved? How would we ever know the truth?

Back on terra firma we found our land legs and our way to Pacha and into the extraordinarily expensive VIP area, which renders you roped off from riff-raff and reality. Still swaying from my ocean adventures I had to duck out early, crawling into my bed and then into the pool the next day. And there I stayed, like a beast in a swamp, occasionally peering from my lair like a crocodile, with only eyes above water, as the shore became populated by succulent promoter and DJ animals, coming to drink and feast at the poolside afternoon barbecue. Promoters like Charlie Chester, Dave Beer and Darren Hughes; DJs such as Steve Lawler and Pete Tong; and kids, everywhere kids, scampering about like Ritalin rabbits.

"Having kids is the new rock'n'roll," said Dave Beer, scruffing up his son's hair and the dyed flames that climbed up the back of his head. Tong had his kids with him, Darren Hughes his, Charlie had his daughter, and they were all in their element — it was their day really — all the pop you can swig and free gaming for as long as you want, with games that will hit the market later this year.

Other journalists sat down to interview Tongy and Lawlery, making me feel utterly inadequate in that I was still in the pool with a cold beer and couldn't — to be utterly honest — really — when it came down to it — you know, like... be arsed. I tentatively asked one of the other scribes what was with all the interviewing, and he replied that without quotes all he would be left with was a bunch of nonsense about pissing around in Ibiza. Jeepers. Better keep quiet, I thought, slipping quietly back beneath the comforting folds of the pool. That was *my* angle.

Discombobulated

*You know you're something special and you look like
you're the best*

Besides which, it was far too much fun in the pool — reclining in the
cerulean clear waters as a couple of the finest females in this fiefdom
poured booze down my throat. Point of fact, I'm not sure I would *ever*
have managed to climb out of that pool were it not for the tempta-
tions of Space, which was hosting a We Love Xbox party with Lawler
and Tong at their controls, the press slowly losing hold of theirs. We
snuggled into another VIP area, another inebriated slouch, as Rich
from *Loaded* mag — who had approached the business of excess with
more gusto than most — mumbled, "Simon, it's not just the drink
talking but... I really think we should go on holiday." If the logic were
a little frayed, as I had known him mere hours, at least the sentiment
was appreciated. As I wasn't far behind Rich in the insobriety stakes,
it set off my own chain of random conversations with other members
of the group. I am now firmly committed to five separate holidays
with people I barely know, ranging from canal barging on the Norfolk
Broads to a week in Centre Parcs.

As midnight approached we left Space for a new location, quite
the most ghetto fabulous villa I have ever been in, with landscaped
terraces leading down to the pool. I settled in, dancing poolside,
drinking with new friends, concentrating on not falling in and thinking over our whole Duran Duran break up conspiracy when I looked
up and swore I could see... Simon le Bon, dancing on the other side
of the pool. And then the hallucination just got more bizarre because
the lady with him looked like Yasmin. And the more I tried to focus
my eyes to cut through the fug, for the life of me I couldn't make Simon le Bon's face go away.

Her name is Rio and she dances on the sand

It was Simon le Bon. Simon fucking le fucking Bon. The full import
immediately sunk in. Christ in a jacuzzi, I'm at a pool party in Ibiza
with Simon and Yasmin le Bon... I'M GOING TO BE IN *HEAT* MAG-
AZINE! It was all I could do not to explode into a thousand pieces

right there, splattering the partygoers in a parterre of goo.

I approached him, crab-sideways. "Simon," I choked. He looked at me silently, suspiciously. "That's a nice name, erm, that you have there." A pause, before I retreated, respectfully, as a courtier would from their liege, mentally beating myself up that those were probably the only words I would ever say to Simon le Bon.

Then all at once it dawned on us — the conspiracy theory! We had only conjured it up yesterday and then — ye gads what are the chances — there's Simon le fucking Bon right there, just begging to be hassled by a tangle of spangled journalists with nothing but mayhem on their minds and chaos in their hearts.

So we asked him.

Strangely, it appears that wasn't quite it at all. Simon very politely explained it was all down to a pork pie. And if you want to know any more you'll have to sit me down one night and ply me with top drawer liquor, because I ain't letting go of information like that unless I'm being recompensed according to an info/ABV ratio of my own choosing.

Oh Rio Rio dance across the Rio Grande

We danced poolside until the sun came up over the hills and shone its rude torch down upon the revellers, incinerating us like insects. Back at the villa, my exit — just like last year — was both stumbling and awkward. A voice in my head whispering "escape, make haste, the villa video demons will byte and smite you if you stay..."

I decided to bunk the flight home and stow away on the island; leave a million euros worth of pool parties and Simon le Bon, on the off-chance of being offered a couch in a worker's flat somewhere in San Antonio.

The shimmering, computer animated glitz of the Xbox world dissolved before me. I always knew that at some stage I would have to switch off the console, leave the virtual villa and all its cartoon animations, and slum it back to some actual game called reality.

I tell you something, I know what you're thinking | August 2003

28
Coolio

THE RAP HEAVYWEIGHT ARRIVES IN THE METROPOLIS OF
MACCLESFIELD; EJECTED FROM VIP ROOM — THREE TIMES (THE
CHICKEN WASN'T EVEN THAT GREAT)

Coolio: the last word of many of my phone conversations, in a bizarre semantic twist, the origin of which is lost on me. An example: "Yeah, I'll meet you at Titty Twisters at eight. Cool-io."

But that wasn't the only reason I wanted to meet the man, although it would have been cool-io to end the interview with the line "Nice to have met you Mr Coolio. Cool-io." Nope, in a world of Wrong Side revelry this one had to win the Wrong Side award for the most twisted of Dispatches, as accepted by Gwenyth Paltrow, in a tidal wave of tears fit to sink the Titanic.

Macclesfield is a place known mainly for notorious Macc Lad antics but is now becoming famous for a funky little joint, Bar Cuba, which sticks out like E.T.'s sore thumb; a throbbing tropical island paradise in a sea of Cheshire countryside, serving the moneyed burghers of the area... and we're not talking Big Macs here, or even big Maccs.

The venue is chic and sultry, with fibreoptics around the bar, imported Cuban cigars fatter than Bill Clinton's erm, forearm, and a dining area that serves up wonderful Caribbean cuisine. It looks like a place Carlito Brigande might manage but is in fact run by Gerry McKenna, who previously enjoyed a life as the head of the U-Bahn clothing label. The reason journalists and PR folk can put a spin on Cuba faster than your nan's washing machine is that the Macclesfield bar, with a capacity of only a few hundred, has already played host to the likes of De La Soul, the Jungle Brothers, Alexander O'Neil, Jocelyn Brown... and the list goes on, ending with Coolio. -io. And that I just gots to see. Coolio. In a Gangster's Paradise. Otherwise known as Macclesfield.

The whole thing did seem rather far-fetched and through bitter experience I know how breasts up these sort of things can go, but I was assured that it was a bona fide vibe and that my interview was sorted for 7pm. So I gets my ass to Cuba at 7pm only to find that my homeboy had already soundchecked and promptly fucked off back to his hotel. OK. No worries. Cool-io. I axed if I could catch up with him at the hotel, at some stage during the three hours before he was due to come back for the gig. No, he'd hurt his leg and was looking for a physiotherapist. *He's done a what what and he's looking for a what now?* O-KKK, cool-io. -ish. I still managed to meet up with Anthony Photos and we agreed to disappear, Pinochet style, for a few hours and then come back at ten and catch him before the gig. So we jumped into Anthony's Lotus Elise and sped around the narrow Cheshire lanes at speeds hairier than my aunty Mabel's lady tash, ending up in dead posh Wilmslow where we sank a few dead posh beers and wiled away a couple of hours, before jumping back in the Lotus (at which point I decided I was in the wrong business... me with only a pair of legs for transport) to wend our merry our way back.

Still no Coolio. Now *not* cool-io. With a journalist's uncanny bullshit radar I knew then things were becoming, in the vernacular of *Saving Private Ryan*, FUBAR (Fucked Up Beyond All Recognition). Still, Cuba resident Jack and Mark 1 were rocking the crowd with a chunky funky set and instead we disappeared upstairs to the VIP room. Cautious at first, by eleven we were so hacked off with the situation we tucked into the plate of chicken that was laid out for his arrival, and liberated a couple of bottled beers from the fridge, which I proceeded to open with my teeth (a definite sign of frustration — I don't actually know how to do that). 11.15pm. Coolio was due on stage and he was still not even in the gaff. And then in he strolled, glancing over at us like we were trash before tucking into what was left of his chicken with his posse the 40 thevz (don't these people have a spellchecker on their computers?).

Then some jobsworth of a bouncer approached us. "You have to leave now."

"Pardon?"

"Go. Move."

Charming. So we were shuffled downstairs on the promise of a post gig interview, which sounded like a crock of shite for a kickoff as I had been reliably informed that Coolio didn't do interviews after the gig as he liked to entertain laydeez. In fact I had been told that he had actually requested extra security because he wanted to, and I quote "!!&%$ white women" and needed the security to sling them out when he had finished. Renaissance man, or what? So anyway he appeared on stage with his "bad leg" working surprisingly well and the first thing I noticed was that his hair was indeed as dodgy as I remembered, which was something of an achievement for someone who owned a hair salon. He sang all his "hits" — that "classical music" one, the "Michelle Pfeiffer in the video" one and the "Ooh La La" one but it still made me chuckle when the bad boy from LA said things like "HOW ARE YOU DOING, MACCLESFIELD". Marvellous. Rap version of *Spinal Tap*, anyone? To be absolutely fair the music was OK, the performance was OK but by this point I couldn't give a budgie's right bumcheek for any of it.

And then it was over. We headed back upstairs for our interview, queuing behind a line of white girls seeking their sexual destiny and were eventually called past them and into the room where some fucking muppet of a manager was running around in a vague attempt to conjure up some sense of importance. Pretty soon I knew what was coming.

"You have to leave now."

"Pardon?"

"Go. Move."

So we're back downstairs and I'm trying to drink myself calm. I don't particularly want to come over all Anne Robinson and *Watchdog* here, but a couple of points of view have to be made. Obviously the lives of meagre writers and photographers pale into insignificance beside those of men with dodgy haircuts and dodgier attitudes but this was quite clearly taking the piss. Aside from Coolio, it was the fuckwits around him that were really doing my bonce in: the management/PR/spin doctors, usually just back room people with a mobile phone and a bag of Daz Automatic, pissed off at not being famous convinced that fame may come by association if they hang around enough famous people and act like arseholes. In a culture of public relations, these people would be hard pressed to relate to a cabbage.

Gerry and the people at the club did their best to pull the situation around and eventually we were all ushered up AGAIN, stepping over the 40 thevz who were in the club dancing with the nearest white women (and there weren't forty of them, neither). Upstairs Coolio was giving it the old ELO (extra large one) and it was all starting to go PT. More food had been brought up, so I tucked in, before the inevitable happened.

"You have to leave now."

"Pardon?"

"Go. Move."

When you get kicked out of someplace *three times* you start to kind of get the hint. If I was an intrepid investigative journalist I would have stayed back and followed the story through to the bitter end but that's not what Dispatches is about and I was bored and pissed and maybe bored some more so I left Coolio to his life (one wife, seven kids and more, it would seem, to follow).

But I would never want to let down the many avid readers of Dispatches, so when I got home I decided, instead, I would interview the back of Coolio's album covers. Which, at about a quarter of an inch thick, seemed to contain a lot more depth. So can we get this started please?

"*Let's Do It.*"

"OK, Mr -io, can I start by saying I'm disappointed in your behaviour. I knows you iz a bad bwoy an' all 'dat, but I just wanted a chat wit ya."

"*Nature Of The Business...*"

"Yeah but it sucks."

"*Thought You Knew?*"

"Well, yeah, I knew, but it still fucking fucks me off big time."

Discombobulated

"*Ooh La La.*"

"Don't take the piss Mr -io. Don't make me come round there and bust a cap in yo ass... whatever that means."

"*Can I Get Down?*"

"OK, OK. Questions... erm, so what's it been like getting to wherever it is you think you are at the moment?"

"*Fantastic Voyage.*"

"Did you get out of your pram one day and start rapping for Farley's Rusks? Who got you started?"

"*U Know Hoo!*"

"No I don't, that's the whole point of this interview. Jesus, don't you know how to do this?"

"*I Remember.*"

"Good, so where does your music come from?"

"*My soul.*"

"But you know what, I've always felt your music is more all encompassing, that it's not so much a case of 'my soul' as 'our soul'. Would 'our soul' be a fair description of you, Mr Coolio? Actually don't answer that. Now then, a lot of rappers have fairly Neanderthal attitudes toward women — so what do you think of the ladies in Macclesfield?"

"*Ugly Bitches.*"

"Charming!"

"*Can U Dig It?*"

"No I can't... many of my female friends have been women. By the way, I'm sorry about eating all your food in the VIP room — did they leave you anything?"

"*Can-O-Corn.*"

"Well, that's alright then. Maybe you could pick something up at the airport when you fuck right off out of this country. What are you going to do at duty free?"

"*Bring Back Somethin Fo Da Hood.*"

"That's very generous of you, Mr -io. So where are you heading after the gig?"

"*On My Way To Harlem.*"

"Interesting. May I join you?"

"*C U When U Get There.*"

"Not if I see you first, son."

Could go on but I'm bored now. So... cool-io. Actually scrap that. Cooli-not, more like. | *April 1999*

29
On the Wrong Side with the Fat Boy

A REFLECTION ON THE CLAN MORRISON... THE "DISCO CLAN";
AMONGST THE HIBERNIANS OF GLASGOW AND
FAT BOY SLIM

I haven't met Fatboy Slim on four separate occasions. Yep, as far as I can remember I haven't said a word to the Fat Lad over four very different conversations we have never had, his attitude to journalists allegedly frostier than a polar bear's left testicle.

Aside from trying to make my mates laugh by mimicking that wobbly legged dance to the Housemartins track Happy Hour, the first time I didn't meet him was at a Manchester University Toga Party in 1992. He was on stage with Beats International, I was dressed in a toga, sliding all over the dancefloor to Dub Be Good To Me, eventually sliding over completely and finding myself unable to get up; choosing instead to lay there semi naked, with a bedsheet wrapped around one ankle.

Next up was Freakpower, who I interviewed sometime in the mid nineties, before the launch of their second album, *More of Everything for Everybody*. Norman was notable by his absence but Ashley

Slater was present — the guy who played trombone as if horizontal, possessed a voice smokier than a pack of Marlboro Reds and a scalp balder than Uncle Fester (on this occasion minus the monkey that so patiently sat there for the video of Turn On, Tune In, Cop Out).

And then that was it until I moved to Ibiza last summer. Norman and Zoë were part of a boat trip that went over to Ibiza's sister island of Formentera. We moored up and jumped off the boats, and I somehow ended up hanging off a lilo with the Fatboy, bobbing about in the turquoise Mediterranean water. Norman encouraged people on the boat to throw bottles of beer down into the water and, finding there were no bottle openers in that part of the ocean, I opened one for him with my teeth, which hurt a lot more than I let on.

Then earlier this year we didn't meet again when I was in Istanbul for the Quake Aid gig, to raise money for the survivors of the Gölcük earthquake. A press conference was held at our hotel. Mr Slim looked shady. He'd been at the Grammy's in LA, jetted back to spend a couple of hours with the missus in the UK and then shifted to Istanbul. He was in bits, poor bloke and could barely gather his thoughts, in front of a Turkish media that seemed to see him as a DJ deity with all the answers, as opposed to a bloke from Brighton who played records. "We're not trying to change the world," he muttered. "We're just playing records and trying to help some people."

Maybe Glasgow would be the place, I pondered, as I stepped off the plane and felt the Scottish air gust into my lungs. Soon enough I was back amongst my people, whisked back to one of my past lives like a scene from the movie *Highlander*. See, "Morrison" is actually a clan name; anyone called Morrison descends from an island on the west coast of Scotland. Back in the day we were known as the "Disco Clan". We would charge over glens and battle our way through heather and high water in order to gatecrash neighbouring clan discotheques — or kayleighs — whereupon we would challenge other clans to a "Battle of the Dancefloor", proving the might of the Morrison clan through a series of complex and frankly devastating disco moves. Wearing skirts.

I was minus the skirt on this occasion but there's nothing like getting to a club full to the neck on food and booze, having enjoyed

Discombobulated

a hearty dinner with the boys from Soma, along with Orde Meikle and Stuart McMillan from Slam. But I could still see straight enough to appreciate that the Arches is some fecking brammer club right enough — an absolutely incredible space, not surprisingly composed of interlocked arches which each form dancefloor cocoons. Slam took over one of the rooms and at the far end of the main area Norman took to the stage and promptly tore the place a new arsehole. He was manic behind the decks, focusing on the dancefloor; connecting smiles with people dancing; crouched over the decks when a mix demanded; dancing around at all other times; his index finger held aloft, Shearer style, at particularly gargantuan breakdowns; underneath the arches, dreaming his dreams away (OK cheap gag but I'm saving for Christmas).

Sneak followed the Fatboy but by that point I was firmly ensconced in the VIP room guzzling everything that was within my radius like a ravenous twister absorbing everything toxic, a real high lander. You couldn't swing a poodle in that room without taking out some member of the London meeja and that's unfortunately when, with a kind of Dispatches inevitability, it all discombobulated as I flipped over to the Wrong Side. The Wrong Side is that hazy place you find yourself late in the proceedings: you don't know how you got there... you sure as hell don't know how you're going to get out... and you're resigned to just kicking back and enjoying the ride. I doubted my ability to talk to the wall, never mind conduct an interview but, having been summoned, I eventually found Norman in a corridor, hiding under some netting: "I've always said that to talk the talk you've got to walk the walk," he said, emerging from his disguise. "And I've always been there, in the clubs, off me nut, everywhere — remembering why we like this. It's like, if I'm sitting at home every night maybe I'd be faking."

Although Fats doesn't play live, the UK gigs are the DJ equivalent of a support tour for the new album, *Halfway Between the Gutter and the Stars*, a mature malt with a strong blend of flavours. "Half of me is on the campaign trail of trying to sell the album, but it's very difficult to do that. I love making records and when I'm DJing I'm just having fun. There's something at the back of my head that says, play your own records, plug the album, drop that in. But you know what, I'm a DJ and... I can't be arsed, frankly."

Honesty from a DJ. How very refreshing. Maybe it's honesty derived from the comfort of having it all: the fabulous lifestyle, the celebrity missus, the impending arrival of Woody, Fatboy Jnr. The future's bright, the phuture's phat. "I'm taking three or four months off to be there," he detailed of his paternity leave. "And after that I kind of re-assess. I have to find this balance between being a good father and still making music. It would be so easy to be a great father but make shit music; and it would be so easy to kind of like ignore my child and just carry on. So anything could happen in the next two months."

But you will carry on...

"I really want to carry on; I really want to do this forever. But there is the risk that you'll end up doing the Frog Chorus."

Ay, there's the rub. What happens when the samples run dry? What happens when the music stops? But I get the feeling Fatboy Slim still has a good few tunes in him, tucked up in the sleeves of his many Hawaiian shirts.

I retired to the sanctuary of the VIP room and dozed off. At some stage someone woke me up and, gathering as much dignity as I could muster I stood up and fell through an open door. Someone asked if I was OK, and then a little more sinisterly if someone should escort me outside. It really is something to be a grown man of thirty and still have to be helped home from a club; but there were no cabs to be had outside and I didn't have the first fucking clue where I was (perhaps not surprisingly, since I had need been to Glasgow previously) and it was totally up to Daniel Photos to aid my stagger back to the hotel. And at some stage on that walk, through the haze of inebriation, I had a Bodhisattvan epiphany: I'm a walking fucking cliché — a writer who thinks too much and drinks even more... just what the world needs. But in the midst of that revelation I was gripped by an ugly belligerence. I think I know when it's time to make my apologies and leave a party but ferchrissakes why the hell shouldn't I be lagging drunk — am I not in Glasgow, after all?

"Did I miss something, Daniel?" I barked, gesticulating at the gut-

Discombobulated

ter and the stars. "Did I sleep through the meeting when we decided to get so fucking serious? When the 'head nod' was voted in as an acceptable form of dancefloor activity? When people were allowed to leave clubs sober.

He smiled and took pictures as I drifted towards the hotel, bouncing off walls as if Glasgow were a ping pong table and I, the badly bruised ball. | *November 2000*

30
Interview with the Gangster

HUNTING DOWN THE MULTIPLE MURDERER AND CELEBRITY
GANGSTER DAVE COURTNEY TO HIS VERY OWN MANOR, CASTLE
CAMELOT; GETTING ON GRAND; THEN DISCO DAVE PULLS A GUN

Dave Courtney lives in a place called Castle Camelot. In Plumstead.

"How we gonna know which one it is?" asked Danny Photos, as we checked house numbers on a suburban street like any other in London, full of semi detached houses rather than castles.

At that moment, through the south London mist, appeared what I can only describe as... Castle Camelot, a shimmering white, end of terrace house — floodlit — with castle walls and turrets running around it. On one side of the building was a mural as big as the house, depicting Dave on a white horse, in a suit of armour with a sword held high.

"I think that's it."

Dave Courtney was one of the country's leading underworld figures. I say "was" because he has now gracefully retired, choosing to use his somewhat colourful life as a launch pad for a media career. He now hosts one-man shows; recently wrote an autobiography, *Stop The Ride I Want To Get Off;* and is pursuing international film opportunities. The Vinnie Jones character in *Lock, Stock and Two*

Discombobulated

Smoking Barrels was based on Courtney. Remember the infamous sunbed slam? One of Dave's, that.

Yep it's been colourful, with perhaps a disproportionate amount of claret. Courtney has been beaten up, shot, stabbed, burnt and once had his nose bitten off. In a sword fight in a Chinese restaurant he sliced waiters into a sweet and sour mess; he has witnessed Triad murders; by his own admission he has killed two people; he organised Ronnie Kray's funeral; he organised Ronnie Bigg's seventieth birthday. If truth be told he very probably organised more than one or two parties that you've been to yourself. If not, you have undoubtedly had to cross him or one of his firm on the door before you got in.

That's all something of a mind melt for me. I don't do fighting. To misquote Michael Jackson: I'm a writer not a fighter. My family's been in about two fights, including the Second World War, and the only real fight I've been in (with bouncers, in Prague of all places) left me with three stitches in my head, a night in the slammer and a lesson learnt. So Courtney's Castle Camelot was truly kooky, a cross between Del Boy and Del Rey; suits of armour, swords and elaborate statues jostling for position with the paraphernalia of average domesticity. A sword in a stone in the garden; a Tardis in the bathroom. As we waited for him in his sitting room, I watched Dave stroll up to his front door on his own security cameras. "Sorry I've been so long, mate," he said, shaking hands. "Bet you want to rip my head off."

"HA HA HA," I laughed, nervously loudly. "Erm... ha?"

He was big and bald. Big and bald with glistening eyes that contained terror and mirth in equal proportion. He led me through to the back room and we sat down at a round table, seemingly buckling under the weight of the biggest, gold, jewel-encrusted knuckle duster I had ever seen. And I'd never even seen any. Dave's wife, a rapper called Jenny made us cups of tea, while another friend was put on joint patrol. The keys to the house were in the lock of the back door, along with a note that suggested if the police wanted to come in, they might consider using the door rather than smashing through it.

The profile the Kray funeral gave Courtney made him a prime target for the police and signalled the end of his "naughty" days. "All credit to the Krays for what they did but it will never ever happen again," he said. "Because crime has changed and because policing has changed it's the wrong era to be a gangster. Gangsters are finished — they've gone out with prize fighting and swashbuckling." The police closed Courtney's cab office, his pub and hit the heart of his operation. Clubland. "They went to all the clubs where I had doormen and said 'if you keep Dave Courtney's doormen you won't have a licence for a fucking telly, let alone a club'." With little left to do, Dave was forced into the crookedness business of the lot. The media. "That's frightened the police to bits," he chortled. "In the popularity race Dave Courtney is in front of the Metropolitan Police. And that's sort of not right... I'm the murderer, they are the British police force but if you went to twenty people they would all rather go out for a night with Dave than Sir Paul Condon."

I wasn't about to pick bones with a man who picked bones out of spines and used them for toothpicks, but it's certainly true the connections between the underworld and clubland are well forged and deep set. As Dave explained: "The underworld have got more money than most people and there's not an awful lot of places to go and spend it apart from the nightclubs. So it's a meeting place, I'm afraid, for numerous naughty people." Moving from the door to actually promoting, Dave brought one of the first raves to London in 1986, under the arches in John Ruskin Street. "I employed Danny Rampling and Fabio & Grooverider for £25 the pair. They wouldn't sell one of their farts for that now, would they?" Currently involved with Terry Turbo in the drum & bass night One Nation, Dave keeps more than a toe in the warm waters of clubland. "The old ones get on with me because of the Kray twins connection, and the young ones get on with me because of the raving thing. I can dance the bollocks off any fucker!"

But as Sir Paul Condon implied when he told people not to read Dave's book, Courtney may be a lot more dangerous now than he ever was then. He nodded. "The authorities would hate the world to know what I know. I know very, very much too much. And can PROVE IT. They cannot allow someone like me to actually tell people what it's like. When they nick me they say, 'it's not about putting you in prison Dave because you'll be a fucking martyr, you little cunt. We've just got to stop everyone loving Dave Courtney because you're a FUCK-

Discombobulated

ING BADDIE and there's A POSTER OF YOU IN SMITHS!'"

Dave Courtney is a master at manipulating the media. I dislike everything that he stands for but he's a funny fucker, and charming with it. Ask him if he is involved in organised crime and he'll say sure, he organised the Kray funeral and that was full of criminals. When Roger Cook burst in on him, he didn't do the old palm-over-the-camera-lens routine, he asked if he could dressed and invited Cook to do an interview on a boat in St Katherine's dock... allowing him to change into the clothes he wanted to wear, sit in an environment that was conducive and also have the time think of his answers. He was the heavy on the Gerry Sadowitz show — all good exposure until, as Dave puts it, "some geezer viciously threw his chin at my fist." Now there's plans for a £12 million movie of his life. And guess who Dave wants to play Dave? "I may not be the best actor in the world, but I play a fucking good Dave Courtney," he smirked. "And America is going to lap me up, matey."

Dave Courtney's done his time, done his tour of duty and he got out. If what he says is true, good luck to him. "I'm better at entertaining than I was as a gangster, to be quite honest. Because I'm quite eloquent and I'm a cocky fucker and sort of pleasing to the eye because I've got a bald head, the media seem to think I shit diamonds at the moment. There's a little bit of Dave Courtney hysteria. I've even started stalking myself. It's easy — I know when I'm in."

The talking over, we stood up from the table. "So you want some photos then?" said Dave, clapping his hands together. He disappeared upstairs to change, returning in a suit sharper than one of his swords and together we walked out into the front yard of Castle Camelot. Danny Photos started snapping Dave next to his mural.

"This will be a good one," I said to Dave and held one of his swords over his head. Danny snap snapped.

"This one will be better," he replied and pulled open his jacket to reveal a gun in a shoulder holster. He pulled out the gun and put it to my head. Snap snap. He then put the gun in my hand and told me to put it to his head. Snap snap. I've fired a few guns in my time but I wasn't about to fire that one. I had absolutely no idea — if I pulled the trigger — whether it would skewer the brains of one of the most feared men in Britain or provide a light for his cigar.

We walked down the drive and took some more photos by Dave's Porsche. "Wave to that house over the road," he said, pointing.

I waved. "Why?"

"I'm under surveillance!" He roared with laughter. Apparently the police had installed twenty four hour cameras in the upstairs room of one of his neighbours. I handed Dave his gun back. "I must be doing something fucking right because they've been looking at me for four years and I'm still here so bollocks. Listen fucking harder!"

We accepted Dave's offer of a lift back to Plumstead station and climbed into his Porsche, Dave pulling away at something approaching warp speed. At the junction with the main road the lion roar of the engine mellowed to a pussycat purr. A man stood talking into his mobile phone turned to look in the car. "Is that Dave Courtney? It is... Dave... Dave.. how you doing, mate?"

"Starving comfortably, starving comfortably," Dave smiled, before gunning the engine and hurtling his Porsche down the road. | *January 2000*

31
Last Tango
in Paris

BIZARRE ENCOUNTERS WITH SUPERMODELS, STING AND
MICK HUCKNALL; ALL EQUALLY GORGEOUS (APART FROM THE
LAST ONE)

... so anyway I was in Johnny Depp's club in Paris, partying with
Sting and Mick Hucknall, and I simply couldn't move for tripping
over supermodels. Darling, don't you just hate that?

The models had gathered in the VIP balcony area, displaying the
kind of collective flocking nature you might expect from a gaggle of
rare and exotic geese. One almost had to wade through them as one
carved a hazardous path towards the complimentary canapés. There
were blondes and brunettes, girls from Poland and Portugal and they
draped themselves elegantly about the place as though part of a pat-
tern of human furnishings. Not that any of them seemed particularly
happy with looking gorgeous — a dour expression was somehow part
of the outfit, de rigeur for that look of Parisian chic, along with the
Stella McCartney frock and the Gucci tomfoolery. I turned to the
guy from *GQ*, who was also at the table. He looked like he'd stepped
straight out of the pages of his magazine: a well groomed and, it has
to be said, thoroughly charming young man. In contrast to my nervous twitch, he seemed to suck up the entire room in his gaze, gorging
himself on the moveable feast before him and I suddenly felt like a
disco hobo from the backwoods of clubland, with booze in his soul
and mayhem on his mind.

"I have a theory," I posited, leaning back to talk from the side of my mouth, seditiously. "A kind of conspiracy theory if you will, that these models have been placed here as an organic accessory to brighten up this club."

"Pardon?" he replied, as though mere words were not enough to cut through the gossamer of his reverie.

"That they're heavenly sirens, encouraging us to dash ourselves on the rocks of a gin & tonic."

"Come again?"

It was too late. I knew then that he had let his gaze lie upon this wealth of beauty too long and that he was lost. I guess that's what you get for working for *GQ* and not *DJmag*; for working in the relatively sober world of fashion instead of cauterising your senses and erasing roughly twenty seven per cent of your personality from a life spent in discotheques. But it was true that the models contributed in a human sense to the feel of the club — the Man Ray, at 24 Rue Marbeuf in the 8th Arrondisement. Once upon a time there was a man, a man called Man Ray, a famous French photographer, and far from my own reticence and misprioritising of booze over beauty, Rachel Photos was straight in there — somehow persuading in mere seconds two of the most lithe and lovely models to recreate a famous Man Ray photograph in which two girls are kissing.

But anyway my disco amigos, to the point! Which was this: I had found myself in Paris courtesy of eurostar who had brought a ragtag gaggle of the press corp out to the city to get le spangled. If you leave Waterloo (*how did you feel when you won the war?*) after 4pm on a Saturday afternoon and get the eurostar back from the Gare du Nord station in Paris before 10am the next morning, it will set you back £35. Now I don't know about you, but on a night out I can easily blow that in cab fares and kebab scares, so changing the scenery of a Saturday night for thirty five sheets has to be a viable option for clubbers who fancy indulging in a little of that chi chi clubbing *a la* Français. Our own quasi-Napoleonic plan of attack was thus: we were to head into the city, tear through a couple of discotheques and then get the rat twat out of there before les Bleus knew what had hit them, or had fashioned any time to make the relevant arrests. A night out in Paris and then straight back to Blighty on the eurostar: smoke me a kipper I'll be back before breakfast.

Taking advantage of the happenchance of possessing sight in both eyes (for now), I soaked it all in. Paris is a beautiful city at night. The street lights illuminate gothic architecture and the broad boulevards that run through the city like a jugular vein, curling and bending and carrying human energy rushing like a welcome drug into the neon soul of the city — junk flecks like us, in a cab that carved its way from the station toward the eighth district, passing both the Eiffel Tower and l'Arc de Triomphe, which meant I had done the sights within the first ten minutes and was ready for naught but nocturnal naughtiness.

There were several venues disco dotted around the eighth district and the Champs-Elysées that cut right through it, full of boardwalk bawdiness. After the first bar we hit it was but a short walk onwards to the Man Ray and the models that it nurtured and fed via the placenta bar in its VIP womb. At some stage they cleared the tables to make way for a dancefloor... oui, clubbing is very different in Paris. My hairdresser told me that — he comes from the city and if I've learnt one thing in life it's that you should always listen to one's hairdresser; you trust him with your follicles, you should trust him with your frolicking. Whereas clubbing in the UK revolves around buildings dedicated to vertical action, Paris seems more about elegant, horizontal, loungecore action — dining, socialising, drinking — with dancing as an optional extra rather than a dusk 'til dawn obligation. So people gradually drifted onto the newborn dancefloor, the DJ cranked it up and... and the music went très merde. Some amazing music comes out of France, some incredible DJs have emerged from the city but, perhaps because of this dearth of dedicated clubbing, the Man Ray's soundtrack was — how shall we say? — *interesting*. Put it this way... I wasn't expecting to hear anything from the *Grease* soundtrack in Johnny Depp's Parisian boudoir.

Despite such scant resources, we managed to turn the dial up to wrong anyway and soon the room was busy and bouncing; in fact so bouncing that we bounced straight out of Man Ray and all the way down the Champs-Elysées to VIP, a club behind some tall gothic gates, down mysterious stairs. This was much more like it — more seedy, more sleazy — a room that opened out and went places: round corners towards bars; downstairs onto dancefloors; into booths where couples snuggled; the Parisian patrons filling out the space like a rich perfume. Some of our group started to fade to grey and I must admit that travelling from Manchester to Paris on two trains to get leathered in a couple of clubs was all starting to take its toll. But I was lifted by the quality of the venue, of the music, and of the people panorama that stood before me, 2D actors on a Parisian catwalk. I danced around the club until I was all danced out, exhausted from movement and gorged to the gills from everything that I had taken in. One could always do with another drink — a last drink for the rail, if you will — but the previous bottle of beer cost £8 and I don't think Louis IX himself would have been getting many rounds in at those prices.

Outside we debated heading further down the Champs-Elysées to the Le Queen, a club with a strong gay element that was supposed to be oodles of fun, but it was starting to dawn on people that it was dawn and that we had to get home. And that meant I was in the wrong country and it was going to take my passport to get me back to my bed. We drifted in groups back to Gare du Nord and gathered on a terrace outside a café already open and serving black coffee and warm croissants.

It was gone six in the a.m. when we stepped back onto the train and gone two in the afternoon when I climbed back into my bed back in Manchester; so exhausted I could no longer feel my ears and the sheer indulgence of climbing back into my own bed was like a million feather down highs. I had just closed my eyes and drifted into the welcoming arms of Morpheus when the phone rang.

"Get your skates on, I've got tickets to the United game."

I tried to explain to my friend that I had been out in Paris the night before... with Sting and some models... in Johnny Depp's club... but it was all so dreamy and surreal that, looking around my bedroom, I had to convince myself I had... hadn't I? In no small agony, I climbed back into the same trousers, concluding that: if the French have contributed anything to culture it's my favourite word in the world, "discotheque." It had been good to check a couple more off my list. *Vive la différence!* | *November 2001*

32
Take That
and Party

The scene was twisted, no doubt about that. It was like one of those
fucked up dreams that overpower you in the half light of dawn; as you
awake from a night when you haven't so much slept, as fought with
the duvet dwarf demons. If you'd like me to surmise, it goes something like this: I was embroiled in a wonky scenario involving a bottle
of Bacardi, a cup of tea, a detached house in Stockport and a member
of Take That

If you would like me to paint in a little more detail, then drop
from the clouds of reality, gentle reader, and fall into the pages of
this book — towards sunny Stockport and the suburb of Bredbury;
and closer still towards a detached house in a row of similarly detached houses; and further still into the kitchen of that house, where
you'll find yours truly, drinking tea with erstwhile member of Take
That, Howard Donald. Pretty kooky, eh? Perhaps now you get what
I mean... in all those years spent watching Take That on *Top of the
Pops*, I could never possibly have conjured a time slice in my future
that would consist of me and Howard drinking tea in the kitchen of
a detached house in Stockport. But the teacups felt real enough so,
in the increasingly blurred world of reality and fantasy, I guess we'll
have to chalk this one down to the Wrong Side. To my side of the
tracks.

For those of you who had perhaps taken up residence under a rock for the entirety of the nineties, Howard was the one with the dreads, the one who peered out from between the twisted limbs of the follicly blessed creature that lived atop his head and kept him company when he was on tour with the boys. But those day are long gone. "I see Gary a lot, because he's got his own production company now," Howard remarked of his ex-colleague and band alumnus, "and I saw Jason and Mark quite a few weeks ago." One name was conspicuous by its absence but then the lives of Robbie Williams and Howard Donald have taken very different tangents since we "took that" and they "did one". Whilst Robbie has gone on to do a very good impression of a pop star, Howard has come over to join us on the Wrong Side, on the dancefloor. Yep, Howard Donald is a DJ.

I can see all the way from here that the word "gimmick" has just appeared in flashing lights before your eyes — neon lit, with pyrotechnics and fireworks going off in the background. But you just hold your horses there, big fella, and lay aside the suitcase of cynicism that's weighing you down, because there's more. Howard Donald *can* DJ, which is more than can be said for some of the limp wristed jocks currently ruining your Saturday night. And perhaps your overly refined, early twenty first century scepticism may be further abated when you learn that Howard didn't, in fact, take up DJing last Wednesday. He was a DJ *before* Take That. "I started collecting records in 85, soul records and stuff like that," he recalled, sipping his tea. "And then I've been through all me techno, and me electro. I started properly in 89, then obviously Take That came along in 90 and took six years of my life away."

He chuckled the chuckle of someone who has come to terms with a very strange thing that happened to him once; something that he can now step back from and smile about. Because when you're a part of a well lubed machine like Take That, it's going to be hard to wield your own influence on the sound. "I was always doing it behind closed doors and stuff but I never really introduced it into anything to do with Take That," Howard said, almost whispering this terrible, hidden disco secret. But despite hiding his dance leanings beneath a pretence of pop normality, Take That were nevertheless young northern lads doing what young northern lads do. "Yeah, whatever country we was in, we'd go to the clubs in the local area, try and find a good one. Not all of 'em were good, though." He collapsed into another fit of giggles, as though the words had triggered a memory in the darker recesses of his dreadlocked memory.

So, after briefly dipping his toes into the warm waters of international superstardom, Howard has gone back to his roots: two decks, a dancefloor and a boxful of records. Unfortunately what he also now carries with him like his own excess baggage is the triple barrelled strap-on surname "ex-Take That", lurking within parentheses — the remnants of that boy band idyll. But on the plus side it's got to open doors. He paused. "It opens and closes them really. You've got a name and you've got to advertise your name to a certain extent to get people in the clubs and things. But eventually I'll hopefully lose that tag." He put down his cup of tea to continue the train of thought. "Because like I say people are obviously gonna think that I jumped on the bandwagon doing DJing but no, I've always wanted to be a DJ, since the very early days. Every week I used to go to Shelley's in Stoke and Bugsy's in Ashton-Under-Lyne, where Sasha used to play. So that was a real inspiration for me, watching him."

People should be allowed to shed their skin and evolve but the great British public seems singularly unable to cope with that. After all, Sasha wasn't always the closely cropped, progressive house, super-serious muso that he is now... once upon time he had the full ponytailed mane of joy and spent his weekend playing plinky plonky Italian piano house. And let's not forget the murky pop pasts of both Boy George with Culture Club and Jeremy Healy with Hayzee Fantazee.

At that point screams erupted from the livingroom next door, overwhelming our polite conversation in a sonic rush of female shrieks, which woke me up to why we were here in the first place. It was all the result of a competition run by Key 103 radio in Manchester. And the prize? A party — in your own home — organised by the clubnight 2Risque, Bacardi and Key 103 — broadcast live across the city. With Howard Donald from Take That. Now I remember lasses back in the last century who would have gnawed their own arm off for such a prize, and the house was indeed full of totally bemused females, trying to come to terms with the fact that someone from Take That was drinking tea in their kitchen.

The party people scurried between rooms as if the house were some kind of hobbit's hole; as if they'd coincidentally found themselves lost in the same dream as me. And I wouldn't want you to feel left out, so take my hand and I'll show you around the place. Bacardi had transformed the front room into a full-on bar, with barmen flaring with bottles, spinning them to the ceiling and the stars beyond. I ordered a Bacardi with a cup of tea chaser — you should try it sometime, it really hits the spot. At the bar was a battle weary comrade from the Disco Wars: David Dunne. If Howard Donald is ex-Take That, David Dunne is pretty much ex-everything else; if it involves decks or a radio station, he's been there. He was to DJ at the party and the one, in fact, who had invited me along but let's leave Dave at the bar and climb the stairs, where we'll find bedrooms and people sprawled over the beds; then wind back down the stairs, past the door to the kitchen and into the back room, dark and full of people, with the decks set back against the patio doors to the garden. The party was now live on air, the screams from the livingroom carried right across the city of Manchester. The DJ cued Relight My Fire (the Take That version, of course) and that house in Bredbury visibly shook, the sonic aftershocks rippling out as far as Tesco in Hazel Grove.

From a jet set lifestyle to a livingroom in Stockport... and yet Howard seemed remarkably balanced about his change of pace, his change of gigs: "Some places you go to, you've got a DJ playing cheesy trance before you and you think, Jesus Christ I'm gonna go down like a lead balloon here. And you normally do." He grinned. "I get fifty per cent great clubs and fifty per cent crap clubs and I don't mind that because it's a learning curve for me — you get the rough with the smooth — you can't expect everything to be amazing like it was in Take That, when you got the best of everything."

Howard was already getting ready to head out into the night, to a gig booked in Hereford, but I had one question I wanted to ask before he left. I asked it as he was heading out the door and it went something like this. "When you think back over those years: the gigs, the

Discombobulated

adulation, the screaming girls, the being part of the biggest boy band in the world... what does it feel like now?"

"A dream," he smiled, and walked down the front path of the house, waiting patiently as the entire female contingent of the party queued to have their photo taken with the DJ Howard Donald, who used to be in some boy band.

And while they took that, I took off. | *January 2002*

33
Ibiza with Judith Chalmers

DISCOS IN IBIZA, AND SUMMER HOLIDAYS WITH THE FIRST LADY
OF FAMILY TV; WISH YOU WERE HERE?

This one time — a few years back — I was sitting outside Café del Mar
after a particularly ferocious long night's journey into day, when I noticed a discarded postcard lying underneath the table. A regular tourist postcard (some photo of a beach, maybe donkeys wearing hats), it
only turned weird when I read the message on the reverse, scrawled
in the handwriting of a condemned man, as though scratched into
prison walls with his fingernails. It read, simply: "Dear mum... help."

These Dispatches remind me of such postcards from the edge.
Life, with all its punky permutations, can fling up some pretty random circumstances for you to cope with; sometimes it's hard to capture them within the dimensions of a Dispatch, never mind the confined corners of a postcard. How, for instance, when someone asks
what you're doing for the weekend, do you reply you're going to Ibiza
with Judith Chalmers? It's just wrong... right?

Señorita Photos and I caught the red eye flight from Manchester
and by the time we arrived at the villa Can Mateo it was pretty much
deserted; save for a couple of souls sinking scoops out on the stoop.
It was gone 6am by the time I turned in. I was sharing a room with

Discombobulated

Nick from *Mixmag*. Although he was out at Pacha, he had already claimed the one supersized bed by the cunning, colonial use of a carefully placed bag — the luggage equivalent of planting a flag — leaving me to sleep on quite the most rickety looking contraption I have ever encountered. Now I'm the first to accept I'm not as lithe as once I was, but I swear I just sat on the thing and the top end collapsed, as though booby-trapped. And I'm there trying to reattach that end, when the bottom end collapsed as well. It was like one of those clown cars that blows up and falls apart at the slightest of touches. All I needed was a set of red slippers the size of flippers and one of those side horns to squeeze. Honk bloody honk.

It was mid afternoon when I awoke on my clown bed. I grabbed some fruit from the kitchen... and strolled down to the pool... and there she was. Judith Chalmers, the cellular embodiment of thirty years of celluloid TV. I was slightly nervous of meeting her but the good lady Chalmers was fabulous. By the time we got to lunch, at the Jockey Club on Salinas Beach, she was offering advice on everything from relationships to cricket.

Of course by this juncture it might be pertinent for you to ask: What in the name of light entertainment programming was I doing in Ibiza with the First Lady of holiday shows? Well, then, let me tell you, disco amigos: Judith has become the face of the Nokia N-Gage, the hybrid phone that is part communications device, part games console. Now I've got a serious question to ask you here: Do you remember the last time you were bored? Really thoroughly bored? Because I can't — truly, I can't. I mean life is hectic enough when spent up to one's neck in dwarves and yoghurt but honestly, even in those moments waiting for trains... planes... more dwarves... you can now hold a complete entertainment device in your pocket — and fellas, I'm not talking bones, I'm talking dog & bones.

"It's been a thrill, I really am delighted," Judith eulogised as we cracked crustaceans over lunch, the slightest of breezes wafting in from the sea. "To be asked to get involved with something for the young market of gaming people is marvellous." I'm guessing at this point that Judith does irony as well as ironing. "There's a bit of tongue in cheek," she agreed. "Here's this bird who's not in her thirties, who's not quite a young chicken, by far... but she's a trusted person."

Plus, the lady knows her discos from her frescos. "The party scene has developed here in the last ten years particularly," she reported, across a table that had transmogrified into a wooden TV screen between us. "You can see the competition between the clubs when they all parade through Ibiza Town and show what they do — for instance Manumission — competing to get the visitors. They put on these special nights, they have the special DJs and it's a real business."

Yowzers. If the language was mild mannered, the understanding of the machinations of clubland marketing was bang on. And Judith was also warming to the Jockey Club soundtrack. "I like that laid back house," she grinned. "It's marvellous. And everybody on the beach is moving to it — it's an integral part of a holiday here — so many people come for the music. I love it. I really love it."

Here's another picture postcard moment for you: drinking Moët & Chandon on a yacht that creaks its way across to Formentera as Lottie DJs behind some decks assembled on the... well, deck... and teaches Judith Chalmers the rudimentaries of DJing. Life really does get curiouser and curiouser — when reality involves raving with Judith Chalmers is it any wonder my dreams are populated by pinstripes and pensions?

After a massive paella on Formentera we sailed around the westside (*aaaiiieee*... check 'dis) of Ibiza — past Es Vedra, the lost beach of Atlantis, and towards the low slung concrete milieu of San Antonio. At Mambo the beach seemed to ebb and flow with waves of human beings, gathered for the Radio 1 weekend. What else for it but to moor up and move in, with Judith causing quite a commotion amongst the booze addled revellers, as though their brains couldn't quite compute what they were seeing — blue rinse amongst their blue smurfs. To paraphrase Pink Floyd, spangled ones: "Planet Earth... wish you were here".

"Tonight was absolutely marvellous, Simon, wasn't it... at Café Mambo," Judith enthused, back at the villa. "To see those... what was it... two or three thousand people standing on the beach and listening to Pete Tong, going out live to 4.5 million people... it was just so thrilling. It topped the whole thing off." We sat on the villa's terrace as that

Discombobulated

deep velvet cloak of nighttime dropped gently over the shoulders of the island. "To come back at the end of the day to this villa, to the peace and quite of the countryside of Ibiza, and yet know the party scene is there... there's an answer for everybody here really."

There is indeed. Say, for instance, you needed a lesbian ballerina of diminutive stature, where else could you go but Manumission? The name itself derives from the latin verb "manumit", meaning "freedom from slavery" — or at least freedom from Manchester, where the club began, back in 1994. Man U indeed. So that night was Manumission's tenth anniversary, a special one-off Friday party for the club known more for its happy Mondays. I once accused Mike Manumission — in print — of being made of jam, and subsequently, of talking to trees. He collared me soon afterwards and said that he wasn't made of jam, he was made of space dust. Mike is a man who makes you believe in such cosmic confluences — after all, Judith met Mike when filming *Wish You Were Here?*, without realising who he was AND both Judith and Manumission started life in Manchester. Coincidence... or should I lay off the Red Bulls for a few rounds?

Walking into Privilege is, indeed, a privilege, especially when shown to a table on the VIP balcony, overlooking the biggest club on the planet, full of the strangest, freakiest creatures ever to stalk a dancefloor. The aforementioned dwarf ballerina did high kicks along the gangway over the pool; 2ManyDJs splashed sonically around in the DJ booth; a massive doll's house, complete with rooms and stairways and a six metre doll with a spliff in its hand, occupied the stage; Quasimodo chased ladies around the place; the band Electric Six played three songs: Danger! High Voltage (which, rather neatly, featured on the 2ManyDJs album), Gay Bar and then Queen's Radio Ga Ga.

I was perversely straight, yet my powers of perception had been warped, interfered with by some higher force. What next? You could imagine Freddie Mercury himself returning to the very stage where he sang Barcelona. Girls held up cards counting down the ten years as the resident DJs span a song from each of those years, a little psychedelic postcard from another time and place. Howard Marks did his best to evade Al Qaeda. (Has he finally rolled a spliff too far?) A massive cake was brought onto the stage, from which erupted Mike and Claire like human lava. Happy Birthday, Manumission, you wonderful, gorgeous kooks.

It was late when we returned to San Mateo.... or rather, early... or rather, that time when you're not sure which is which. We lounged by the pool like sleazy, drunk geckos. Judith returned to the UK. Before she left she wrote a postcard to my folks, which read "Wish your were here. Love, Judy."

And you know what, I wish she was. | *September 2004*

34
From Dusk till Dawn

TWISTED ADVENTURES IN THE TITTY TWISTER; AMONGST
VAMPIRES AND SNAKES, TWO BROTHERS GO TO THE BAD PLACE

Sit down with Buddha long enough and apart from getting a sore butt
you know what he'll tell you? Nothing ever stays the same. Impermanence. It's one of his phattest beliefs, and if you follow it through to
its natural conclusion you'll find there's no point deciding who are,
because you won't be that person in a day's time anyways. Love sub-
sides, life moves on. You get to grips with that and things are pretty
much a breeze from then on.

I'm no Buddhist. Sure I have a tattoo of a Buddha on one arm, but
then I have a tattoo of an angel on the other and I ain't no Christian
neither. I just want all bases covered when I shuffle off this mortal
coil and gatecrash life's afterparty — when I hit those pearly gates
I need to be on as many guestlists as possible. If the club's called
Heaven, well then I flash my left arm; if it's Nirvana, my right. If it's
Hell, then I merely set fire to my pants and jump in. But I know these
Buddhists are onto something with this impermanence ticket. I've
shapeshifted many times. In Sydney, Australia, I was Andrew. In LA,
I was Charles... or Chuck, once you got to know me. Each time I had
good reason for living under a false identity and facing deportation
on a daily basis — once for a girl and once for the discos.

My kid brother, Jonny Bing Bang, was with me in LA for a while.
We're kind of business partners, you might say. He's joined me for a

few of my jobs and shares the memories as much as the scars. We'd just pulled one last gig and were heading our separate ways — at least as far as business is concerned... I guess you don't get much choice when it comes to the family stuff. Me, I was thinking of getting into the property game; my brother, well he had a jonesing to become a librarian. He was always something of a loose canon, that kid — shoot first, ask some questions, then maybe shoot a little bit more. He'd started the shooting on this last job as well — bam bam bam — and the end game of his trigger happy bullshit was that he had a hole the exact same size as a bullet through his hand, and I was the klutz that had to put him back together. Just like the first time he got drunk at our mom's house and filled up a sink with chunky sized sick and I had to put my hand into it just to flush it out, to save her finding it and whooping us till Tuesday.

Always with the patching up. —How's it feel?

—How ya think, it hurts like a son-of-a-bitch.

—I bound it tight enough to last the night.

All we had to do now was get to some bar over the border and stay put, long enough to meet Carlos and make the exchange. Bada-bing bada-boom then lickety split we shake hands and make like parallel bananas.

So we pulled up at this joint and the first thing I heard was the dull crunch of knucklebone against flesh, like someone crumpling up a grocery store paper bag. Guy crumpled like a bag, too. Above, a neon sign blinked "The Titty Twister", the walls almost pulsating from the loud, raunchy music within. Other signs read "BIKERS AND TRUCK-ERS ONLY", "MONDAY NIGHT BOLLYWOOD NIGHT", "THE SLEAZY TITTY TWISTER DANCERS", STUART AND HIS AMAZ-ING ANGLE GRINDING CROTCH", "TEN NUGGETS IN AND ALL YOU CAN DRINK" and "HOMEMADE FLAN".

I turned to Jonny. —Okay, this is the home stretch. Here's the deal; this place closes at dawn... so we're gonna go in there, take a seat, have a drink — have a bunch of drinks — and wait for Carlos. You... be cool."

Jonny nodded in the direction of the doorman stood between me and my drink like a misplaced wardrobe. —This place is fucked up,

Discombobulated

he whispered.

—Aww, whatsa matter, is this little baby too afwaid to go into the big scary bar? Shit, I been to bars in 'Beefa make this look like a fuckin' Methodist youth club. We hang around here for a coupla hours, in all likelihood we'll get fucked with, so get your shit together, brother.

—My shit is together.

I locked his eye to make sure he weren't bullshitting me, then we bumped fists and I turned to the door, dropping the bouncer with an uppercut and stepping over his limp body and into the club.

It was like walking into an orgy of flesh and alcohol. Faces peered out from the walls and the pillars of the club; locked in a perpetual gurn, their faces warped in the final spasm of their high. The tables rested on stiff snakes. The walls, the ceiling, everything was a deep blood red. It was like being inside some kind of pulsating human organ, the plasma dripping down the sides like magma. It was the sort of joint where, come closing, you just sweep up the teeth and hose the place down.

—Now this is my kinda place! I could become a regular.

We walked to the bar, ordered some drinks, had a look around. For the first time I noticed there were no windows — no windows to the street, no windows into the souls of the clientele. Then, everyone's eyes turned to the stage. A dude was making sparks fly from his crotch. To the other side, a slim, blonde chick appeared, one snake wrapped around her neck, curling around her in a slim cuddle, another wrapped around her wrist to form a moving bracelet.

—Bravo! That's what I call a fuckin' show.

Jonny was entranced, so involved he didn't notice the bouncer I KOd walking back into the bar, wiping the blood from his mouth.

—Surf's up, I said, tapping Jonny on one shoulder.

Slowly, together, we climbed up from our bar stools and trod quietly into battle — a good old fashioned bar brawl — chairs flying all about the place, heads cracked open with pool cues, guns going off, naked strippers fighting. It was kind of cool. Me and Jonny stood on the bar, letting fly at whatever flew by.

Pretty soon there was blood up the Ying Yang, which was when I noticed the snake lady lick her lips, fangs growing down from her mo lars like calcium stalactites. Before I could change the clip in my gun she grabbed Jonny and sunk her fangs deep into his shoulder. He let out a scream. She drank heavily from his neck. I fired the whole clip through her and her snake, which fell from her body and twitched spasmodically on the floor. The angle grinder dude turned to face me, his eyes like a cat's. OK, so the shit had turned weird. Things had gone wrong for me in clubs before, but never in my life had I witnessed ravers turn into vampires.

—O, Brother, where are thou?

I had one of the vampire chicks by the throat. —You wanna suck something, suck on this! I screamed, thrusting the gun into her mouth.

We beat a retreat, holding them trapped in a corridor behind a door.

—Do you know what's going on? Jonny asked, a hungry look in his eye.

—Yeah, I know what's going on. We got a bunch of fuckin' vampires outside trying to get inside and suck our fuckin' blood! That's it, plain and simple.

The hunger in his eyes was palpable and I knew he'd gone to the Bad Place; transmogrified into a bloodthirsty, hell crazed librarian. Without thinking I grabbed a stick and holding him to the ground, thrust it through his heart.

—I love you little brother, I'll miss ya bad.

I let his body fall to the floor, just as the door to the room caved in and I was quickly surrounded by a strange crossbreed bat/devil/Crasher Kid kind of creature.

—Fuck, piss, shit! Motherfuckin' vampires!

A strange Mexican stand-off ensued; they closed in.

—You are all gonna fuckin' die! I'm gonna fuckin' kill every last one of you godless pieces of shit.

Closer, closer still, until I could feel the rank stench of death on their breath, hanging between us like a rancid mist. I closed my eyes and waited for the thud. Instead — hellish screams, as holes were blasted through the walls of the club by shotgun blasts, releasing shards of bright daylight into the room, incinerating the creatures as

Discombobulated

soon as they were touched. Those that could move, or at least limp away, melted into the nooks and crannies of the room, as it caught alight, the drapes carrying the flames to the ceiling.

Crash! as the front door of the club was violently kicked in. Carlos. And the bastard was even smiling.

—How are 'tings, sweetpea?

—Peachy, disco amigo! The world's my oyster, except for the fact that I just rammed a wooden stake in my brother's heart because he turned into a vampire. Aside from that unfortunate business, everything's hunky dory.

He helped me out into the warmth of the virgin daylight. I knew then that I believed. I believed that you could walk into a club one person and walk out another, transformed during the long night's party into day. Impermanence. Things change. People change. Clubs change. Night changes into day; dusk into dawn. | *November 2002*

35.
The Blair Crasher Project

A JOURNEY INTO THE CYBER HEART OF GATECRASHER; ADOPTED
BY THE CRASHER KIDS; ONE OF THEM NOW

"In April of 1999, a writer disappeared in the woods near Snake Pass, Yorkshire, while writing a story.

"Four months later his journal was found.

"My name is Heather Donahue. I am a student from the University of Manchester's Anthropology Department. For my final year thesis I took a special interest in the Blair Crasher Project. Some time around April 24, 1999, a young writer by the name of Simon A. Morrison went over the Pennines into the depths of Yorkshire to investigate the cult of Tony Blair who, he believed, had witch-like powers. Because Tony Blair was dynamic, in with the kids, and frequently to be found 'aving it large at Gatecrasher, Mr Morrison thought that club would be a good place to start.

"He never came back.

"In fact, his disappearance is only detected at all when *DJmag* stop receiving the drunken dribblings that he passed off as his Dispatches; and Manchester brewers detect a sharp decrease in profits.

"During my research I trace Mr Morrison's last known steps, along the road known as Snake Pass. It is then that I find a duffel bag

Discombobulated

(DKNY) containing his journal, buried under the foundation of a 100 year old cabin. When sections of the evidence are examined, Sheffield Sheriff Ron Cravens announces that the evidence is inconclusive and the case is declared inactive and unsolved.

"The journal is released to the family when the legal limit of its classification runs out, on September 1, 1999. Meg Morrison, mother, contacts *DJmag* with a request to examine the journal and piece together the events of April 1999..."

April 24th 1999
10:03pm
God damn. God donkey bonking damn. I can't see straight from last night's boozing. My body feels like some scally's broken in, kicked the shite out of it and run off with my soul.

I'm driving to Sheffield with Rachel Photos. She's talking to herself again so I thought it would be a good chance to jot down some notes about Gatecrasher and get my head round it all. Place sounds funkier than a game of strip Scrabble with S Club 7. Aside from the venue Republic, there's the albums — *Red, Wet* and *Disco-tech* (that's their titles, not a description of a steam bath with John Travolta); there's the nights in Birmingham; the new venue in Sheffield; Millennium party at Don Valley stadium; the T-shirts, merchandise, cuddly toys. Paul Van Dyk has made the club his home. Judge Jules seems to be perturbed about the Crasher Kids' sense of fashion — I'm sure tempers will fray at some stage over the summer.

10:38pm
Bloody hell, I just I asked Rachel why the road is called Snake Pass and she looked at me like I'd asked her to have sex with a tin of biscuits. God she's a weird one, that Rachel. But it's kind of spooky actually, carving your way through the Pennines in the darkness, watching Sheffield appear in the distance, glistening like a knife's edge.

11:13pm
Check into the hotel and set about the business of getting spangled. We manage with surprising ease.

12:08am

We are met at the door of the Republic by an extremely pleasant young lady who thrusts a fistful of drinks vouchers in our hands and wishes us a good night.

I surreptitiously make notes as I walk around. I want to somehow capture in words what I can almost taste on my tongue. It's brighter than a thousand explosions... more colourful than a child chucking up a curry.

Two steps into the place I bump into a girl I know from Ibiza. That sets the course for the night. People have gravitated to Gatecrasher from all over the world — I meet people residing everywhere from Basingstoke to Birmingham to Bumblefuck, drawn towards the club as if by a strange kind of kinetic energy, like dayglo moths drawn towards the light at the end of a dark clubland tunnel.

1:37am

I creep around the club like a disco Dickie Attenborough, studying the habitat and behaviour of these creatures. Tiesto is DJing, the music forms trance food for the dancefloor monster. The revamped venue is gorgeous: it's smooth and easy to wander around, through three rooms populated by some seriously kooky Crasher Kids. One girl is dressed in a dalmatian skin bikini. Others are in fancy dress. At least I hope they are, otherwise there's a hospital nearby short a couple of nurses. I approach one, eager to see if she'll assist in fulfilling a fantasy which involves her, three tins of Dulux paint and several small farmyard animals. She asks me to wait for a moment and then comes back with a funky female friend.

"Who's this?" I ask.

"My patient," she replies, smiling.

I'm about to go into the details of what I have planned when Rachel Photos makes an inopportune appearance. She says it's taken an hour for her lens to de-steam. I'm about to remark that I couldn't give seven flying fucks, when I turn back and both nurse and patient have scarpered. But Rachel has a point. The club is so full of people that the energy seems to burn out of them, turning into soul steam reaching for the heavens, as if exorcised by a DJ deity.

Discombobulated

2:49am

Tall Paul is DJing. He leads the crowd into a breakdown that the AA couldn't recover. On the back balcony a reveller holds aloft a card that reads "TUNE!" It's so well thumbed it comes apart in his hands. His face is full of devastation, as if his pet hamster just died, and people put their arms around him for comfort. Another podium bunny has a T-shirt that counts down from 60 to 0. Over and over again. What purpose this has I have no idea but I'm transfixed. 23... 22... 21... the inescapable inevitability as each number turns draws me in until I realise I am in the middle of the dancefloor, heads bobbing like the crests of waves across an ocean, my own head a transcendental part of it all.

4:21am

Everyone's hair is spiked into concrete, Bauhaus structures, except that instead of grey, the follicle frolicking contains every colour known to man and Rolf Harris, often atop the same head. It has a dazzling effect on my eyes — a human test card — and I start to feel both woozy and wonky, a swirl of colour orbiting my body as if the room were melting.

I think maybe the room *is* melting.

5:32am

Jules is on now. When he thumps in a large track, a man holds aloft two packets of Tunes, assembled in a T. T for Tune. Makeup is caked on as if people were trying to pebbledash their faces in psychedelic colours. Some of the Crasher Kids seem to be caught in a whirl of hippy nostalgia. One guy holds aloft a piece of paper emblazoned with the aphorism "there would be a lot less war if everyone went to Gatecrasher". Other people seem to be have regressed even further, with dummies planted firmly in their mouths in an attempt to disco dumb down, to return to a childlike state of blissful ignorance. Others have gone even further, snuggling up warm within a Gatecrasher womb.

5:49am

It's really starting to go squiffy. More people from Ibiza... and Sister Bliss from Faithless. I'm not even sure how we get onto the subject but it transpires we went to the same school — Latymer, in North London. She was in the year below me. I sing her the school song:

"*Sing it Latymer, loud and long.*

Song of Latymer's deathless throng..."

I can remember no more. A thousand million assemblies ground to dust. We talk about our English teacher Mr Binding, who we once made cry because he was so into reading and writing; something I thought was funny until I found out I was as well. Things are now getting twisted into a tight tangle. Ex Latymerians. Me, Sister Bliss... and Bruce Forsythe. I quickly dart my head about the club, like a twitchy Meer cat, to check he isn't there. The only person I can see is Rachel Photos.

"I'm going back to the hotel. Are you coming?" Her voice doesn't seem to come from her mouth but just appears in my head, cutting through the fog of the air and my own inebriation.

"No," I reply, very deliberately. "I need to stay here. Yes, stay here. Make notes. Research, you see."

I watch her leave, then turn to witness the Crasher Kids ascend to further luminous, spiritual planes. One guy has glo sticks stuck through his hair, through his ears. Another guy walks by, just about every flange of flesh in his face pierced. He's the bottle collector...

6:23am

I walk towards the dancefloor, passing two people sitting under the stairs, both in cycling clothes.

"What are you doing?" I quiz.

"Sitting under the stairs," the male cyclist replies.

"Sitting?"

"Yes. Sitting," says the girl. "Do you want to sit with us?"

"Yes. I would very much like to sit with you."

I sit down. They smile. I smile back. I'm one of them now. I've been absorbed into the Kult of Krasher, gatecrashed another plane of existence. I cast aside my worldly trappings and — in gaffer taping

Discombobulated

an inflatable dolphin to my head — give myself freely to the cause (I would prefer to give myself freely to the Corrs, but you can't have everything).

6:44am

I leave with the Crasher Kids and journey into the woods outside Sheffield, along Snake Pass, casting aside everything as I go. Well, everything apart from this DKNY bag... oh God, all right then. I'll just bury it somewhere. Hmm, this handy 100 year old cabin seems perfect. Right then, I'll sign off. No need for writing now — I will communicate only through space writers, flatulence and by means of glo stick semaphore.

I start spiking my hair for the Millennium party, preparing to gatecrash the next century in style. It will undoubtedly take me the rest of the year to get into these lycra shorts.

But I am happy. I am amongst my people.

This is my family now.

The trance. Oh God, the trance.

It will always be with me.

"I, Heather Donahue, would like to assure everyone that following the discovery of this journal, I will be returning to Yorkshire to investigate Simon's whereabouts. If I find him I then intend to persuade him to bloody well stay there." | *October 1999*

36
The Donkey Show

WHAT HAPPENS WHEN YOU CROSS STUDIO 54, WILLIAM
SHAKESPEARE AND A DONKEY? QUOTING SHAKESPEARE AND BEE
GEES, MEASURE FOR MEASURE; KICKED OUT OF ARDEN

Ahhh... Dispatches. It's like climbing into some comfortable slacks, easing back into my favourite armchair, lighting a pipe and sucking those all too familiar fumes down into my soot blackened lungs.

For those of you new to *DJmag* or this column, the ethos is as follows... essentially I stick my proboscis into the most pungent corners of counterculture and have a good sniff about; insert a finger into clubland's sweatiest crevices and have a fiddle. You can only go so far with two decks and a dancefloor. I want chaos, in big fat portions; I want havoc and I want it supersized and I want it NOW. And perhaps one of the finest purveyors of both is a man by the name of Toni Tambourine.

I first met Toni in a force nine gale on a boat to Hamburg. I was wearing an orange Hawaiian shirt with pineapples on it and was utterly, utterly arseholed. He was helping to organise a party on the boat and offered to buy me a drink, which seemed a remarkably civilised idea. So I graciously accepted, whereupon he stood up, fell over, and proceeded to do the front crawl across the carpet to the bar. Halfway across he seemed to founder but, after a rest, completed his voyage with the cunning use of the breaststroke. At the bar he asked two people to pull him up by the armpits so he could order the drinks,

Discombobulated

then crawled on his hands and knees onto the dancefloor and began barking like a rabid hound. This kind of behaviour is only going to guarantee my life long friendship so it was good to get the call from Toni inviting me to something called the Donkey Show at London's Hanover Grand. Admittedly, the last time I went to a show with donkeys in it I was in Bangkok, so I was somewhat hesitant but Toni promised me it would be worthwhile. The idea? To take the Shakespeare play *A Midsummer Night's Dream* and set it in New York's über-famous nightclub Studio 54. And that kind of lunacy sounded just delicious to me.

So here we go: I'm the boozy breathed, incontinent old guy in the comfortable slacks, regaling you with tales that you don't want to listen to of daring do during the Disco Wars; inviting you to hop on his knee, excuse, if you will, that faintly stale smell and tune in your ears as we go back... way back... to New York in 1979.

Well you can tell by the way I use my walk, I'm a woman's man, no time to talk / Music loud and women warm, I've been kicked around since I was born

Awake the pert and nimble spirit of mirth / Turn melancholy forth to funerals / The pale companion is not for our pomp

I was a regular at Studio 54. No shit! I once banged Grace Jones over the bar while snorting cocaine off of Mick Jagger's bits, then hung out with Andy Warhol, talked movies with De Niro — sure, all of that. So it just flipped my flan that they'd resurrected the spirit of Studio 54 right here in the heart of London in merrie olde England and thrown a Shakespeare party. You remember Shakespeare... he's that crazy cat who wrote plays and shit. The Spielberg of his day, only with a smaller beard.

So anyways, I pulled up at the Hanover Grand — downtown on Hanover and Regent — and the club's promoter, Toni, he met me at the door. We talked a while and watched as the queue grew long as a line of human cocaine. That's what I love about Studio 54 — the magic starts before you even gets in. It is all about the queue, about whether you were gonna get in at all, about the size of the V in your VIP. An old bag lady kept axing Toni questions. Man she was old; she was like, two days older than dirt, and this bouncer cat had to move her on. Well, I didn't much like the look of him either. Anyone who stands in the way of me and a dancefloor ain't ever gonna be my pal, but Toni got me in OK.

"So what's the deal here, Toni?"

"These actors visited us and noticed that this venue is very similar to the Flamingo, where they'd had the play in New York for two years. And I was like, what is it? And they told me it was a disco show and it had a donkey in it. And I thought… superb, we'll try it out."

Inside it was difficult to tell where the punters stopped and the actors started. Crazy stuff was going on all around me. Toni asked if I wanted a drink. I asked for a beer and he got me a vodka Red Bull. That's what I like about Toni. Next time I asked for a vodka Red Bull and he brought a bottle of champagne. I slid slowly into a groove.

And you come to me on a summer breeze, keep me warm in your love then you softly leave / And it's me you need to show, how deep is your love

I never may believe / These antique fables, nor these fairy toys / Lovers and madmen have such seething brains

Nightclubs are like, crazy ass places. They're theatre anyways. What's that Shakey line? "If all the world's a disco, let each man bust a groove." Believe — in discos across the planet, each dude is playing their part. I'm particularly fine in the role of Incoherent Boy. And here, the boundaries were blurred further still as the disco took to the stage, as theatre snuck past the bouncers and onto the dancefloor, mixing it up into some unholy disco smudge.

The Dream evolved as it revolved around me. Oberon had turned into the owner of the joint; Titania focused on the first three letters of her name and was all kinds of naked; Puck was a rollerskating, cocaine dealing freakoid; and the fairies, well let's just say they were bent as a seven dollar bill. Us people in the club, we was part of it too,

Discombobulated

dancing and romancing beneath a mirrorball moon, spinning at the centre of this disco universe. I won't tell you too much of the story (read the fricking play, why dontcha) and anyway I was too sozzled on the sauce to take a lot of it in, but it was a helluva lot of fun. After the show finished with a big Broadway climax, everyone carried on dancing. I snuck backstage to talk with Jordan, who played one of the Vinnie characters and Anna, who played Titania.

Oh say you'll always be my baby we can make it shine / We can take forever, just a minute at a time

Love looks not with the eyes, but with the mind / And therefore is wing'd Cupid painted blind

"It goes back to William Shakespeare."

I looked at Jordan. "No shit. But he didn't set it in a disco, did he?"

"No," Anna added, patiently, "but he set it in a forest; this crazy forest where everything happens magically. You're not expecting people to fall in love but there are love potions and everything."

Strange dramas take place between the walls of a nightclub, trust me, buddy, I've been there, mad passions and violence; qualudes and comic interludes. Maybe setting Shakey in such a club is just a way of — I don't know — exposing that and 'fessing up. End of the day, Studio 54 was all about dressing up and taking theatre onto the dancefloor... this was just the same. People can be so precious about this guy Shakespeare and they can be too damned precious about discotheques — it's all entertainment, right bud? Popular culture. The themes of Shakespeare go beyond the border of the five boroughs... they are universal, right? And so are those of those furry guys, the Bee Gees — the biggies about love and such like. The Bee Gees wrote music for the dancefloor, Shakespeare wrote plays for the stage. Nightclubs and theatres, they're all places to escape from the crap in our everyday lives.

Anna nodded. "It's for people to enjoy themselves, to forget themselves, to abandon themselves and leave the world behind."

The Donkey Show

*Ears are to the ground, there is movement all around / There is
something going down / And I can feel it*

*I can no further crawl, no further go / My legs can keep no pace
with my desires*

If "to be or not to be" is the question, then here is the goddamn fucking answer. Shakespeare is disco and disco is Shakespeare. Could it
be any clearer?

Man that revelation has like, totally messed with my head, Dad-
dio. Why's that bouncer looking at me funny? Who let these fairies
in here?

"I'm afraid I'm gonna have to ask you to leave."

"Yeah buddy, what-ev-er. I've been thrown out of better clubs
than this, you schmuck."

That told him. It used to be my teenage ambition to get to every
Hard Rock Café on the planet. Now it's my ambition to get thrown
out of every Home nightclub. But that's cool. I'll just come right back
and bust a cap in his ass, just as soon as I find out what the hell that
means. I began walking away and then turned back.

*Now to 'scape the serpent's tongue /
We will make amends ere long.*

True dat. | *November 2000*

37
Fear and Loathing in Stalybridge

THE GOOD DOCTOR HAS FINALLY PASSED OVER TO THE WRONG
SIDE; A PERSONAL EULOGY

We were somewhere around Droylsden on the edge of Greater Manchester when the drugs began to take hold.

I remember saying something like... let's stop at the Asda in Ashton and get supplies. Wrong move, Bubba, wrong move. The supermarket was far too bright, as though a nuclear bomb had detonated in aisle five, just by the frozen veg. Hurriedly, we bought cigarettes and bourbon and wine and John Smiths. Truly, it was going to be a long and brutal night.

"Do we need cake?" barked my attorney Antony, far too loud for the environment.

"That's hard to say," I muttered under my breath, an unlit cigarette hanging limp from its holder. "Depends how deep undercover we plan to go."

Ye gads, what was the point in even thinking? What depth is there other than deep? The check-out chick looked us up and down, as though we'd parachuted in from outerspace. Things were degenerating rapidly, unwinding like a ball of wool. How did it come to this?

Fear and Loathing in Stalybridge

I remember when I started this column — six or seven or who-the-hell-knows years ago — and I made preparatory notes. One was about the tone it should take and it read something like "a cross between *Fear and Loathing* and *Withnail & I*, between Hunter S. Thompson and Richard E. Grant". That's where I wanted to be: halfway between the decadence of the US and the dandyness of the UK, that mid Atlantic point symbolised by the out-to-sea, castaway nature of the collective middle initial. S.E.A.

My company for this mission into the savage sweet heartland of the Wrong Side was a brown seventies Mercedes called der Fraulein, a Stetson I bought in Vegas, several pairs of increasingly ridiculous sunglasses, and a bootful of various uppers and downers and lefters and righters and pills and thrills to take you every which way and loose. And, a cardboard cutout writer in the passenger seat.

Our first point of call had been to drop by the surgery of Dr Herman, proprietor of Manchester's finest head shop. The good doctor — a prescription for every occasion. Our medication included Trichocerus Peruvianus (aka Peruvian Torch cactus), Columbian mushrooms and several Hawaiian Baby Woodrise Seeds. Now, pimped to the max, we were driving through green countryside, like the cue ball in some game of surreal pool, the green felt countryside like baize beneath our wheels.

Hunter S. Thompson changed everything, turned everything on its head. New Journalism. Gonzo Journalism. It's guiding principal: fuck the story, unleash the mini bar. Requirements are simply an ego the size of a Zeppelin, its engine fuelled by chemicals. The point of the story is an irrelevance, an intrusion, an annoyance. Simply climb in and start drinking until things start to go wrong. They always do.

In the dark ages Stalybridge had just one club, called Shades. The town soon became known as ShadyBridge. Then they opened another one and lo, there was much rejoicing. The locals got kind of carried away with themselves and a local radio station christened the place StalyVegas (pronounced Stay-lee-vay-gas). It's a strange

Discombobulated

town — the very edge of Manchester, nestled in the shadow of the hills and Saddleworth Moor, where green turns to grey. Stick to the roads boys, stick to the roads. We drove der Fraulein through downtown, past the shimmering glitter of Cosmo Bingo, cricking our necks to drink in the neon, plastic splendour of a Tuesday afternoon in Stalybridge. Could life possibly be any sweeter?

Well, the only hotel in Stalybridge is called Thompson's. How strangely beautiful is that? Thompson's Cross. The one I have nailed him to, now he is dead. Christians have their Bible; my good book is a first edition of Fear and Loathing in Las Vegas *that I bought from the States and had shipped over. Everything you will ever need to run your life is within those pages. My attorney swung der Fraulein into the carpark and turned off the engine. We were here now, there was no going back. We had long since dropped off reality's freeway, many exits back.*

Dr Hunter S. Thompson. Of course, I never knew him, but I read him enough to maybe know him a little. Without him there would be no Wrong Side. He broke all the rules, broke down the fence and let the cattle run free. If you want serious stuff, kindly turn the page and move on. Keep turning, Travis. Quick quick, your kind aren't welcome around these pages. Still here? Is everybody in? Is everybody... in? The ceremony is about to begin.

We checked in and I phoned Alix Walker — a friend, a DJ, a dapper gent and, more importantly, a local of StalyVegas who wanted to show us around town. He knew the kooks and korners of its mean streets, but none of that mattered now I had settled on my plan. He arrived, sober and straight.

"Alix, my plan relies on your ability to accelerate from zero to idiot in about the time it takes you to ingest one of these mushrooms and wash it down with this here can of John Smiths."

His eyes lit up. I knew he'd be in. "I'm in. What's the plan?"

"The plan? We go... nowhere. What do you think? It's beautiful, right? My only thought is to stay within the comfortable pink walls of this little girl's room, consume the entirety of the booze and po-

tions we have brought with us, next level everything, talk bollocks until the sun comes up, and then set fire to Hunter... "

"Torch Thompson?"

"Sure, why not. It's an obituary."

"And then?"

"Then? Then... and this is the truly beautiful part... we get off. Hightail it for the hills and never look back, not even for the memories."

The plan was beautiful in its symmetry and simplicity. I had my whole record collection in a little white box on the bedside cabinet; I had the company of good people; and the fuel to keep the engine of the evening running. Everything I wanted, and needed, was within the four walls of this room.

Hunter knew he was an idiot. People think I'm an idiot and, of course, they're right. An imbecile with a pen and a bottle of booze and the goodwill of a publisher to puke that heady cocktail up onto the page. I never wanted to join a provincial newspaper in Bumfuck Egypt and write stories about cats up trees. I wanted to sit still and take so many potions the top of my head would flip open like a bottle of Heinz and all this goofy gonzo juice would pour out in glorious Technicolor, like thought ketchup upon the page.

Baggy thoughts, loose times and good vibrations in this doll's house in StalyVegas. Christ knows what madness lurks outside, what beasts roam these moors in March. In this guesthouse bedroom we are kings.

The hall toilet flushed. There were other people in the rooms of this guesthouse. Civilians. I could imagine them holding a glass to the wall, trying to make out what sounded like... well... like three idiots, high on booze and mushrooms, toasting a cardboard cutout and giggling like schoolgirls. Never, in their wildest imagination, would they be able to get a handle on what madness was unfolding, or be able to explain what they had heard on this Tuesday afternoon in Stalybridge. The truth would be too brutal for such a fragile imagination, the ring of horror would make it shatter like a chandelier.

Discombobulated

My ambition in writing is only this: that the best I have ever written could somehow share company with the worst of the Doctor's. That our fictional personas could possibly be imagined sitting together in some fabulous place, tucked away in the pages of a bar built from words.

Staying in is the new going out. Why go out for burgers when you've got steak at home, right Bubba? We had a case of beer, wine and bourbon. The mushrooms had gone but we had the Matucan cacti, and after that was done in, we still had the pills. The evening had only just begun. I wanted a cigarette. I haven't smoked in years but the occasion warranted it.

Hunter S. Thompson, sixty seven years old, shot himself in the head and ended it all. *Res ipsa loquitor*. Let the good times roll. I miss him very much.

Some time around dawn we left the room, and took Hunter down to a disused railway line, beneath an old brick bridge. I poured lighter fuel over the cardboard and set alight to the Doctor and he was soon consumed in fire. The surgery is closed, but the Doctor is always on call. A loco locum. Selah, and so much for all that. Thank you for the words and the stories you wove them into, and for the nonsense and the chaos.

Thank you for the Fear and the Loathing. | March 2005

For Hunter S. Thompson, 1937-2005

38
Moscow

*38,000ft up in British Airways Club Class. I'm watching Will &
Grace as the extremely attractive airhostess, her Muscat blonde hair
tied neatly behind her slender neck, asks if I would like a second bottle of Piper Heidsieck champagne. I nod a polite affirmative, then
stretch out my legs.*

You know what? Getting deported ain't as bad as it's cracked up to be.
Not too shabby for Simon. I have been refused entry to a club before
but it's all a little different when it's an entire country, especially a
superclub like Russia. It would seem that lacking the right visa is the
geopolitical equivalent of having the wrong shoes. And to carry this
rather tortuous analogy forwards, what happened next was the inter-
continental version of going home, changing into the right shoes and
trying it on again a few weeks later, hoping it's a different immigration bouncer at the gate.

The Russians have a phrase for such tight situations: "It's impossible but it's possible." For the next attempt at entry, I had apparently
become a student at the University of Moscow, there was a visa in
my passport, and I was with the Gallery's John Askew, watching the
in-flight movie and trying to recall whether it was Oscar Wilde who
penned the screenplay to *Dude, Where's My Car?*

I have partied in Moscow before — a good few years back — when

Discombobulated

I went over with a fellow alumni from the old skool, Mark Luvdup, who graduated *cum loude* from our local DISCOmprehensive. I'd met some real good people back then, including a DJ called Gregory and his friend Andrei. It was my plan to get their numbers from Mark but I hadn't had time. And then who should be there to meet us at the airport but...

"Andrei, man, fucking hell, how you been?"

It was a Friday night and light was fading over Moscow like a dimming bulb. We stopped at a backstreet bar for fish and beer and conversation, then headed over the river to the club Fabrique. The back end of the club also doubled as a restaurant; steps led down to private dining booths, separated by curtains, a glass floor overlooking the club below. We joined the club's manager, Ilya Kochevrin, at his table. The lighting was low and dark, giving the place a feeling of svelte, understated class; the club swelled with humans and music.

Many alliances are now being forged across Europe. The Gallery night of the club Turnmills has hooked up with Fabrique; John's label Kompressed (part of the label stable of Tall Paul's Duty Free) has an almost Soviet identity — their first signing was a track by Russian act Sensorica. "They're really into the Gallery here," John shouted above the noise of the club. "I think they keep an eye on the line-ups and stuff. So they booked us to do a Gallery night, we came over and it really fucking rocked.

"Ah yes, would that be the time a dapper young journalist got knocked back at immigration?"

John grinned. "Yes, unfortunately the KGB had been keeping an eye on his movements."

The noise made it difficult to hear clearly. "The cagey bee? What, a bee who keeps his cards close to his furry little chest?"

"Yeah, he's quite cagey. He's been to self-help classes to build up his confidence but you can never tell what he's up to."

Yoinks, only a couple of drinks in and already our conversation swayed like a sidestreet drunk. Personally I don't do vodka — but then try telling that to a Russian as he slams a round of neat shots down in front of you. The world quickly became soft and giddy. After dinner I followed John into the booth for the beginning of his set, built from the real deal trance, not the kiddy stuff. "The music we're playing here is pretty much exactly what's played at the Gallery." John pulled his headphones around his neck and shouted in my ear. "The harder it is, the more they love it."

He played more than ten of his own productions — either his own tunes, remixes or re-edits. I continued to confuse laga and vodker. The club was difficult to negotiate; the darkness concealed little steps and passages leading off in convoluted directions. Eventually I gave up and leant against a wall by the bar and that's where I found my old disko comrade Gregory, his smile as wide as Siberia. Gregory was to follow John and finish off the night. I was pretty much finished off anyway.

I opened one eye. Someone was poking me. I was lying in bed... dressed only in my boxers... and someone was definitely poking me. And I don't mean the good kind of poking, I mean someone was in my room, poking me in my side with their finger or a stick or some such poking device. I rolled over and opened up the other eye. Stereovision. There was a woman, as wide as she was tall, in some kind of pseudo military chambermaid outfit. Three other similar women were standing behind her. Either that or I was seeing quadruple.

For some reason I started laughing. "Is there any chance one of you might like to tell me what, in the name of Lenin's little beard, is going on?"

"You pay," she smiled, in a way that contained no semblance of humour.

She poked me again.

"Enough with the poking already!"

I swung my legs out of bed, walked out into the corridor and knocked on John's door. "Johnny, there's four Olgas in my room. I think we're being kicked out."

A muffled soundtrack of grunting and groaning, then the door was flung wide. He was also in his boxers.

"Try calling Andrei," he coughed, his eyes only half open.

I walked back to my room, to find the door was now locked and my key fob no longer worked. Olga was standing in the corridor, still

Discombobulated

smiling. "You pay," she repeated.

So I'm standing there in the corridor of a Moscow hotel, dressed in my pants, wondering how she exactly expects me to do that?

"This is ridiculosovich," barked John, in a rather neat bit of bilingual invention. "We're leaving."

Olga allowed me into my room to dress and pack my bag. I have never stormed out of a hotel before. It was rather exciting. To be honest our exit may have been more dramatic if we'd actually left the building, rather than making it as far as the lobby bar and then staging a sit down protest, which basically involved ordering some beers and giggling.

Kicked out of my room... kicked out of the country... you know, a guy like me could really grow to like Russia. It's my kind of town. The lobby bar beer was like a breeze blowing the cobwebs from the derelict mansion in my head, allowing fragments of memories to enter like the silver ghosts of strangers. Andrei joined us and, with a look that said how-weird-are-you-exactly, swiftly paid for another night. Our revolutionary tendencies now placated by a combination of tiredness, resignation and lager, we carried our bags back to the exact same rooms we had just stormed out of.

Our personal little Boxer Rebellion had cost us most of the morning, but when we did get out onto Red Square the sun was still high in the sky over St Basil's cathedral. In Moscow there are things that are impossible that are possible; there are cabs that aren't cabs. It's all very Kafka. Hold out your hand and any old car will stop for you. It's a cross between a Hackney cab and hitching. After a day's Moscow mooching we re-assembled at Fabrique, but as John and I approached the door we realised neither of us knew the Russian for "we're on the guestlist". The bouncer just held the door open, grinning through gritted teeth, "please, no drinking for you guys tonight," accompanying it with a look that suggested he knew a lot more about last night than we did.

"Yes, well I rather think we'll be the judge of that, my good man."

We found a table towards the back of the club and Andrei ordered food, which we washed down with tall, cold glasses of beer. The dancefloor swelled once again, as though stung by a cagey bee, throbbing with the music. At around 4am we left to check out a couple of other clubs: one called Zeppelin, with all manner of mischief and mayhem unfolding over several floors; then a smaller, seedier after hours joint, full of the weird, wired and wide-eyed. At whatever o'clock we caught the subway back to Red Square, the early morning sunlight whitewashing Moscow in a bleached out patina; empty, save for a few lost souls and the lonely chattering of birds high up in the trees.

Later that day we made a dash to the airport in a cab-that's-not-a-cab, our lackadaisical attitude rendering any likelihood of making our flight absolutely impossible. But possible. | *June 2004*

39
Cologne

NAZIS, SM FETISH PARTIES, BOMBS AND SKELETONS; COLOGNE
HAS AN AROMA ALL OF ITS OWN

1913. The grand opening of a chi chi cigar club in Cologne. Two gents approach the door, looking forward to inhaling the best Cohibas Havana has to offer.

Friday night my date cancelled and out of joy or despair, I'm not sure which, I drank two bottles of wine and passed out on the couch. Next thing I knew the apartment intercom was buzzing like a bee on Benzedrine and it's this cab dude telling me he has to take me to the airport. I yawn-swept the cobwebs from my head, smack-puckered the goom from my lips and checked my watch. Just gone 6am. I gathered whatever was within radius, chucked it in a suitcase and hightailed it down the stairs.

1920s. People think that, since the cigar club closed, this place is empty but head down some stairs... and then some more... and you'll see leering men leaning over a balcony as two guys wrestle without rules. This is Fight Club.

So I made it to Cologne and was feeling pretty damned chuffed I'd managed that, when the batteries of my PDA died and I suddenly had no information about who I was seeing, where I was staying or when the good people of Cologne would like to see the back of me. Nothing, other than I was to meet a man known only as Dr Walker.

1930s. Two students approach a doorway, looking behind them to check no one has followed. They support the ideas of a little man with a little moustache, and have come to debate them with other Nazis.

All out of moves, I dragged myself up onto a nearby barstool, ordered *ein grosse bier* and attempted to get a grip on things. A couple of sips in and a big bear of a man appeared, dressed in long shorts and tattoos, introducing himself as Dr Walker. He led me to a car driven by a stoned Parisian, his eyelids heavy as boulders. Dr Walker would have driven but they'd both got so smashed the night before he can't remember where he left his car.

1940s. An RAF bomber reaches the skies over Cologne. The mission is to drop bombs on a building thought to be a tank factory, but last night the crew got into a mess in the mess and they miss. It lands on a tall, thin building down an anonymous sidestreet.

A lesser man may have cracked at this point and run screaming to his shrink; or at least his manicurist. These are mangled times so if you're gonna go nuts, you might as well do it with neat nails, right amigos?

1950s. Cologne is devastated. Just rubble. A woman takes owner-ship of a building and uses it as a shop from which to sell black mar-ket goods, mostly fags and booze, smuggled in from Belgium.

For these are indeed pugnacious times and we need to get our kicks before the whole powder keg goes up. Goodnight Vienna. Kaboom Kabul.

1970s. The hardcore music makes the leather bound chaps sweat, the moisture dripping from their chunky moustaches. Two men are falling in love for the night and decide to take a room in the gay brothel upstairs. This is Fuck Club.

Discombobulated

We swayed into Cologne, pulling up near to the building Dr Walker calls home. Down a side alley there was a doorway, set away from the street...

2004. A hungover, unkempt journalist, a supine Frenchman and a Teutonic titan approach the door of a building with great history, a building he now owns...

At street level you have two choices. Downstairs is the club Camouflage, tucked away and hidden, a stealth disco. Upstairs is the artist's hotel, Monte Christo. I checked into my room. The walls were a deep and comforting blue; depictions of Jesus stared down from a myriad of pictures and gauche statues; a tacky statue of the Virgin Mary sat above the sink; a chocolate bunny on my pillow.

"We have a theory," said Dr Walker, the hotel's proprietor, sometime later, walking me down into the club, "that it's not healthy if the distance between a beer and the second beer is more than seven minutes." The good doctor has it all under this one roof — his home, hotel, bar, club and studio. "For me it's important not to have much of a distance between bed and PlayStation and synthesiser and club and fridge."

The club had a low ceiling and long history. Dark recesses shadowed secrets, camouflage netting made the place feel like a bunker far behind the lines in these Disco Wars. Through a corridor and down some more stairs was the subbasement. Dr Walker pointed out the line that formed the old balcony where punters would look down on the illegal fights. In rebuilding the club they had dug down into the concrete, and uncovered human bones from the time the building was bombed in WWII. "It was like opening a grave," the Doctor recalled. In every stage of rebuilding the place, they had uncovered another level of history, another story in an evolving, archaeological narrative. Now Dr Walker was part of the story, the next chapter in the history of the building. "I didn't find this building," he deadpanned. "This building found me."

Up one level to the club, and we were joined by Cem Oral, Dr Walker's partner in their production outfit, Air Liquide. Formed in

Frankfurt in 1991, their new album, *Let Your Ears Be The Receiver*, will be their eleventh — real eclectic electronica, built for the dance-floor — which is kind of understandable, as it was literally recorded *on the dancefloor* of Camouflage, the very place I now sat with Dr Walker and Cem, amongst the ghost echoes of bombs and violence and sex.

Over the years Air Liquide have made a lot of different noises. "We've made totally experimental records," Cem explained. "We've made techno-y records, then we've had some hip hop style... ambient. And this time it's four-to-the-floor."

The Doctor concurred. "After we got the club... we wanted to do a club album."

Whilst the guys got ready for the evening I took a walk along the bank of the Rhine, along the eau de Cologne, flooded with thoughts as though the river itself had burst:

"Strange days. Even now my countrymen are in a desert someplace shooting at people until they understand the concept of freedom; deposing a torturous leader so they can show them how it should really be done."

I scribbled such thoughts as fast as my pen would move, sitting in a place called a McCafé (I guess to give the Golden Arches a sense of the cute and continental) and even that got me thinking: maybe the clown in the red pants could suggest to the clown in the White House that he sponsor the games in Iraq. McPeace. And maybe Bush could be the supersized McUnt. Whole thing is as tasteless as one of their burgers.

Order the happy meal, people! Look how far we have come in Europe — even that night's party took place in a WWII tank factory, over on the other side of the Rhine where, once upon a fucked up time, the grandfathers of folk like Dr Walker made tanks to shoot chunks of metal over fields at the grandfathers of folk like me. Very strange then, to be partying and drinking and meeting people (including, bizarrely, a buzzing bee on Benzedrine) under the self same roof of what is now an arts space called Kunstwerk which, come to think of it, is probably the German translation of Operation Iraqi Freedom.

But anyway, let's leave my festering, pustulous rage for a moment

Discombobulated

and get back to the good and pure business of hedonism and electronic music, which is how I spent the night, partying to DJs that included le stoned Francais and Christopher Just, before Air Liquide took up position behind a bank of wires and equipment, so entangled it looked as though a mislaid shell had detonated beneath a Dalek. They played a mix of material, manipulating music before it was pumped out to the punters — retro-electro squelches, acid pianos, vocoder vocals, a real rave aesthetic.

Back at the hotel the party rumbled on in Camouflage. When I awoke the next morning it was Easter Sunday and Jesus stared down at me from all walls, already awake after his three day cave kip. And still a beat resonated up through the floors, as though a rusting generator sat in the basement powering the cogs of this concrete machine. Tempted to head back into the fray, I made it as far the club's door, overcome by the fear as strange and pale, golem-esque creatures emerged from the stairwell of the Monte Christo, a hotel like the Manumission motel, like Hotel California, like the Morrison Hotel... like any motel, hotel or Holiday Inn that has provided a sanctuary for the spiritually unhinged and culturally perverse. | *May 2004*

40
Shanghai...

BROTHELS AND NEONS TWINKLE IN THE HEART OF THE ORIENT;
BAD KARAOKE AND EVEN WORSE DISCO DANCING

... SUPRISE! OK, me old china, these may well be cheap jokes, but I'm saving to pay for the sackful of sneakers I bought in Taipei. Dispatches seems to have turned into a game of "Where's Waldo," recently — "Where's Wrongo," perhaps — and indeed here I was, amongst the shimmering chimera of Shanghai, a city that stretches out in every direction, including up — as if to tickle the heavens with its glass fingers.

On the twenty-something floor of La Residence hotel, in the livingroom of my suite, we recombobulated — the DJs Iain Taylor and 4, promoters Turtle and Alex, and myself. Turtle ordered Chinese food and we talked about the Chinese dance scene, still nascent in its punky, pubescent beginnings; still a rave against the machine, against the Mao Man who doesn't want big groups of people getting together, for dancing or sedition.

"They're afraid of it," said Iain. "They've got a right to be."

Turtle tucked into the food, his chopsticks doing a Riverdance between his fingers. "You've got to work with the government — you've got to make the party some fucking stupid Shanghai Tourist Cultural Exchange shit. Put that in the name and you'll be OK."

Of course, you cannot legislate against the need young people have to connect with other young people around the world. Confucius he say, clubs are the planet's playground... records are the swings and slides. Confuscious also he say... once the Chinese market truly opens

Discombobulated

up... it's boom time in the boondocks, folks.

"It's important for the artists," Turtle said, as he click-clicked his chopsticks, "especially with a place with 1.5 billion people. It's potentially the biggest market in the world. And they just want to party — they're so eager to catch up, you know. They want the UK sound because it's very hard for them to go to London, it's very strict."

Well, if the mountain won't come to Muhammad, better take the disco to the disciples. The second Check-In party was at the downtown club Pegasus, set out on two floors. Entry was free for me, two days' wage for the average Chinese, yet it was already busy when we arrived. A couple of drinks in, DJ 4 and Iain stepped up, spinning back to back as I span my own neat Arabesque betwixt dancefloor and bar. The room swelled with a rum old mix of locals, Brits living the ex-pat life, other Europeans and Shanghai Shermans. A big Chinese guy stomped across the stage in a ten gallon hat, big buckled belt and cowboy boots, looking like some Asian parody of a Texan. It transpired he was, indeed, from Texas.

Then I was talking to this one girl, I forget how or why. She was also what they call an ABC — American Born Chinese. She asked if I wanted to dance, and I did, so we're dancing and talking and... you're just going to have to trust me that this next bit is true because... she was there to cast the final role for a movie and needed a drop dead gorgeous Chinese female lead. So while we danced she asked me to scope out the ladies: I picked out the ones I thought were cute, and she went over and asked if they wanted to be in a movie. I'm not proud of myself — it was sleazy, low down work — but goddamn it I didn't do it for me... I did it for the movies.

Iain was up to his gills in the party, dancing around behind the decks as he DJd, scratching, shouting "show me some ass!" to no one in particular, as had become his wont during the weekend. Elsewhere it was some guy's birthday; he filled up my glass with Jack and pushed me over the edge. The rest is mere party paraphernalia, a gaudy umbrella left lonely in the cocktail glass of an evening. We were in another club called Guangee at some stage. Iain still had his records, so he got up and played and I partied with Turtle and Alex until they, too, left and it was just me and Iain and the morning sunlight, hydroponically warming the clubbers who basked in a nearby park, re-energising themselves like lounge lizards lazing on rocks.

I woke at about 3pm the next afternoon and lay in bed thinking... shall I get up and get out into Shanghai, one of the jewels of the Orient — or shall I continue to lie here watching *Undercover Brother* on HBO?

In the end it was a bit of both. Iain met me in the hotel lobby and I told him a joke I had made up that night in my sleep. It goes something like this: "Did you hear about the Chinese law firm called "Sosueme"? Iain chuckled, then told me Rennie Pilgrem already had a record label called that. It seems originality is hard to come by, even for the drunk and unconscious.

The afternoon unwound with us trying to seek out "the real Chinese shit" and ended up with us in a shopping mall. And I'm looking around thinking... hang on... there's Starbucks, there's McDonald's... we are in China right, not China White? Where are all the peasants in tunics riding around on rickety rusty bicycles like they show you on telly? This place has five-buck beers and rip-off shops and feels just like home. It would seem that the US has accomplished commercially what we were told communism would do ideologically: reducing the world and even my writing to some homogenised cultural yuk. Oh the irony... Michael Moore, get over here, I need a word.

Shanghai has glass skyscrapers that huddle together to carve an urban landscape as stunning as Manhattan. The main square may be called People's Square, but it still winks and glints with neon advertisements. I had to have a sit down with myself to get my head around it all. Of course we need to balance this polemic with the fact that Shanghai is unique in mainland China in that it's commercially similar to Hong Kong (apparently your average Chinaman needs a permit to even come to the city and have his pure brain warped by such vulgar western decadence) and the government is undeniably hardcore elsewhere. Just that day there had been comments about the Taiwanese election and tension hung over the place like smog. But bottom line: Ronald McDonald was not what I had expected given what I'd been told by teachers, the media, even the government. In fact, George Orwell, get over here I need a word with you, too.

Discombobulated

As these issues queued to be considered like thought traffic at synaptic traffic lights, my phone beeped and I got the outright weirdest text I have ever received. It said, simply: "Turtle will take you to dirty place."

The dirty place in question was an establishment just out of town, one of several KTV bars; kind of like KFC only they serve chicks not chicken. The whole thing was a David Lynch experience: the walls of the upmarket, private rooms dripping with warped surreality as you are introduced to girls, who sit with you, hold your hand, play drinking games with you, serve you food and — this is the killer — sing karaoke to you while cheap videos play on widescreen TV. And that's as far as it goes, unless you want to next-level it with one of the girls, but that's a whole different ball game (literally) and I was happy with the hand holding. So I was talking to this girl who patted out the small talk and giggled at everything I said. She seemed fascinated with my eyes, which are blue, although not bright as they once were, before the pressure of booze and bohemia dimmed their light.

"Show me your arse," she said.

I spat my drink over the table and chocked up an "excuse me?"

"Show me your arse," she repeated, squeezing my hand, reassuringly. All this was like a red rag to the bull for Iain, who had overheard her comments and had his pants down before you could say Chairman Mao. She screeched in horror. "NO! Your eyrsh... show me your eyrsh!"

"Dude, trousers up, she means eyes."

Fortunately she seemed to see the funny side — a breath of fresh air, one would imagine — after seeing the backside.

We'd done the sights. Almost. We still needed to see the Wrong Side so, deciding it was too early to call time on the evening, myself, Iain and DJ 4 (a deep hearted Judo champ, hip hop DJ, kind of a kooky cat) went for a few drinks down some other sleazy alley, patrolled by cops and hookers and lonely ex-pats looking for a few minutes of squelchy love and a cuddle.

And who can blame them? Humans want to connect (and music is the glue that binds us). Whether governments tell us we are capitalists or communists; fascists or orthodontists, it's inherent in the human condition to strive for community and companionship. Michael Moore was entirely right when he said that the currency governments deal with is fear, what they trade is anxiety. But at street level there's a lot of love going on. | *July 2004*

41
24 Hour Party People

CLIMBING INTO BAGGY, LOOSE FIT TROUSERS AND FLOPPY HATS;
TRIPPING DOWN MEMORY LANE TO MADCHESTER; PLAYING THE
PART OF YOURSELF: AN EXTRA IN THE MOVIE 24 HOUR PARTY
PEOPLE

Fuck. Ing. Hell. Last Friday was one of the kookiest nights of my klubbing kareer. And believe me, that's going some. I was an extra in the making of *24 Hour Party People*, a movie about the explosion of the MADchester scene. I spent the night on the dancefloor set of the Haçienda — essentially playing the part of me, twelve years ago — an extra in that scene on the dancefloor of the actual Haçienda. The fact that a movie is being made about a chapter of cultural history I inhabited is a mind bender I have yet to properly navigate (let's just say Steven Spielberg has yet to show interest in shooting a movie about the London suburb of Palmers Green in the seventies) but MADchester is now seen as important enough to warrant being committed to celluloid. For me, art is now indeed imitating life.

After spending the previous six months in Australia, I touched down on Planet Manchester in 1989 thinking I was moving to your bog standard northern town. What I found blew my brains straight out my ears. I arrived sporting a corduroy jacket with leather elbow

198

patches and a red cravat — a uniform that I thought was de rigeur for a pretentious student of literature — and found everyone else peering at me through the curtains of their hair, from under the shadow of their hoods. I remember having to ask someone what "stone roses" were, since those words featured on everyone's T-shirts; Mondays had never been happy for me. I was nineteen and in trouble. Sucked out of real life as a would-be teacher, I was quickly hurtled through a chemical vortex of clubland anarchy and spat out the other side as a disco desperado, possessing a propensity for nothing other from lounging around in discos. Don't blame the parents. Blame Manchester.

Almost subconsciously, the fringe grew down over my eyes, the width of my jeans widened, my walk melted into a floppy swagger, the music wriggled down inside of me and life came into focus for the first time. Around that point, in almost conspiratorial whispers, people started talking about a club: a mad disco laboratory where deranged experiments were conducted in fusing dance and indie music, creating in the process Frankenstein monsters like Shaun Ryder and Bez. So somewhere during the very last few months of the eighties, I ventured down.

The Haçienda put the "disco" into discombobulated. I remember every nasty nook and corrupt cranny of that club cathedral, even the cloakroom sign that read "Cloakroom Full", complete with those Peter Saville yellow and black industrial stripes. One day I went to hang my coat and the sign had gone, replaced by an altogether less stylish bit of A4 paper sellotaped to the counter. The sign never reappeared until, one night, a few dates into seeing this lass... The first night she asked me back to hers. There, in her bedroom, above her mirror, was the sign... which she'd nicked. I thought she was the coolest creature I had ever met.

Over the years these experiences have multiplied. I've been out for a drink with Gary Whelan from the Mondays and Andy Rourke from the Smiths; been introduced to Mani from the Stone Roses; chatted to Liam Gallagher at the Haç; sat on a beach in Ibiza nattering with Shaun Ryder. Despite having a vicar at the head of my family, I have never had a religious, indeed moral, fibre in my body but these events

Discombobulated

are the closest I will ever get to God clapping his hands and saying "right then lads, what we 'aving?"

So we had the club, we always had the T-shirt and now we have the movie. Whether this is the movie of the T-shirt or the other way around I have no idea; quite frankly the whole thing has flipped my flan, big time.

I went down to the filming with my kid brother Jonny — six years my junior — who had never been to the Haç. Dressed for the occasion, I wore a top that read "Mancunian", given to me in 1989 by the editor of my first publication — the student newspaper of the same name. I lent our kid an original Identity T-shirt, with the words "On the 6th day, God created MANchester". We pulled on a pair of floppy hats, left the office where we work together and walked around to the warehouse in Ancoats where the Haç had been re-built for the night.

As I walked in and saw the set my brains spilled from my ears all over again. It didn't just look like the Haç... it *was* the Haç. I walked through the crowd, mostly dressed in period gear, many of the faces familiar, many of those same people back again and I thought: you're *not supposed to be able to do this*; you're not supposed to climb back into your past and bounce around again. Everything was in the same place: the cloakroom, the toilets, the balcony, the DJ booth, and of course, that infamous first alcove, moodier than a midnight picnic in Beirut, where I found the actors playing the Mondays.

"Is that supposed to be Rowetta?" I said to my brother, from the corner of my mouth.

"That is Rowetta," he replied.

Reality and illusion were merging and mixing in ways I found hard to comprehend. Peter Hook from New Order turned up and the look on his face as he gazed about the club he part owned was priceless. He chatted and chuckled with Ralf Little, from *The Royle Family*, who was playing him in the movie; John Simm walked by, already a clubbing movie legend via *Human Traffic*, now playing the part of New Order's Bernard Sumner; then Steve Coogan appeared, playing the part of Anthony H. Wilson, owner of Factory Records and part-owner of the Haç. On the dancefloor the energy was all too familiar — a curvaceous ocean of floppy hats and Joe Bloggs jeans. One film unit grabbed hold of Jonny and dragged him onto the dancefloor to film him dancing in his top, which is just typical, lend some fucker your T-shirt and they end up in the movies...

Back at the bar that wasn't a real bar, of the Haçienda that wasn't the real Haçienda, I found Graeme Park queuing next to me (he was real at least). Parky was resident DJ at the club for more years than he probably cares to remember and what he said summed it all up: he was there the day they knocked the actual building down (allegedly to make way for an apartment block to be called the Acid House) and his last memory of the Haç was rubble. Now, playing here, would go some way to restoring things in his memory — *this* was the closing party, the proper disco funeral, that the Haçienda deserved. Personally, I can pay no greater compliment than the fact that, when our kid turned to me and said, "so what was the Haç like then?" I looked around and replied, "it was like this."

All those gargantuan tunes were dusted off and allowed to shine once again, spun by Haçienda DJs like Dave Haslam, Jon da Silva and Mike Pickering, and I bounced around like a teenager, which is probably dangerous when you're as unkempt a human being as I now am. The actors playing Bez and Shaun Ryder vibed everyone up and at one point Ryder connected eyes with Jonny and started screaming "C'MON!" while Bez did his freaky dancing behind him. By the toilets were what looked like gangsters, or actors playing gangsters, it was becoming increasingly difficult to differentiate.

Eventually it was time to leave. Me and our kid walked back through the dark, damp Manchester streets and for some reason opened up our office and carried on drinking. Outside, the view over Ancoats and the Northern Quarter confirmed the fact that Manchester isn't always the prettiest town. Since living here I've been mugged, robbed, had my house burgled and was all too recently evicted. I felt safer out of my head wandering around South Central LA asking tramps if they knew the way to the disco. Aside from La La Land I've lived in Sydney, Amsterdam and for the last two summers in Ibiza and I've always come back home to Manchester. I don't know why I wax lyrical about this city, just as I don't know why Mancunians aren't always explicit with their affection. It's really impossible to ex-

Discombobulated

plain in 1,500 words. I would write a book but Haslam's already done that. Maybe, as I always suspected, the answer is now to be found in the movies. | *March 2001*

> *The children need to go back to their roots, back to the green, green grass of home, back to the Haçienda. The Haçienda must be built.*
>
> *Situationist International Manifesto, 1957*

42
Sex and
Sexuality

WE ALL DO IT. ALLEGEDLY. BUT WHAT'S IT ALL ABOUT THEN?
AND HOW DOES ONE GO ABOUT GETTING SOME?

Strange ways, here we come...

It was a scene of carnival carnality that might have spurted forth from the quill of the Marquis de Sade: *A dancehall in central Manchester — Canal Street, I think. Men — working class men — are dressed as women, their skirts lifted to the heavens to reveal thick, furry legs. Music fills the room as acts of random depravity take place around every corner. Just when it seems the party has reached a rude crescendo, the doors burst open and the police steam in, their truncheons drawn, swiping at the punters in an attempt to beat down the merrymaking.*

So where am I? Somewhere in Manchester's gay village, made famous by the Channel 4 show *Queer As Folk*? Some corner of the mardi gras? Well maybe the question should rather be *when* am I, because that's the right place, wrong time. For I have climbed aboard my trusty time machine once again and travelled back, not to the 1990s, but the 1890s, when parties such as this took place in and around Piccadilly. Believe, my friends — you didn't invent the cocktail of "sex and a dash of clubland". You didn't even come close.

"Manchester is a fucking twisted place," remarked Luke Cowdrey, as we sat stewing in the sun, outside a bar on Canal Street. Luke is a DJ, promoter of Electric Chair and something of a clubland historian

Discombobulated

who has agreed to join me in this investigation into the role of sexuality in clubland. "The gay scene in Manchester in the fifties and sixties was connected to the underground criminal scene, by virtue of the fact that the cabaret clubs were the only late night clubs. So you had your old school Manchester gangsters next to the drag queens. So there's always been this mad fusion of people."

Sex. We've all done it. I did it once, although thinking about it I was drunk and confused at the time and may have accidentally gone Crown Green Bowling. But let's face it, if you're up for a bit — whether straight, slightly concave or bent double — you're unlikely to find any down the back of your bedsit couch. Sex in itself implies another person, which is why a room full of sweaty, semi-naked human bodies gyrating to polysexual, pulsating music holds a powerful sexual allure. Sexuality, like clubland, is essentially tribal, which is why it doesn't take Sherlock Holmes to trace house music back to the gay, black clubs of New York and Chicago. Listen to *French Kiss* by Lil' Louis. Case closed.

For instance, have you ever gone to the lav in a disco only to hear strange noises emanating from the next cubicle? At first you think it's someone trying to expel something particularly repugnant from their digestive tract, until that solo tenor is joined by a staccato falsetto, just a beat behind. Number twos that is not, disco amigos; that is a couple making whoopee... nookie... the beast with two backs... bumping uglies... engaging in the kind of horizontal folk dancing you are unlikely to see on the dancefloor, unless you're at Manumission and Mike's got the Viagra falls again. But even then, the word "Manumission" comes from the Latin "manumit", a freedom from all kinds of slavery, and we know the Romans didn't need asking twice when grapes and groupies were on the menu.

For many years the tribal instincts of both clubland and sexuality led to a kind of disco segregation: if you're gay you hang *here*, if you're straight you hang *there*. I'm something of a discoptomist in that I'm hoping there's a phallic, pendulous swing to the middle — surely we'd have the most fun if we all partied together? "Some people are threatened by ambiguity," Luke argued. "But ambiguity is a wonderful thing. I love going into a place where you don't know whether the woman next to you — who's absolutely beautiful — is gay, straight, lesbian, AC/DC or whatever." I guess my point is that life is so much more tasteful when it's mixed up, into the sort of heady human soup that takes place during mardi gras, when every description of human being walks down the catwalk that is Canal Street. Even during my game of conversational ping-pong with Luke, the people that walked past... well, they'd make your toes curl. Which, depending where you've put them, may be no bad thing. Step forward Sarah Ferguson.

While the twin horrors of homophobia and rampant heterosexuality are still somewhat uncouth, I think at least some of the battles have been won. After all, we're in the noughties and the whole concept of segregation seems so... well, just so damned last century. "To be absolutely honest with you, I think some of the straight clubs have become more progressive than the gay parties," Luke added. "I think some gay parties have become a *Queer As Folk* fucking Ikea float of conveyor belt nonsense. The gay scene has gone literally right up its arse." In a sense the explosion of club culture has blown away a lot of the cobwebs that suffocated British society and we've realised that at the end of the day, sexuality is more rainbow coloured than black or white. Heterosexuality is not a 100 per cent open and shut case, just as bisexuality doesn't sit astride a fifty/fifty fence (as sexually appealing that may be to some people). Rather, there are 100 different percentages, and that's what makes clubs so vibrant.

Clubs like Manumission — which began life just off Canal Street — just happen, they can't be forced or contrived. "You can't put two drag queens with two grammes of coke up their arse on the door of Po Na Na and expect to create that vibe," said Luke. "It's got to be natural." There is an electricity created by sexuality which is ignited in the test tube of the dancefloor by a spark of house music. Think of fetish clubs, where people like nothing better than to be strapped to a fridge, interfered with by dwarves armed only with yoghurt and bad intent, then left to mull it all over for a fortnight.

I agree that glitzy clubs are anathema to real sexuality. It's impossible to sanitise sex; it's almost self-definably unsanitised. But while the Ritzy, alpha male mentality of our youth may have been relegated to the subconscious by the sheer weight of evolution and matura-

Discombobulated

tion... it's still there, lurking like a caged beast, waiting to be set free, to take the controls of your conscience when, through a combination of heady emotions and Bacardi Breezers, you let down your guard.

The mardi gras brings them all out, and Luke gets them all in... into his club Homo-Electric, the philosophy of which is that there shouldn't be any. Homo-Electric is the real deep down, sleazy deal. Down some anonymous looking stairs at the arse end of the gay village (if you'll excuse the turn of phrase) and into Legends, a scene opened up to me just as the Moss Eisley Cantina did to the young Skywalker in *Star Wars* — host to every twisted, gorgeous brand of life form you could ever possibly wish to share a beer-and-a-boogie with. Further into the club, rooms opened up behind curtains... down stairs... truly, it was a wonderful kind of scene; wall to wall smiles worn on faces of every sexuality — everyone getting on grandly, at least within the bounds of this nightclub.

The first flyer for Homo-Electric was a call to arms for "heteros, lesbos, homos, don't knows". In Luke's words, "everybody who was nice". He continued: "I've see straight guys copping off with men; some of the combinations of humans in the toilets have been amazing. To me, the people who find that threatening, whether gay or straight, are as pathetic as each other. Some of the best clubs I've been to have had some of the roughest people and some of the gayest people at the same time. The glory of acid house was uniting the roughest bastards in town with the queens — where everything became an irrelevance apart from the fact that you loved the music."

There was definitely a pheremonal scent in the air. I connected smiles with someone; the music quickly dissolved, became soundtrack to my interior thoughts — of us on a Hawaiian beach, high on life and margarita, the moon illuminating the tops of the waves as they crept gently up over our bodies. By the time I opened my eyes it was plainly evident I had played my usual trick of getting so mongled my legs were sitting at a different table from the rest of my body and I was only able to talk in an obscure dialect of Cantonese. But that's just it: the dancefloor really can be a human lonely hearts column. Dancing, as they say, is the vertical expression of a horizontal desire. It tends to follow that if you can wiggle your hips, you can wiggle your bits. Whether you're gay or straight, Ewok or Wookie; whether you're a line dancer in Nebraska or a brown bear in Alaska, it's all part of an animal mating ritual, a fertility dance. Just be thankful we're not scorpions — you really don't need someone trying to sting you to death as you enjoy a postcoital cigarette. Mind you, I did know this lass once. But that's a different story. | *August 2002*

43
Top of the Pops

Ner ner ner ner ner, duh duh duh, duh duh duh

It was 1986, I was sixteen and looking good. My tie was secured the wrong way round, so that the thin bit was on the outside; blonde streaks ran through my hair as if a cat had urinated upon me from a great height; my trousers were thin. Me and my best mate Darren had formed a band called The Cry and recorded our first demo on my four-track, entitled The First Tier (which we both agreed was a genius play on words), mostly consisting of songs about girls who wouldn't go out with us. We wanted to be pop stars and as part of our strategy we blagged tickets to see *Top of the Pops* being recorded, figuring that being near pop stars was pretty much tantamount to being one.

Walking into the *TOTP* studio (back then at Television Centre) was like climbing inside the box of my telly; it really did seem that small, that messy, that full of wires and electronics. Once inside, I straightened my tie and checked my flick was at the correct tilt, overwhelmed by the same nerves that plagued me when I was near Mandy Williams* in English class — that flickering energy that made your skin tingle. The warm up guy told some jokes and then had us dance to some track that was big in the charts, to see who moved OK. Me and Darren danced together, in that kind of twitchy epileptic way your body moved before you discovered booze, drugs and reggae. And yet despite that, the guy walking through the crowd picked on us, and asked us to move behind the stage, onto a raised platform, to dance behind the first act. And that was how me and Dazzer came to be behind Yazz, as she sang The Only Way Is Up, pointing our arms "up" at the appropriate moment. It was without doubt the coolest moment of my teenage life; and that includes getting jiggy with Mandy Williams out of Mr Binding's English class.

Darren is still a musician and we are still close friends — he writes R&B stuff for people like Romina Johnson now, which is kind of odd because on the night I returned to *Top of the Pops*, Mark Hill from Artful Dodger was on, another producer who's worked with Ms Johnson. I've lived almost another sixteen years since the last time I brushed cheeks with the show — I haven't learnt much more than I knew then — and I still watch *Top of the Pops*. It's an institution. The Queen Mum, HP Sauce, cricket, *TOTP* — it's all part of our cultural heritage, of the rich tapestry of English life. *TOTP* is something dependable, something you can rely on in the brutally twisted times in which we live — a fact reinforced by the news that both Redman and Linkin Park had pulled out of their appearances because of the 9/11 tragedy in New York.

I mooched around backstage, checking Melanie Blatt as she applied her makeup; peering into the various rooms trying to find Shaggy, Mr Lover Lover, who looked like he might be good for a chuckle. In one room I found Mark Hill, the Artful Dodger himself, relaxing in what appeared to be a broom cupboard (backstage at *TOTP* you'll find that, outside of the glare of the spotlight, the great and the good of showbiz hang out in broom cupboards). "It's pretty grim," he agreed. "It's 'orrible. But it just wouldn't be *Top of the Pops* otherwise — to see all these flash people like Shaggy walking around back here — it's so much smaller than you expect... and so much grottier."

It's the dream of every kid who has stood before their bedroom mirror, tennis racket in hand, strumming the power chords to Bohemian Rhapsody; of every girl who has held their hairbrush to their lips and mimed the words to Like A Virgin, to one day appear on *Top of the Pops*. It's the same deal as Christians and heaven. "Even when I

Discombobulated

was a little kid, this was *the* show," Mark continued, "there was nothing that came close. Then the first time we went to Elstree to do Rewind, all my illusions were completely shattered, completely fucked."

Ah, yes. Does anyone remember the first time Artful Dodger appeared on *TOTP*? Recall Craig David giving it some up front as the two corpulent lads behind the keyboards stepped out to bust the strangest moves ever witnessed on terrestrial, nay, extraterrestrial, TV? I felt compelled to bring that up. "Ah shut up!" he retorted, chuckling. "Whatever! We never thought we'd be in the public eye again — we thought we'd get away with it — do our thing and fuck off and nobody would ever see that again or care. We didn't realise we'd have more hits and we'd have to live up to that — do interviews a year later and have to explain it."

Well can you explain it?

"It was someone else's idea, of course."

Of course. I left Mark to his preparations and continued poking my proboscis into random rooms, generally getting under people's feet, including those of presenter Josie D'Arby. "I'm from the Anthea Turner era," she quipped, a smile racing across her face, "she's the first presenter I really remember watching. And I still have tapes of Debbie Gibson doing Shake Your Love — I played them last Christmas, it was great!"

It's a long and winding road from Debbie Gibson to Spiritualised, but they were up first, doing the mournful, smack addict bit. In complete contrast Shaggy followed, with quite the loudest shirt I had ever seen in such a built up area, mumbling his low rumblings. Alien Ant Farm were great value and the show's climax was from the last remaining Artful Dodger, with the lithe and mellifluous Melanie Blatt on vocals. But unfortunately this was *Top of the Pops*: strapped tight to an agenda — that of the vagaries of the top forty... and Bob The Bastard Builder was number one. Now I don't give a cat's cock how pre-pubic, ill formed and ill informed are the kind of Ritalin choked brats who buy this sort of shit, but they are encouraging sad twits to make more of it, and for that alone they should be rounded up and deported to Camp Euro Disney. Josie made something of a statement by dropping a Bob The Builder effigy on the floor, though personally

I would have preferred it if she'd gone a little further and scooped out his eyes with a rusty spoon before stringing him up from the *TOTP* neon sign.

It's just one occupational hazard for the show's hirsute producer, Chris Cowey: "It's important that we reflect the charts, and if something like Bob The Builder gets to number one, it's very difficult not to have it on. However, I can make a lot of choices and quite often we're making a damned good music show despite the charts, not because of the charts."

Dance music has always had a strange kind of relationship with *Top of the Pops*, making for slightly uncomfortable bedfellows. Essentially, club culture has changed the rules of just about everything and when it comes to telly, it's hard to convey music in the context of a pop show when it's probably been made by some spotty guy in his bedroom who hasn't seen sunlight for a fortnight. More often than not you end up with telly baggage — dancers, someone miming the words and, if you look very closely, the actual producer guy in the background, cowering behind his keyboard. "It was difficult for dance acts for a while," said Chris. "But now, if people think about it and come and talk to me, I don't think there's any excuse for people in television not being able to do dance acts well. You've just got to look at dance culture and accept the fact that bands don't just consist of drums at the back, guitar on one side, bass on the other, vocalist front and centre. We've got to be able to do different kinds of music in different ways and that can only happen through collaboration with the artist."

I guess you could flash-dance-back to the concept of chicks wiggling around to a record in a kind of synchronized disco fandango. Remember Pan's People? Legs & Co? All I remember of those girls is of a standing joke between my parents every time they appeared, which I never really understood. But as Chris remarked, sexuality... fashion... these are all intrinsically tied in with pop music. "That's why I often have the camera men do a thorough investigation of people's footwear or jeans or buttocks or whatever... breasts, certainly. I think popular music and sex are completely, inextricably entwined — always have been. Rock'n'roll... jazz... these were African American terms for sex. And I think it's still true. It's all tied up with sex and teenage angst and boy meets girl."

My teens have long gone and I'm left contemplating if there will ever come a time when you stop watching *Top of the Pops*? If someone from, say, Age Concern comes visiting, kindly suggesting that you might like to leave *TOTP* to the young folk and move on to something a little more appropriate, like *Antiques Roadshow*? I'd just like to sign off by saying if anyone ever pulled that crap on me, I am quite prepared to slap them rudely about their ears and then set fire to their knees. The day I stop watching *TOTP* is the day I hang up my dancing trousers forever, and retire with my monkey to the alien ant farm. | *September 2001*

* The year after this story was published, Simon bumped into Mandy online, after fifteen years without seeing her. They married in the summer of 2008 and a daughter, Emma, was born. On September 11 of that year.

44
New York
Stories

A SUITE AT THE CHELSEA HOTEL; A LAPTOP AND A BOTTLE OF
SCOTCH FOR LUGGAGE; INVESTIGATIONS INTO BEATIFIC NEW
YORK

"George Segal stayed in this room last night," the bellboy sweet-noted, putting down my bags and switching on the lights in room 325.
"He was filming something right here in the hotel."

"George Segal. Wow. *The* George Segal." I tipped him and shut the door. Who the hell's George Segal? No matter — just seeing the room made me smile so hard I thought my face would crack. For a week, this suite at the Chelsea Hotel would be my home in New York, a fact indelibly stamped onto me and my credit card like an ugly blue tattoo.

If you're into beat culture, the Chelsea is somewhere you just have to visit in the course of your life, like maybe Mecca or Graceland. The Chelsea is where William Burroughs wrote *Naked Lunch*; where Arthur C. Clarke wrote *2001*; where Joni Mitchell wrote Chelsea Morning (after which Chelsea Clinton is named). It's the place where Bob Dylan doodled; where Dylan Thomas died. And it really is quite a trip to be sat in the tub reading about how Sid Vicious killed Nancy Spungen in room 100, just two floors down. You'll find that if you tickle the underbelly of American culture, the Chelsea chuckles.

That night marked the launch party of Transatlantic Express — a loose amalgam of gigs, art shows, clubnights and industry flim-flam

Discombobulated

— in the bar underneath the Chelsea. A couple of beers to the good and me and Antony (the shutterbug for this Dispatch) headed over to the building that was once the Tunnel nightclub; no longer much dancing going on, instead an art gallery filled the space. Disorientated, jetlagged and quickly drunk I stumblestruggled about the place and at one point pretty much headbutted an extremely attractive girl which, as far as I recall, isn't the done thing at such swanky art affairs.

The next morning I stepped out onto the street and the sudden impact of sights and sounds was like the rush of a neon drug through plastic veins. My only company for the day was an iPod. We're inseparable. I'm guessing our next evolutionary step will involve being born with one of these things welded to one's hip. It's teaching me loads about both me and my record collection and what I'm principally learning is what a fucking kook I am. I've set it to play on shuffle and it throws up some real delightful mixes: Puccini into hed kandi; Chet Baker into Gatecrasher and, as I stepped out of the Chelsea that first morning, all hungover and discombobulated by the movement of Manhattan, I hit play and first up was I'm Afraid Of Americans by David Bowie.

Mooching around Manhattan is probably my favourite pastime, short of anything involving Kiera Knightly or the Arsenal midfield. No guidebooks, just letting the shifting of the traffic lights dictate direction, as though carried on a downtown stream. Manhattan is nothing short of steel and glass poetry and recently that has been a poetry of pain. It was hard to figure whether I wanted to go gawp at Ground Zero — it's a pretty tacky thing to go look at — or rather, to *not* look at. Doesn't that strike you as strange? That tourists, in staring upwards, are not actually looking at the presence of anything, but the very absence of something? When I looked up to the sky I could almost still see them, the sometime great glass double digit, penetrating deep into the rumble sky.

That evening I met up with Antony, a designer called Nick Fry and other northwesterners at their hotel, the Maritime, and after some bickering about IDs (that's identity cards, not Iain Duncan Smith) on the door of this cuddly bar Pianos ("Dude, you really think I'm under twenty one? How sweet!") we settled in for a night of drinking and

music and rabble rousing. It was there I met Marvin, something of
a rude bwoy from the Cheetham Hill area of Manchester, currently
residing in New York, for reasons undefined. We watched a couple
of bands and conversation began amongst the group about heading
over to the Limelight, continuing as we spilled outside and cabs were
flagged, people filling them fit to bursting (Nick climbed craftily into
the boot of one and shut it down on himself) and that left just me
and Marvin, kerb side. Still in the mood for mischief he led me into
Alphabet City, where some nice and sleazy afterhours bars could be
found. By this time it was late... maybe it was early... I forget which,
but I do recall the steel shutters coming down over the windows of
this one place, so that anyone who was in was *staying in*. It was one
of the most ominous feelings I've ever had, caged like a booze beast,
the last slither of daylight disappearing as the shutters rattled down.
I was a mess — eventually prolapsed out of the bowels of some other
pub showing the football into the now bright new Manhattan morning, flagging down a cab and getting home some time around 10am.

I didn't leave the Chelsea the whole of the next day. It worked
out rather well actually because in the lobby, a hybrid formed of half
livingroom, half art gallery, I managed to sit down with Stanley Bard,
the owner of the hotel. "No matter what it is, they never forget about
the experience they had at the Chelsea," he chuckled, his voice reso-
nant as the Manhattan skyline. "Almost from its very inception it ca-
tered to a very elite kind of clientele — very creative, very bohemian
and intellectual."

The history of the place clings to the walls; its memories linger in
the stairwells; you can only guess what chaos lurks behind each of
the locked doors. Approximately 100 people live at the Chelsea all
year round — what Stanley describes as a "community within a community" — in the penthouses and roof gardens of the top two floors.
"Through the years it became known that if you like a certain kind
of atmosphere, go to the Chelsea. There's something very creative in
these walls."

That night, walking alone down 8th Avenue to the Maritime, two
guys approached me in the street and whispered: "What you need,
bubba? We got cocaine, ecstasy, heroin, pizza, cheeseburgers, pret-

zels." Their drug and munchy combo meal deal left me befuddled through much of the early evening, spent with Antony and Nick in an old portside speakeasy called the Ear Inn. Nearby was a club called Don Hills, where the night Tiswas was celebrating its eighth birthday with a Mancs vs Scousers party. The intention for the evening was to have Bez from the Happy Mondays as its host, but he'd been turned back by immigration at JFK. By the time I heard the story, it appeared the problem was that he'd ticked the "yes" box next to the bit about bringing narcotics into the country. They hauled his bug-eyed backside into a private room, checked him, and indeed found *something* cunningly concealed in, wait for it, his pocket. Job's a good 'un. Maybe the story had been stamped on a few times by the time I got to ingest it but that's the way I heard it.

As the hours peeled back to reveal the ugliness of morning, Marvin informed me he would be crashing in my room. A little later he informed me that, actually, there was to be a party in my room and I really should come along. When Don Hills closed he gathered a box of beers, part of the danceflooor and decamped to the Chelsea. And it just went wrong from there: a suite populated by a bunch of UK creatives, three Canadian sisters, a Manchester gangster and a box of Cheerios. By five a.m. I had formed a romantic attachment to the Cheerios, making out beneath the rusting Chelsea sign, still winking against the dirty light of an early dawn.

I had breakfast in a bar that morning. It was Sunday and being something of an unreconstructed romantic, I wanted to kick through the fall leaves in Central Park (amongst other Manhattan clichés). Antony decided to kick some, too. Afterwards, walking back down the gorgeous gullet of Manhattan to the Chelsea, every corner brought some new excitement: Carnegie Hall... Radio City... on 7th Avenue steam erupted from vents in the sidewalk as though deep underneath the crust of New York some great dragon struggled with a tickly cough. Further down I could see the beat wink of Times Square and its advertising signs. Buy *this*... See *that*... Your life ain't worth shit without one of *these*. I got a crick in my neck just from looking up at it all.

At the deli local to the Chelsea I bought some booze to restock the fridge and noted that it was all starting to feel very much like home. I cracked open a beer and lay back on my bed. The Yankees had drawn level, two games into the World Series. | *October 2003*

45
Zouk
Singapore

TALKING WOODSTOCK AND THE SUMMER OF LOVE WITH
SOMEONE WHO WAS THERE; SHOWN AROUND ONE OF THE
MOST FAMOUS DISCOS ON THE PLANET BY ITS ELUSIVE OWNER,
LINCOLN CHENG

I'm going to kick this off with a question, ladies and gentlemen, because it's been troubling me greatly. Why, when you step onto a plane, does the airhostess always — *always* — demand to see the detached stub of your boarding card? She'll take a studied look at it, pause, then gesticulate down the aisle to her left, at which point I'm left thinking... *where else*, pray tell, would you have me go? Because sweetheart, my options are seriously limited here. There's only one guy who gets to go the other way and he's got a badge on his shirt that says "Captain" and a shiny fucking hat so LET ME GET TO MY SEAT I'M SERIOUSLY WIGGING OUT HERE...

...and relax. I found my seat, next to Laura, the saxophonist joining DJ Richard F on this Asian tour. I'd done my homework on the Fresh DJs website (the company that manages them both) and found Laura billed as "the Lovely Laura". A few gins into the nonstop, red eye from Manchester to Singapore and I wasn't doubting that.

It was weird o'clock when we touched down. The air was thick, soupy. The promoter of the first gig at Zouk, Eddie, took us for some breakfast out back of our hotel, on a terrace next to the Singapore River. It was Eddie's idea to incorporate a live element within the gig, flying Laura out to blow sax, and me to blow expenses. "Clubbing has come to a point where it's so obvious," Eddie said, ordering a coffee. "So I think it's important to have an event where a DJ collaborates with live musicians to create more of a spontaneous atmosphere. It's still something new here in Asia."

I couldn't sleep much and wanted, as soon as was politely acceptable, to slip into Singapore time and a Singapore Sling. Laura was up for a mooch, so we strolled along the river towards downtown, approaching skyscrapers that lurched like twenty first century ogres over the riverside shacks of Boat Quay. Laura needed to buy a disposable camera... I needed that drink... so, as the waiter pointed out a nearby camera store, I kicked back with a beer and the unfolding afternoon. Time went by... enough for a beer, then another, then another and Laura had yet to emerge from the store. An hour or so had passed when I caught a glimpse of her, looking slightly concerned, a camcorder in one hand and a suit in the other. "I'm not entirely sure what's going on," she whimpered. Oh, they're good, Singapore shopkeepers. Sleep deprived and jetlagged, Laura's need of a disposable camera had transmogrified into a camcorder and handmade silk suit. When Laura went back to pick up the suit, they talked her into buying another one. They're *real* good.

Becalmed by a Lions Peak long gin at the Fullerton Hotel, we caught up with Eddie at Raffle's, the colonial palace built by Singapore's gentleman thug, Sir Stamford Raffles. Drenched in warm, tropical rain, we then beat a retreat to the hotel and prepared for the evening. Just a few steps down from the hotel on Jiak Kim street, Zouk is one of those places you hear about when you live in clubland; I remember Geoff Oakes from Renaissance once telling me that Pacha and Zouk were his two favourite clubs on the planet. It has long been an ambition to tick the place off my disco checklist, just as I am ticking chronologically through the A-Z of nations whose women I have seduced (propriety prevents me disclosing how far I have progressed, suffice it to say that Abyssinian chick was HOT).

The club's owner and founder, Lincoln Cheng, is something of an enigma — what I would call a Disco Forrest Gump — he just seems to have "been there" at last century's most crucial cultural moments.

Discombobulated

Living through one Summer of Love might be classed as lucky, but two... surely that's just greedy? Originally from Hong Kong, Lincoln's parents told him to get the hell out of dodge during the Chinese Cultural Revolution, so he moved to the States to study at Berkley in 66, just as the hippy movement kicked off in San Francisco. Then he popped along to a little party people were throwing called Woodstock. "We were one of the first groups there," he recalled, granting me only the second interview he's given in ten years. "And once we'd parked our car we couldn't leave anyway because it was all jammed up, so we ended up spending three nights and three days there."

Lincoln walked me around his club — lest we forget, really only bricks and mortar, but Shangri-La, Nirvana and Heaven all rolled into one for Lincoln. The main room was very much like Pacha; the back room, Phuture, more a separate club in itself; the rooms of the Velvet Underground area more salubrious still. Andy Warhol posters ran along the walls. Only, they weren't posters. They were original Warhols. Lincoln collects art and because he'd run out of space to hang stuff at his home, he'd hung it at his club. Somehow I can't imagine original Warhols surviving on the walls of Fabric.

An internal collection of corridors curled like rat runs within the club, allowing secret access to the rooms. One took us out back, where a few of the 200 staff gathered for a break, burning incense next to the shrine built for luck because someone at the club had once won the lottery. Continuing his story, Lincoln detailed how he holidayed in Ibiza through the mid eighties, partying with all those DJs during their infamous holiday, the year Alfredo turned the world onto Balearica. Forrest Gump again. Check the photos — I'm sure if you look closely you'll see Lincoln behind Oakenfold, Holloway, Tong and Fung. He brought that weight of experience back to Asia and used it as the foundations for his own club, which opened its doors a few weeks before Ministry of Sound, giving the whole of Asia somewhere to play. He's now fifty seven and looks younger than me.

"I'd been to the Haçienda, I'd been to New York and when I came back here it was all hotel discos — there was no such thing as a stand-alone club. I got so bored with the music and became frustrated." So he built himself a disco. Naturally everyone thought he was bonkers.

That comes with the territory of being a visionary — everyone else has to play catch up. He had to explain to the builders why the walls shouldn't be smooth, but rough in Moorish, Pacha fashion ("I just told the contractor — give me your worst plasterer"); and he had to explain to his business partners why they couldn't have a karaoke room, or why the club's first resident had to be Alfredo. ("What better than to bring the original master?") My personal tour brought us to the music room, floor to ceiling with records from Lincoln's own collection, donated to his club for DJs to use. "Zouk, to me, is a passion. I started it as a passion, not a business. I just loved the music and really wanted to see the music spread in Asia."

Which brings us rather neatly onto Spread Muzik's Richard F, spreading music in thick strokes across the dancefloor of the main room. We stepped up into the DJ booth. Lincoln took up position behind the lighting desk, playing with his toys, which included a smoke machine and a klaxon that he sounded with boyish joy. Richard was starting to sweat, dancing the head nodding, side stepping dance DJs dance, his hands on the rotaries, a big grin for the crowd. "It's weird playing to a crowd that's not on drugs," he said, turning down the monitors in the booth. "It's like... you better rock it or else we're going home! I felt them out for a minute in the beginning but they were having it, no matter what I played — the shit was off the hook after the fourth record. And when Laura came on with the sax the place erupted. Definitely one of the biggest highlights of my career."

As this was something of a *DJmag* party, I'd brought over loads of *DJmag* slipmats to give away, which I proceeded to spin like rubber rings out to my shipmates floundering in the choppy seas of the dancefloor. The Lovely Laura stood on a nearby podium, nestling into Richard's music, blasting jazzed up, tangential sax breaks into the crowd, rhythmically kicking out one leg as if to power up her lungs. The night had one big smile across its face.

When it ended, Lincoln demanded he drive us all of the twenty or so yards back to the hotel. We had it all to do again the following night and before that we had to get to Kuala Lumpur. I climbed into bed, my ass firmly in a Singapore Sling. | *September 2004*

No W46ax

DO WE REALLY NEED RECORDS TO DJ? IN A DIGITAL AGE DO WE
EVEN NEED DJS? IPOD SNOBS AND MUSIC SLOBS UNITE!

Shuffle is the new random.

For you to comprehend just how ill I felt the morning after this particular night, I need to take you back through a series of random, yet deeply connected butterfly effect happenings and circumstances.

In the week running up to No Wax I had been to the doctors because a rash had erupted across my body like some kind of plague. He proceeded to prescribe a bunch of various and nefarious pills, ointments and tinctures, like a travelling medicine man or snake oil merchant.

To comprehend that, you need to go even further back to a plate of shellfish sat in my fridge for far too long, that I'd um'd and ah'd over eating but ultimately did — drooling Homer Simpson style — because there was fuck all else in there aside from the obligatory tub of mayonnaise and four-pack of Stella. And the football was on.

So flash forward in time and you may possibly be able to rustle up an inkling of how bad I felt that morning, trying to figure out why God had cast me down with this combination atomic/bubonic hangover when I reached blindly for the packet of pills the doctor had prescribed and checked the box. Sure enough, that crippling alliteration: "Avoid alcohol."

Random is the new order.

I reached over to the bedside cabinet for my headphones and

plugged myself in, hoping music would carry away the pain like peace pipe smoke dispersing into a digital spirit world. Only my iPod could save me now, for my relationship with my iPod is as fond as that between a human being and a pet, or perhaps a new parent and their progeny — tickling its plastic white belly, gurgling "you're so cute... yesh you are... yesh you are!"

People who truly, passionately and to the point of utter deranged irrationality *love* music, will always have this innate need to share that music, to use it to communicate with others. When I was a kid I was forever taping compilations on D90s for school friends, forcing my taste down their ears, like a demented fascist dinnerlady might force semolina pudding down your throat (something that also happened to me at school). I believe that exact imperative to share music with other human beings is what lies behind the desire to DJ. I personally never went down that path because I had no patience for it, and it smacked of being the disco equivalent of designated driver. But I do have decks and have previously played as DJ Wrong so, to paraphrase my spiritual brother Mark, the invitation to spin MP3s at No Wax was the perfect opportunity for the Return of the Mack.

No Wax (a pun on James Lavelle's Mo Wax, for those of you who may not be aware or are else pun-phobic) began in London. The clue is rather in the name: this was a clubnight *sans* vinyl, purely digital, handing the precious reigns of DJ power over to the dancefloor. Truly then, this is disco anarchy, or perhaps a kind of dancehall utopia where everyone takes communal ownership of the evening: both the methods of control and the means of production.

The London No Wax is currently monthly at 333, but two MP3 fanatics, Jonathan Brown and Neil Williams, wanted to bring the idea to Manchester, and started a funky franchise, moving it around the city so that it became a Romany amongst nights. In a world of plug and play, it seems even the venues are on shuffle. They set up in peoples' houses in a kind of impromptu digital folk aesthetic; then a bar called Centro in the Northern Quarter (Manchester's version of Shoreditch), followed by one-offs at Baby Cream in Liverpool and In The City; and now the svelte surroundings of the basement nightclub of the rather wonderful Rossetti hotel.

Discombobulated

So I arrived, armed with my little box of joy... my beaten up 15GB... my mega mega white thing... into a room busy with digital boys and girls, each with a universe of music burning holes in their pockets. I soon bumped into Neil and he led me over to the "decks" to instruct me in the ways of No Wax: First, you take a ticket (as you would at the meat counter at Tesco) and then wait your turn... for your number to come up on the screen.

Neil and John DJ together as Plastic Surgery Disaster and they set the mood, before the public with iPods join in, throwing their sonic car keys into the pot for the ensuing digital orgy. And that's the fabulously empowering, liberating thing about No Wax: the lunatics really have taken over the asylum and power has been devolved to the unwashed masses of the dancefloor. Anything can happen... and probably will. The whole room had become an organic, throbbing jukebox.

I stepped into the booth. John was acting as a kind of old skool MC, instructing the blue corner and the red corner that they had just three rounds to spa *one-on/one-off*, feeding off what the other pugilist was playing.

Of course you can't legislate for taste and whilst my nerves jangled at the prospect of having the destiny of a dancefloor in the palm of my hands, a previous DJ played something approaching Leonard Cohen, killed the mood and gave me a hungry dancefloor with which to work. "That's the joy of No Wax, really," said Neil. "You've got to be willing to accept those random tracks because it's a nugget thing — you may have to sieve through it to hear something you've never heard before. I'm not just a 4/4 junkie — it's quite nice to hear old sixties psychedelia or something."

MC John took a harder line: "It's a nightmare if you get someone coming down who wants to play S Club Juniors. That's when we're gonna have to get tough."

Yep, you have to take the rough with the smooth. I kicked off with the Dimitri mix of Stetsasonic's Talkin' All That Jazz, because (a) the shit rocks and (b) the lyrical content seemed to fit the occasion, in the sense of what it says about dance music and sampling.

As my DJ spa countered, I cued up my second offering, which was more risky and esoteric, but with a good backstory. (If you're not pre-disposed to such stories, here's a good time to put the metaphorical kettle on:)

I was out on the razzle dazzle in New York a few years back and my pals had dispersed into the heart of a Manhattan night (one stowing away in the boot of a yellow cab), leaving me with the change from the evening and a gangster from Manchester who took it upon him-self to drag me backwards through every sleazy bar he knew and right out the other side into the guts of morning. So I'm hanging off the counter in this one place (in Alphabet City, I think) as the shut-ters came down for the lock-in — one of maybe four or five stranded barflies buzzing round the counter at dawn. Then this voice ema-nated from the shadows at the far side of the bar. "I know you," it said. And he did, an Irish DJ I met in Dublin or maybe Cork, and before I knew what was going on he was loading me with booze and new music, including a promo CD of an album called The Sound of Young New York, *which I carried all the way back to the UK and my stereo, where it stayed for some time.*

(Has it brewed?)

It was a strange and random link, which connected me to an even stranger track called If I Gave You A Party by Syrup. Indeed a party was pretty much what I was trying to give and lo, the dancefloor did receive with thanks. It's a real warm buzz in the cojones to figure out in your head that a track will turn a dancefloor on... and be right.

My third track had never been played in a club before and an even greater risk for my curtain call: a take no prisoners floor stomper called I Like To Rock by an outfit called Arouser, which, apart from being a certain brand of dildo for the better pleasurement of ladies, is also a production name for DJ Graeme Park. He gave me the track on CD-R. I Like To Rock consists of distorted growling guitars over low slung, botox basslines and a screeching vocal sample from a heavy metal hero. Think BodyRockers but better. I looked across the dance-floor and... blow me down and set the Arouser to "pneumatic drill"... it *did* like to rock. Those were my three strikes and then I was out, set

Discombobulated

free to do the No Wax shuffle amongst the DJ denizens of the dance-floor, my last lingering thought only this: To drink where it was dry... and to scratch where it was itchy. | *April 2005*

Afterparties 47

A THOROUGH UNDERGROUND INVESTIGATION INTO THE MURKY
WORLD OF AFTERPARTIES; WHAT HAPPENS WHEN THE NEEDLE
HAS LEFT THE RECORD?

This story starts not at the beginning, but at the end of the beginning or, perhaps, the beginning of the end. There was an awards ceremony. It happened. It's over now, gone. It is of no consequence here. Our story starts.

Now.

"Wasssawallawassgoinon?" My eyes peeled open like skin envelopes gummed shut with sleep. I rubbed my face awake and looked around. A tube train. OK, need more information. Piccadilly line, full of commuters, Friday morning. Judging from the proliferation of pinstripes it was somewhere approaching 9am. Train pulled into a station. South Kensington. South Fucking Kensington? Hang on a bastard minute — if anything, I'm supposed to be north, at least east — this, this is all wrong. As the train pulled out I lifted my head from the glass pane pillow. Booze sweated through my pores like mercury droplets from shattered glass. A gold plastic medallion hung around my neck, inscribed with the metaphysical question: "Who's The Daddy?"

Christ on a spacehopper. The disgust of the commuters was palpable; it filled the carriage like smoke. Next station: Knightsbridge. Hang on a cotton picking minute: *I AM going east...* how the hell does that work? The rusted cogs in my brain crunched into clock-

Discombobulated

work action and this is the net result of what they computed: I had been asleep for hours, bouncing up and down the Piccadilly line from Cockfosters to Heathrow like a holy human yo yo. The full realisation hit me, as though being slapped about the face with a wet haddock on a damp February morning in Cleethorpes: *I am that guy on the tube that everyone tut tuts at, before sitting as far away as possible. I AM THE TUBE DRUNK!*

Gadzooks, how did it come to this? Who did this to me? Who perpetrated such a moral rape upon my saintly soul? Savages. *"ALL OF YOU!"*

Christ, did I say that out loud? Hyde Park Corner. I sat up a little straighter and smiled weakly at my fellow passengers. Eighteen stops before Oakwood (presuming I didn't fall asleep again), at least that gave me time to get a fix on what the hell happened. (If this was a movie, the screen at this point would go all fuzzy as we go back... back... *back...*)

"Where's this fucking bus?" Rachel Photos stopped still in the street outside the SE One nightclub. She had that look in her eye that spoke of chaos and unchecked violence. I guess that's the thing about afterparties: the clue is kind of in the title. They necessarily imply you have been somewhere previously and that crucial fact, in my own enfeebled case, means that I will absolutely, without a doubt, be goosed before I grace the doors.

The afterparty was supposed to be in a strip joint, which seemed an eminently sensible idea. Westminster Council didn't, however. They objected and turned down the licence which, I have to say, is the right and proper decision. You'd *hope* Westminster Council would object to a *DJmag* party. I hope they would object to me, to be honest. I want my social life to be illicit, immoral, depraved. I want society to raise an eyebrow to my very existence — it's rather comforting being objectionable. So the party switched to a north London boozer, and Clubs Editor Ben Edwards was charged with the job of herding people onto the bus to transfer them there. The double decks soon swelled with bodies, like some kind of weird school trip from St Wrongians. Buckle up, baby — this is the Antics Roadshow.

*Covent Garden. The shoppers get off. I try to keep my eyes open.
The tube heads into the tunnel like a rusty needle into a junky's vein.*

The pub throbbed with an extremely rum mix of revellers and music industry heads; the kind of sleazeballs and ne'er-do-wells that get attracted to such lascivious late night affairs, slovenly moths stumbling toward a seedy red light. If you want to throw an afterparty — or an after hours in general — don't expect to get nice people through your doors. Afterparties are for low slung scum like me. This is my world, and you're in my house now...

...Big, brave words, for a man who was already having stability issues (vertical is such an overrated trajectory, don't you think?) But no matter — on to the good and pure business of getting me drunk — who wants to go first? My disco amigo from the north, Oliver Lang, was already way ahead of me, talking in tongues with a pal of ours from Ibiza, Gordon Trumpetman. There were a few other Ibiza heads around — Pete Gooding, and the likes of Jason Bye and Steve Lawler — DJing on decks in a corner on an old table. To be sure, it was a real old fashioned, late night, lock-in of a knees up. Drunken, rude, wrong.

King's Cross. When we were kids we'd say: Yeah I know he is, but how's the Queen? The memory of that makes me smile. I think about taking the medallion from around my neck, then think fuck it, it's hardly going to make much of a difference now, is it? Plus, it helps me in my quest to be objectionable. Tube train tourettes. But where the hell did it come from? Did someone on this very carriage put it around my neck like I'd won some Olympic gold medal in stupidity?

Deputy Ed Tom Kihl had a bag full of nonsense with him, Christ alone knows where he got it from; weird props to prop up the surreality of proceedings. The further the *DJmag* kooks descended into drunkenness, the more feathers and hats they seemed to acquire. I could probably figure out some mathematical equation to demonstrate the theory, were I any good at maths — or could be the least bit bothered — but who needs numbers when you've been given a pink feather boa

Discombobulated

and a gold medallion?

Music Boss Carl assisted me on my mission oblivion; Lesley the editor tore through the room like a bijou blonde tornado, leaving anarchy and destruction in her wake. Some guy came up to talk to me, slightly miffed that I didn't remember him. Well I kind of did. I used to be a lot more together until I lost fifty per cent of my memory and a large proportion of my personality in a cruel and unfortunate Cluedo accident. To this day I have a miniature spanner lodged in my frontal lobe.

Arsenal. Here's a tube fact for you: Arsenal is the only tube station whose name has been changed for the local football team. The station is actually called Gillespie Road. Seriously... you can still see the old name in the wall. True, but kind of boring. I've bored myself actually. My eyes drift shut...

"Come on Rach, like Uncle Jim used to say — where's your will to be weird?"

There was no talking to the woman. She exited the party. Soldier down. I didn't last much longer, to be brutally honest. Sometimes you eat the bar, sometimes the bar eats you. This time the bar burped me up upon the street, and I headed aimlessly towards a tube station, my goldie looking chain clanking loudly against my top.

Arnos Grove. The train pulls out of the gloom of subterranean London and emerges into the brightness of an autumn morning. It's like coming up too fast from the bends. I twitch with the rave ravages. Not far now...

I tell stories. I peddle narrative like a shadowy, street corner dealer, with wraps of memories and baggies of anecdotes. And as I had time on my hands — trundling through north London in the empty, early hours — you can have this hit for free: It's beholden on everyone who can, to say thank you and farewell to John Peel, especially as he formed part of one of the most special moments of my time in the music media. One afternoon, I was sat in a bar on Whitworth Street

West in Manchester, interviewing Andy Rourke — the bass player from the Smiths — for a radio programme I was making about the Haçienda. "There's John Peel," he said quite suddenly, pointing at a shrugged up figure shuffling down the road outside the bar. "All the help he gave the Smiths and I've never even met him."

I couldn't let that one go. I got up, legged it down the road, caught up with Peel and, trying to look as least like a mentalist as possible, gasped "John, I know this sounds mad, but I'm sat in a bar back there with Andy Rourke out of the Smiths... you want to meet him?" Peel came back with me, and I found myself uttering the frankly surreal line: "John, this is Andy from the Smiths."

Already it seems like someone turned the volume down somehow. But, if life truly is just one big disco, then it follows, logically, that heaven is nothing but the great afterparty in the sky. And you know someone up there just turned the volume up to 11.

I smiled and fell back to sleep, the tube train rattling ever further into north London. | November 2004

48
D.O.N.S.
D.I.S.C.O.

STRANDED ALONE; LOST IN THE HEART OF GERMANY IN THE
MIDST OF A RUSSIAN WINTER; A LIGHT OFFERS SANCTUARY;
THROWING ONESELF ON THE MERCY OF A GIMP WITH A HEART

This is where it ends. Fuck. This really is where it all ends. Wherever this car is going to... that's where it ends for me.

I scanned the situation for some semblance of an escape route. OK, in the back of a car with Jimmy the Hat being driven into the hills outside Leipzig in the depths of a winter night by a homosexual German with a Machiavellian plot and God knows what else hatching within his lederhosen. The car window was but a movie screen showing a bleak, Bauhaus film entitled "Oh Fucking Hell We Really Are Fucking Fucked."

The car shuddered over a bump. I wondered whether the drugs they had plied us with had taken hold — whether it was safe to close my eyes; or, if I did, whether I would ever open them again. And so this... this is how it ends.

It had all panned out as these Wrong Adventures in Discombobulation so often do: First you must combobulate; then you go to a disco; then you *disc*ombobulate. And then you get kidnapped by gay Germans.

Fittingly, we started the Dispatch by flying into entirely the wrong city — Leipzig. From there it was a case of negotiating the German rail system and, after a conversation with a fraulein who spoke no English, we ended up with what looked like tickets to Dresden but may well have been a phone number and a map to her house. Wunderbar!

Talking of wonderful bars, our hotel bar was svelte and stylish and it was there that we sat down with the D.O.N.S.: DJ/producer Oliver Goedicke and diva extraordinaire Terri Bjerre. After dinner we retired briefly to a hotel room to do what journalists and DJs do in hotel rooms...

....conduct an interview, silly! What do you take me for — some kind of powder guzzling, slack nostrilled ne'er-do-well? Honestly, after all our times together, I thought you knew me better than that.

But here's something you may not know. Yeah, D.O.N.S. scored big with their remix of Pump Up The Jam in 2005 but they originally remixed Pump Up The Marmalade back in 1996. It's fast becoming their musical ball and chain, their disco Stairway To Heaven. "I always loved the track," Ollie detailed. "To be fair it's still one of my all time favourites, even though it's hard to listen to the song after so many years."

That track is his sonic fuck buddy; that someone you just can't delete from your life or mobile because you know they're always there and it's always fun. (I'm speaking to the ladies in the house now as well... you knows it!) Ollie will *always* go back to her. "Maybe I can do another remix in six years. Maybe a rock remix!"

Terri is Ollie's stage buddy although, when first we meet, Ollie tries to persuade me she's his cleaner, and lives in his basement. "Actually I love cleaning for Ollie," she purred in a gorgeously deep soul voice that would shake the snow right from the eaves. "Buuurt... that's not what I typically do on a Monday."

Terri came from the States to work in K-Town (Kaiserslauten), where many of the Americans forces are based, but always knew the action was in Hamburg. "I was really a hustler — always out singing on stuff. I didn't know what a 'project' was, I was just singing in the studio and trying to get better." Terri is a pair of lungs for hire, and one of those projects was D.O.N.S. — taking it out on the road, wherever that may be. "We have no fixed set up, it depends on the atmosphere of the club," she explained. Tonight's club was in Saxony. And if the Saxons partied half as well as they rampaged, we were in for a good night. "In East Germany the people party pretty good," Ollie smiled, conspiratorially.

The club was Arteum, a multi-room discotheque, all in Pacha white, with cargo netting, booths and occasional beds spread about the place. One room was hidden down some winding castle stairs, others peeled off around random corners. In the main room Ollie set up behind the decks and kicked off with some chunky, electro-tinged, Saturday night house music. After an hour or so Terri joined him on stage, grabbed a mic and freestyled with the crowd, mixing vocal lines from the likes of Depeche Mode and the Eurythmics with D.O.N.S.' tracks, including the next single (a fabulous take on Big Fun).

Having a diva like Terri on stage gave the dancefloor something chunky to grab onto. She be one funky mama! And when that alone didn't push Terri's buttons, she was down on the dancefloor itself, right in people's faces, shaking booty with the best the dancefloor had to offer. Terri launched into the acapella of Pump Up The Confit and it was anarchy on the dancefloor. Jimmy pretty much fell off the stage and into the arms of two young local ladies. We wound the night up with the four of us canoodling in some random coffee house.

Next morning we bought Frankfurters from Frauleins and tried to keep out of the intolerable cold, even if that meant hiding in coffee-shops with old folk and generally goofing around Dresden until the football kicked off and we could find a bar that would show Man Utd vs Liverpool and serve cold beers until the train back to Leipzig, and the hotel that would house us until our 6am flight home.

Back in Leipzig both light and temperature dropped alarmingly as we caught a tram in the direction we thought we should we going. We found Rossplatz right enough and found the hotel, Zum Weissan Ross, and therefore, with some justification, simply couldn't understand why it stood empty and boarded up. The enormity of just how fucked we had got ourselves started to dawn on me. My itinerary was so creased one digit from the hotel's phone number had been erased. It was late on a Sunday night — there was not a soul on the streets, nor light in a window. The Russian winter that had already taken more than a hundred lives in Moscow had drifted west and it was minus fifteen. My ears, nose and cheeks had frozen and my hands were contorted so viciously I couldn't even hold the kebab I had bought to warm them, which dropped clumsily to the street floor.

Jimmy the Hat proffered mere mumbles. I turned to him and said, slowly: "Jimmy you der-don't understand. If we don't find this h-h-h-hotel, soon, we are g-g-g-going to fucking DIE RIGHT HERE, RIGHT NOW."

Disorientated, we had now meandered off the main drag of Rossplatz and were down a narrow sidestreet. Jimmy motioned to a bar, with a light on. "Why don't we try that place?"

With no other option we pushed open the door and threw ourselves on the mercy of the people within — one man at the bar, one man behind it. I approached, and gave it my best *sprechen zie English?* routine — scratching the darker recesses of my memory for two school years of German — when Jimmy elbowed me in the ribs and side-whispered: "look at the postcards on the wall." I looked and, like Indiana Jones falling into a pit, then lighting his torch to illuminate the snakes that slivered all around, I suddenly realised there were pictures of penises on all four walls.

Oh dear God.

The two dudes started babbling to each other in German, then reported that it was indeed the right hotel, in the right street, but entirely the wrong town. The hotel Zum Weissen Ross we wanted was in a different Rossplatz, 20kms away.

Oh dear God.

"Gentlemen, have one of these drinks," the bartender smiled, passing them over the counter. "We will call our friend. He will drive you."

Oh dear God.

He handed over two vials of brown, syrupy liquid in individual miniature bottles. I was so tired, so cold, I had to all intent and purpose given up my life. If this is how it ends then so be it. I've had a good innings. I knocked mine back in one, and waited for the gimp to emerge from the cellar. Yoinks. I never knew Rohypnol had such a fiery kick.| *February 2006*

49
Dave
Beer'd

GLAMOUR AND EXCESS WITH THE LEGENDARY PROMOTER OF
BACK II BASICS; CAN ONE MAN SURVIVE A WEEKEND IN LEEDS
WITH MR BEER? SETTING FIRE TO BARS AND FIGHTING WITH
BOUNCERS

I recently calculated that I am somewhere between seven to eight per cent completely insane. Having come to that somewhat perilous conclusion, I can only assume I am holding it together at all because sanity remains such a major shareholder in my psyche. But the balance can always be tipped by people with their finger on the trigger and it was therefore with considerable trepidation that I accepted the first Dispatches assignment — a weekender with the founder of Leeds über-club Back II Basics, Dave Beer, who doesn't so much have his finger on the trigger as a bazooka on his shoulder.

It's now Monday. I've just woken up and I'm trying to feel my way around my head and work out exactly what the chicken scratch is going on up there and it goes a little something like this: I feel like I've been sucked backwards through a black hole; driven through a moral carwash in a convertible with the roof down; forced to do a tour of duty in Vietnam armed only with a ham sandwich; been inappropriately interfered with by the Cheltenham & District branch of the Women's Institute. I have been well and truly Dave Beer'd, Beer'd up beyond all comprehension and we got on like a bar on fire — which, as I seem to recall, there actually was at one stage.

Dave Beer'd

I first found Dave at his office, above his bar the Lunar Rooms, and together we walked into town, managing about five yards before the barmaids of the first hostelry tempted us like boozy sirens to dash ourselves upon the rocks of a double scotch. The town centre was busy with parasitical Christmas shoppers, and besuited people who bounced off one another and hurried on before they had time to apologise. It was early afternoon but Leeds was already drawing a warm, nefarious nighttime cloak about itself, the Christmas lights shimmering like cheap jewellery, forming images of green trees and fat men in red suits above interlinked shopping arcades that twisted like retail snakes. Leeds was lascivious and my mouth was getting dry. We found lubrication at the bottom of the Victoria Quarter arcade, outside Indie Joze, beneath the protective shadow of a Christmas tree.

"So how would you sum up your own role in the scheme of things?" I asked, eager to fulfil my journalistic responsibilities before I lost the ability to speak.

"I'm Dave Beer and I do parties. I see myself as a purveyor of good times. I like to make people happy."

Fair fucks. It's not rocket science, it's not brain surgery, it's throwing a party — even if it sometimes goes wrong and costs you a small fortune. "Let's face it," I said, as we chin-chinned our bottles, "as long as you've got enough cash in your pocket for a beer and a Big Mac you're OK, right?"

"I don't need any more than that," Dave replied. "I don't want any more than that. I have the love of a good woman, a child and a lot of people around me. I'm wealthy in love and that's important. People might think it's a bit hippy, but without your friends and without your posse and without love around... you've fuck all."

"People born round don't die square..."

"I'm Dave Beer and..."

"...You're looking at him?"

The corners of his mouth turned upwards at the reference to one of his records. "I've been through the mill and back again, you know what I mean, and my views have changed."

Dave looked at his watch, checking the time against the loony toon itinerary he had planned for us, checking what stage we were at

Discombobulated

in our downward spiral through the varied layers of Dave's inferno, the heart of which proved to be Call Lane, where it proceeded to go somewhat avocado-shaped. Call Lane is a tight knot of independent bars — all aesthetically pleasing, all intoxicating in their different ways. We drank for free in every one, Dave greeted with the kind of reception saved for such barroom Bodhisatvas as Norm at Cheers.

"I was on my arse," he said. "I lost me club. And I could still walk into any one of these places and they'd buy me a drink. They wouldn't take me money. They'd be too busy saying 'Dave, here, have a drink. And by the way, get yourself fucking busy'. And that meant a lot."

Praise the Lord and pass the ammunition. The first cocktail of the evening was sunk at Oporto. The barman was almost alone in his bar and insisted on fixing us something small, toxic and on fire — the booze equivalent of Kylie Minogue. We knocked it back and he fixed us another. We knocked that back and Dave dragged us across the street to the bar/restaurant Soho, where we made short shrift of a bottle of Rioja, handed to us gratis by the owner of the establishment, complete with a little sentiment at the bottom of the bottle: "As you've seen, everyone you've bumped into today, everybody's mates," Dave said. "And if they weren't mates in the first place, they're mates now."

We entered Norman, if you'll excuse the turn of phrase — a funky place with doors made out of toast, washing machines, TVs in the walls and stools that looked like the phallus of some angular alien. We drank and talked to other promoters — all keen to stress the community vibe of the city and the battle lines being drawn between the independents and the corporates — the forces of good versus the dark side.

"As far as I'm concerned, Leeds is fighting the world as far as the corporates go," said Dave, waving his drink around. "We've grown up, we're all older and we're having a crack at it and Leeds is one of the few places where there are independent operators. The corporates are coming in to have a go at us and at the end of the day they probably will get us because you can't beat that. But right here right now there's a fucking love thing going on with everyone in town and everyone looks after each other."

Another guy whispered that "the man" wanted to place a Yate's

Wine Lodge at the end of the street, which is the pub equivalent of a forty stone incontinent rhinoceros crapping on your backyard.

"We know those bastards will get us one day," Dave reflected.

"Don't let them grind you down," I replied, ruefully. "And pass the beer nuts."

Once again the demands of my stomach dictated my movements and we stumble-strolled toward the Townhouse, a three-floor development somewhere nearby, for dinner. In keeping with the tone of the evening the manager brought us cocktails. God alone knows what they were. They had an umbrella in, I think. We were joined for dinner by Everton from the clothes shop Hip, not that I recall much about the food, save what Dave Beer racked out on his plate as a side order... talk about speciality of the house, it would be enough to make your nose — I mean ears — bleed. I was suddenly and inexplicably reminded of a passage from the Bible, specifically Psalms, Chapter 16, Verse 6 through 8, which reads: "the lines are fallen unto me in pleasant places." Pleasant indeed, but by this point real people were sitting down for their evening meals and we were inextricably lost in a very loveable brand of chaos, managing to stay inebriated enough to keep everything just ever so slightly out of perspective.

Then we were somehow at the Elbow Rooms, a venue doing its best to make the sports bar acceptable once again. Perhaps — because I like to spend so much time around bars — pool remains the only game I can play with any proficiency; the pool table like a bar alter to me, a shrine that draws the reverential to pay homage — staggering, boozed up bar warriors ready to do battle, ready to fight for anything from honour to a packet of ready salted. The baize of our pool table was a lush, deep purple and I felt compelled to don my magic yellow glasses. Through the tinted lenses the world took on a kooky hue and through the bottom of a beer glass it was distorted further — fractured, bent out of shape so that I couldn't even remember who won the game. Or who I was playing. And then we weren't even there at all, somewhat compelled to leave in circumstances I am not able to go into — save they involved Dave in a fury, and a bouncer at Elbow getting the elbow.

"Now this is my favourite bar," Dave intoned mischievously, outside a place called Mojo. He opened the door and we were greeted by a wash of rock music and the glorious sight of bulging shelves sweating with the finest boozes in all Christendom.

I stood wide-eyed, like a kid with the keys to the candy store but Dave had more pressing matters, busying himself with a bottle of brutal and poisonous looking fluid which he proceeded to pour along the bar. He struck a match and put the light to it, sending a searing, beautiful line of burning fire the length of the counter. It was at that point, as Dave poured the same vile liquid down his throat and breathed fire to the heavens, that I was forced to conclude, through the fug of my own stupor, that here I was dealing with one debauched libertine, a mythomaniac whose own life was testament to what W.H. Auden called "the right to frivolity."

Avoiding the flames as best I could, I stepped up to the bar. "Have you been trained in the sacred matters of alcohol preparation?" I enquired of the barkeep on the business side of the counter, willing only to put my liver and life in the hands of a professional.

"We're probably the best outside of London," he replied, at Dave's instigation throwing multicoloured potions around with loose abandon.

"So how many drinks do you know how to make," I continued, over the shriek of electric guitars.

"500," he replied, casually.

My mind ticked over the plethora of ways you could get yourself twonked, trolleyed and otherwise frazzled in this Shangri-La of bars. But after only a few mind-crunching drinks, Puff The Magic Dragon belched his last and suggested we retire to his office, where he got on the phone to do business and I flew a model of the Starship Enterprise around his head. I was then introduced to a life-size cardboard cut-out of Dave Beer, a doppelgänger that proved to be surprisingly entertaining company for one so flat, as we continued to read between the lines...

"Where next?" I mumbled, more than willing at that point to catch a trolleybus to Bumblefuck if there was any more fun to be had at the end of it.

"To the club!"

Mint was a cute and cuddly locale. Justin Robertson span for most of the night, the soundtrack to my stagger — occasionally hip-twitching, occasionally chit-chatting, but mostly just wandering... and wondering through yellow-tinted glasses that life was indeed a strange and crazy place to live. At some point in the early a.m. the club closed and I met up with the photographer, Dawn Photos, beginning to understand that I was miles from home with a head steeped in a noble rot, on my umpteenth can of Red Bull, nodding my head to music that had long since finished. Somehow a lucid thought got through, as I noticed Justin Robertson at the decks and it registered that he lived in Manchester.

I walked over to him, struggling to maintain a demeanour at least in the same ball park as Sanity FC: "Just-*iiin*...how are you getting home?"

He smiled and cleared a ride for me and Dawn with his driver.

As we readied to leave I passed Dave by the exit to the club. "Stay for a 'one for the road' drink?" he chirped.

I contemplated the appealing prospect of another but was swayed by the ethereal light of the exit, which suggested the possibility of home and reality. I declined. I have no doubt that if I had said "yes" that man would be dragging me round bars even now; maybe I would have never made it home again. But as we hummed along the M62, my mind slowly unravelling, discombobulating, the one jagged thought that kept turning over like a B reg Maestro on a January morning was... well... maybe that wouldn't have been such a bad thing after all. | [*The first Dispatch*] *December 1998*

50
The Last Supper

SAN FRANDISCO; NOWHERE LEFT TO GO IN THAT GREAT
WESTWARD EXPANSION; THE LAST SUPPER; EATING, DRINKING;
DISCO DANCING AND BACKDOOR WRONGNESS ON THE
DANCEFLOOR

I woke up in a disco. Not in a disco daze you understand, but a bon-afide disco. I blinked my eyes a couple of times to make sure it was true: A disco in San FranDisco.

Californian sunlight streamed through a skylight illuminating a blue, pink and mauve room — a cross between a storeroom and a little girl's boudoir. I swung my legs out of the makeshift bed and opened a window onto the streets of San Francisco. After all these years, it had taken until my final Dispatch for me to awake, complete-ly alone, in my very own nightclub. A kid in a candy store. A Disco McCauley Culkin.

Through one door lay the changing rooms for the dancers; through another, the office; down some backstairs the club itself — the Sup-perclub — entirely empty, save for the armies of bottles standing stiff in perfect ranks behind the bar. Sweet Mary Mother of God these wonderful people had locked me up and let me loose in their very own gorgeous club. I recalled some muted mutters about leaving a renowned booze fiend home alone in a clubful of premium liqueur with, let's face it, good reason. But they had taken pity on this home-less hobo and to take advantage would be unkind.

How I came to be alone in San Francisco is a tricky tale. Myself and some disco amigos had been in New York for the week and the plan was for myself, the Hustler, Jimmy the Hat, Marco di Marzo and Chicago Carlo (aka DJ Swank) to catch the same flight over to San Francisco. However, by the time I got to JFK, for whatever reason, only I actually made the flight. So I touched down in San Francisco one morning (my first ever in the city) with no plan and no information save for the address of the Supperclub and a name. Michael Anthony. I arrived at their doorstep with a suitcase and a smile and, in a quasi-religious move, threw myself upon their mercy.

They let me drop my bags and left me with the day and a deep desire to get out into San Fran. The place has a real resonance for me. When you are into Jack Kerouac, the Beat Generation and its bebop soundtrack, San Francisco is a key place on the map. And it's a beautiful city: Hills lumbering up from the Bay are liberally lined with wooden houses of all hues, as though someone had been playing pick up sticks from on high. I walked up to Union Square and through Chinatown; bought a map and was attempting to locate Jack Kerouac Street when I stumbled right upon it. Next on my beat pilgrimage was the infamous City Lights bookstore, so I took a right down Jack Kerouac Street (really only a small alley), found a store at the end, walked in and asked about its whereabouts. The lady behind the counter looked at me as if I was cerebrally challenged. "You're standing in it," she said.

Counterculture indeed. Call me a kook if you will, but I think there's some kismet in arriving in a city for the first time, wandering off in an entirely random direction and colliding with the place you want to be in. Upstairs in the reading room, windows opened over rooftops where Kerouac's beatific words once hopped like a cat between the eaves. Outside a bar on the North Shore, I sat with a beer and my books and watched the trolley cars trundle on past.

The Supperclub is about as fabulous as life gets. The concept started in Amsterdam: You kickback on beds, while food and wine are brought to you and performers and actors weird you out. Because you recline supine and are lubricated by booze, everyone relaxes into a shared groove. Once desserts are dispatched, the DJ cranks up the music and everyone is ready to party. It's the art of going out lying down.

Michael placed me on a bed with a delightful group of Chinese bi-curious swingers. I kicked back with them and drank champagne until I couldn't feel my toes and then stumbled backstage where all the artists and dancers were changing. Desperately trying to stay awake, I lay back in a storeroom and, amongst the bass thud and low chatter of their conversation, drifted off right there where I lay.

So strange to fall asleep amongst the hullabaloo of a party and wake up alone in an empty nightclub. My morning solitude was eventually interrupted by some commotion on the street. I pushed open the window and there, on the sidewalk, stood Jimmy the Hat, grinning like a street urchin and laden with luggage. "Let us in!" he shouted. Accompanied by Chicago Carlo, we three amigos strolled down to Fisherman's Wharf, overlooking Alcatraz, chugging chowder and beers before climbing up to the very edge of the Golden Gate Bridge.

Jimmy is a regular DJ at the Supperclub, we have partied together at the Amsterdam venue, and San Fran was pretty much the same deal. That evening we lay back on the beds, joined by Michael and the guy who brought the Supperclub concept to the States, Alex Lustberg: "Because of cultural differences in Europe and the US, we've adjusted the formula a bit," said Alex. "For instance, Americans aren't used to having a meal take four or more hours, and we tend to offer a bit more programming on any given evening."

Dinner at the Supperclub makes the Madhatter's tea party look like a kid's do at the Wacky Warehouse. After the first course, a strange medical team passed by: a pseudo doctor taking notes on a clipboard whilst dragging behind a human experiment on a chain. One girl was having a birthday, so they laid her out on a hospital trolley, pushed her around the place and invited people to slap her tush (that's American for posterior). "It really is a fully immersive experience," Alex continued, "in which all five senses are stimulated. It's about experience, creativity, freedom, and love. That's what people respond to."

Boy, they were responding to something. As booze brought the barriers down people started chatting to the folk in the bed next door;

in our case, a pair of Dutch sisters. As Jimmy DJd in the main room and Swank in the back, I wound up dancing with one of the sisters, a twinkle of utter naughtiness in her eye. (Readers of a nervous disposition may want to avert their own eye from the following exchange.)

"You know what you are," I whispered. "Trouble."

"You know what you are," she smiled, "more trouble."

"Well, you know what happens when trouble meets trouble..."

"Yep," she replied, "I usually end up with a fist in my ass."

Jeepers! I like to think of myself as a liberal chap but that fair made me choke up my G&T.

Soon the Supperclub swelled with revellers and together we partied through the night, out the other side and into the twilight of these Dispatches. And I think it somehow apt that, after eight years and 155 adventures, they should come to their conclusion here in California, the following afternoon, as the sun set and we sailed under the Golden Gate Bridge. Because this is where it really all started for me. California is the edge. The very edge between the Right Side and the Wrong Side. Certainly my edge, during my time living in LA. These, from 1998, are the very first words of my first draft of my first Dispatch:

> A few years ago, I spent an eventful period living on the Wrong Side in LA. I have since managed to pull myself back from the edge because, as nice a place as the Wrong Side is, I wouldn't necessarily want to live there again. But I do like to visit occasionally and these dispatches will form a record of such excursions.

And, I hope, they did. All I ever wanted to do with these Dispatches was to at least try (*try*, dammit, I'm not saying I succeeded) to do what Kerouac did with pot and bebop; what Hunter did with rock and LSD; what my generation did with rave and whatever else was left in the medicine cabinet... to chronicle the culture for the people that grew up with me on the dancefloor.

And in that beatific westward expansion, both geographically and spiritually, California is the last land you reach. Go any further and

Discombobulated

you are going to get very wet. So for this pioneer of the Wrong Side it's time to turn back east, to finally return to the soft folds of the Right Side. To reality. And the one abiding lesson I take with me, my disco amigos, as I sign off for the final time is this:

Life is really nothing more than a disco.

And then there's always the afterparty... | *March 2006*

ACKNOWLEDGEMENTS

These Dispatches originally appeared in *DJmag*.

PHOTO CREDITS

Antony Crook (*cover shot of balcony of the Chelsea Hotel, New York, six o'clock in the morning; fear and loathing in Staylvegas; Nick Fry on early morning Manhattan street; writing in the Chelsea*); Rachel McHaffie (*Take That cuppa; 24 Hour Party People; From Dusk till Dawn; Foo Foo's boudoir; in the pool; fukdup with Luvdup; Crasher Kids; Egypt, Las Vegas*); Jimmy Bell (*Golden Gate Bridge*); Daniel Newman (*Dave Courtney*); Ian Sansom (*bum up a tree*); July Van Der Reyden (*crashed out in Serbia*)

AUTHOR BIO

Simon A. Morrison has been writing wrongs for some fifteen years, working for everyone from *Loaded* to the *Manchester Evening News*, as well as presenting TV and radio. Highlights include editing Ministry of Sound's magazine on the party island of Ibiza for two summers and writing two long-running columns — Dispatches From The Wrong Side and Around The World in 80 Clubs — which appeared in *DJmag* and took Simon everywhere from Beijing to Brazil, Marrakech to Manchester.

Having grown up in London and lived in Ibiza, Amsterdam, Sydney and Los Angeles, Simon sees himself as something of a citizen of the global dancefloor. More recently, however, his life has become more sedentary... he currently resides in Stockport with his wife, four children, three chickens, home brewery and psychotropic ailments of varying degrees of magnitude.

A HEADPRESS BOOK
First published by Headpress in 2010

Headpress
Suite 306, The Colourworks
2a Abbot Street
London, E8 3DP, United Kingdom

[tel] 0845 330 1844
[email] headoffice@headpress.com
[web] www.headpress.com

DISCOMBOBULATED
Dispatches from the Wrong Side

Text copyright © Simon A. Morrison
This volume copyright © Headpress 2010
Layout/design: Joe Scott Wilson & Bianca Curacao-Nicholls
Cover design: David Kerekes
Headpress diaspora: Thomas Campbell, Shelley Lang,
Dave, Caleb Selah, Giuseppe Iantosca, Dylan Harding

A CIP catalogue record for this book is available from the
British Library

ISBN 9781900486736

www.headpress.com

Printed in Great Britain by the MPG Books Group,
Bodmin and King's Lynn